CW00432218

FRIENDS LIKE US

The Unofficial Guide to Friends

By David Bailey and Warren Martyn:

Goodnight, Seattle

FRIENDS LIKE US

The Unofficial Guide to Friends

Jim Sangster & David Bailey

First published in Great Britain in 1998 by
Virgin Publishing Ltd
Thames Wharf Studios
Rainville Road
London W6 9HT

Copyright © Jim Sangster and David Bailey 1998

Reprinted 1998

The right of Jim Sangster and David Bailey to
be identified as the Authors of this Work has been
asserted by them in accordance with the Copyright,
Designs and Patents Act 1988.

ISBN 0 7535 0223 2

Typeset by Galleon Typesetting, Ipswich
Printed and bound in Great Britain by
Mackays of Chatham PLC

This book is sold subject to the condition that it shall
not, by way of trade or otherwise, be lent, resold, hired
out or otherwise circulated without the publisher's prior
written consent in any form of binding or cover other
than that in which it is published and without a similar
condition including this condition being imposed on the
subsequent purchaser.

Contents

Acknowledgements

The authors would like to thank the following for their support, love and proofreading for free:

Eric Aasen, John Ainsworth, Matin Akhtar, Liz Ashford, Alexander Graham Bell, John Binns, Louisianna Boulton-Mudd, Fleur Breteau, Helen Buckley, Darryl Butcher, Flora Collingwood, Peter Cooke, Nick Cooper, Paul Cornell, Neil Corry, Martin Day, Ellie Eaton, Fido, Marie-Helene Gauthier, Marcus Hearn, Ian Hodge, Rob Jones, Katherine Kleeb, Rob and Gemma Lewis, Robin Limmeroth, Steve Lyons, Steven Moffat, Richie Moosbally, Adrianna Mudd-Boulton, Jo Murphy, Tina Nellis, Mark Newton, Carrie O'Grady, Kimberley Piper, Geoff Rens, Jim Smith, Bob Stanley, Keith Topping, Gary Wah, Lisa Wardle, Kevin White, Tony Whitt, Rob Wilson, Birgit Zich.

Special thanks to Rebecca Levene, for liking our ideas and encouraging our overenthusiasm; Simon Winstone, for being unbelievably patient; Gary Russell for general advice and inspiration.

Major thanks to Titan Publishing and Sony Computer Entertainment Europe for being tolerant while we worked this through.

David would like to dedicate this book to Melanie Allen, Tettenhall's very own Jennifer Aniston, and to PP Products of Welwyn Garden – the makers of Pro-Plus.

Jim dedicates his half to Paul Condon, Gary Gillatt and Clay Hickman for their eleventh-hour support and to his parents for having him and not scrambling for the receipt twenty-seven years later.

Introduction

(or 'The One With The Guide To The Guide')

Let's start out by saying what this book *isn't*. This is not a
script book or a behind-the-scenes tell-all examination of
how to make the most successful comedy on US television.
Nor is it an in-depth exposé of the lives of America's six
most popular young actors. What this is, in its most basic
terms, is a *fan's* guide, an episode-by-episode *aide-mémoire*
to *Friends*, the hit Warner Bros sitcom shown on Channel 4
and Sky One in the UK.

In some fan cultures, the fans can be caricatured as geeky
or nerdish by the way they dress up in costumes and wear
T-shirts with slogans such as 'Live Long And Prosper' or
'The Truth Is Out There'. What distinguishes *Friends* fans
from the rest is that the characters we all know and love are
not some visiting alien or a conspiracy-driven FBI agent.
They're people just like us, people who wear T-shirts and
jeans when they hang around the house, people who fall in
love, people who have crappy jobs and bitch about them to
the only people who'll listen – their friends.

How to use this Guide

Well you *can* use this book any way you like, just as long as
it's your own copy and not one that you've borrowed (and if
that's the case, GET YOUR OWN COPY!). But basically,
this is a tongue-in-cheek reference book, containing a listing
of every episode, grouped into four seasons.* This is for two
reasons: first, to make it that bit easier to find your favourite

* The term 'season' is used to describe a single transmission run of episodes,
with 'series' being used as a description of the programme as a whole.

episodes; and second, to reduce, as much as we can do, the possibility of spoiling episodes for those fans who have yet to see them.

Anyway, the format goes something like this:

Episode number and title: Each episode has been given a three-figure number – the first figure tells you which season the episode was transmitted in and the next two refer to the episode's transmission order. So 'The One Where Rachel Finds Out' is episode 124, the 24th episode of Season 1. Each episode is listed by episode title, which as every true fan should know is usually prefixed with 'The One Where . . .' or 'The One With . . .' (sometimes abbreviated to 'TOW'). As these titles never appear on screen (they usually appear only in listings magazines), we have had to rely on a number of sources to pin down exactly what each episode is called, but generally we've just stuck to the ones given in the Warner Bros press releases. There is, as always, an exception to the rule. Whereas the first episode is known to some as 'The One Where It All Began', we've elected to go with the title that Warner Bros use, 'Pilot'. Finally, we've listed the production number given to the episode, which shows us that some episodes were shown in a different order from that in which they were made.

First transmission dates: The date the episode was first transmitted on NBC in the USA and on Channel 4 in the UK for series 1–3. The satellite channel Sky One managed to jump in before Channel 4 and show Season 4 first, so we use these dates for episodes 401 onwards.

Guest Cast: *Friends* has more than its fair share of celebrity guest appearances, but we don't stand on ceremony – they're lumped in with the rest of the supporting cast.

After all the technical stuff and the summary we've included a few categories that may need further explanation. We dip into these pretty much as and when we feel they're appropriate . . .

Poor Ross: Those moments when life just craps on Ross from a great height.

Freaky Monica: Every time Monica proves she's that much more obsessive than anyone else.

Spoilt Rachel: Moments when Rachel realises just how protected she was by her daddy's wallet, or proves just how bad a waitress she really is.

Phoebisms: Examples of that unique view on life in glorious Phoebe-vision!

Slow Joey: When Joey completely fails to get the point or realise what's going on. Which is, like, always.

Chandleresque/Chandler's Job: Killer one-liners, witty repartee and summations of life in general. Also, there's much debate in the show about Chandler's job. We don't quite know what he does (apart from 'data processing'), and apparently neither does anyone else, but if he gets his ANUS or WENUS out, we'll let you know!

The Ballad of Ross & Rachel: No matter what other plotlines are running, this is one story that just keeps coming back. Well whadda you expect – they're lobsters! We chart the highs, the lows and all that bitchiness and point-scoring in between.

Parents – Who Needs 'Em?: From the very first episode we see Rachel having problems with her father. Episode 102 introduces the inimitable Geller parents, each with their own pearls of wisdom and complete lack of insight into their children. Whenever the parent of a Friend pops up, you'll usually find a reference here.

Ugly Naked Guy: The continuing story of the semi-regular character who we really don't *want* to see but still find strangely compelling.

Just Plain Weird: All the strange events and obviously deranged people who pop in and out of the lives of the Central Perks gang.

Generation X: Cultural references and homages are a major part of the whole 'Generation X' (or 'twenty-something') way of life, and *Friends* is full of them. Of course some of the American culture references are completely wasted on us Brits, so we've tried to explain them whenever possible, as well as catching as many of those 'Oh, where have I seen him/her before?' moments as we can. Effectively, this is our translation section for the culturally/transatlantically impaired.

The Story So Far: *Friends* is unusual in the way the long-term story arc is often as important as the plot for the individual episode. **The Story So Far** helps keep track of all those cross-references to previous episodes and to events that happened before the first episode.

French Title/German Title: Just a little extra for all those linguists out there – the titles used on broadcast in France and Germany. How they arrived at some of these titles, such as 'Celui Qui A Oublié Un Bébé Dans Le Bus', is obvious, but perhaps those of you who are fluent in French will be able to tell us how we can translate the title for 'The One With The Boobies' without resorting to crude jokes about fellatio.

. . . Plus loads of other categories as and when they're relevant. We've aimed at providing a write-up that tells you as much as you need to know to remember what happens, without giving too much away to those who haven't seen every episode (particularly the later ones).

Finally, we offer a brief review of each episode, just a personal appreciation of the continuing exploits of our favourite TV people. Just for fun, we mark each episode according to how sickly-sweet it gets, with an **Ahhh Rating** out of five (or an **Aaah! Rating** for those particularly angst-ridden stories). One thing worth noting here, of course, is that on the rare occasions when we might be a little negative, we still think *Friends* is so much better than anything else on TV.

Well, except maybe *Frasier*, at a push. (Did we say that out loud?)

Principal Credits

Regular Cast: Jennifer Aniston (Rachel Green), Courteney Cox (Monica Geller), Lisa Kudrow (Phoebe Buffay), Matt Le Blanc (Joey Tribbiani Jr), Matthew Perry (Chandler Bing), David Schwimmer (Ross Geller)

Yasmine and Dick appear courtesy of Benay's Birds & Animals

Executive Producers: Kevin S. Bright, Marta Kauffman and David Crane

Created by: Marta Kauffman and David Crane

Executive Producer: Michael Borkow

Co-Executive Producers: Adam Chase, Michael Curtis and Greg Malins

Co-Producers: Wil Calhoun, Seth Kurland, Jill Condon and Amy Toomin

Producer: Todd Stevens

Executive Story Editors: Shana Goldberg-Meehan and Scott Silveri, Andrew Reich and Ted Cohen

Main Title Theme: Michael Skloff (music), Allee Willis (lyrics), performed by the Rembrandts

Incidental Music: Michael Skloff

Friends is a Bright/Kauffman/Crane Production in association with Warner Bros Television

The Episodes

(* Just for fun, we've marked up our personal top five episodes in each season)

First Season

101 Pilot
102 The One With The Sonogram At The End
103 The One With The Thumb
104 The One With George Stephanopoulos
105 The One With The East German Laundry
     Detergent
106 The One With The Butt
107 The One With The Blackout*
108 The One Where Nana Dies Twice
109 The One Where Underdog Gets Away
110 The One With The Monkey
111 The One With Mrs Bing
112 The One With The Dozen Lasagnes
113 The One With The Boobies*
114 The One With The Candy Hearts
115 The One With The Stoned Guy
116 The One With Two Parts, Part 1
117 The One With Two Parts, Part 2
118 The One With All The Poker*
119 The One Where The Monkey Gets Away
120 The One With The Evil Orthodontist
121 The One With The Fake Monica
122 The One With The Ick Factor
123 The One With The Birth*
124 The One Where Rachel Finds Out*

Second Season

Third Season

Fourth Season

First Season

1994–1995

24 Episodes

101

'Pilot'
(a.k.a. 'The One Where It All Began' or
'The One Where Monica Gets A New Roommate')
#475085

Writers: Marta Kauffman & David Crane
Director: James Burrows
First US transmission: 22.09.94
First UK transmission (C4): 28.04.95

Guest Cast: John Allen Nelson (Paul – the wine guy),
Clea Lewis (Franny), Cynthia Mann
(Jasmine – credited as The Waitress)

Summary: Monica tells Phoebe, Joey and Chandler about Paul, 'The Wine Guy', a guy she's met, but who, she swears, she's not dating. Chandler, meanwhile, wishes to share a dream he had where he receives a call from his mother via a phone attached to his groin (which he finds weird because 'she *never* calls'). Ross arrives, depressed after his ex-wife finally moved out of their apartment to live with her female lover. Into this mix of emotions bursts a woman in a wedding dress – it's Rachel, Monica's old school friend, and she's just jilted her groom at the altar. Later, back at Monica's, Rachel phones her father and reassures him that she'll be staying with Monica, much to Monica's surprise.

As the guys help Ross put up shelves in his depressingly bare apartment, Joey tries to convince Ross that his belief that there is only one woman for him is ridiculous. Equating women with ice cream, Joey asserts that Ross should just 'grab a spoon'.

Monica's non-date with Paul 'The Wine Guy' goes well, with Monica offering her support when Paul tells her that since his divorce he's been impotent, oblivious to the fact that this is merely a line he uses to get women into bed. Rachel's attempt to find work fares little better, so she goes on a shopping spree instead, using cards paid for by her father. Monica and the gang urge her to stop relying on others and start fending for herself – and the first step is to cut up all her credit cards. That evening, at Monica's apartment, Ross and Rachel are left alone. Ross confesses that back in high school he'd had a crush on Rachel, though Rachel tells him that she'd known all along. He tentatively asks Rachel if he might ask her out sometime. Rachel seems pleased with the idea, so Ross tells her that maybe he will. As he leaves, he smiles to himself in realisation that he's just 'grabbed a spoon'.

Spoilt Rachel: Rachel soon regrets telling her father that maybe she doesn't need his money: 'Wait, I said "maybe"!' she cries as the phone goes dead. After Monica asks if Rachel managed to get a job she joyfully tells her that she'd been laughed out of twelve interviews as she's 'trained for nothing'. She cheers herself up by buying Joan and David boots on sale, fifty per cent off, yet sees no problem in the fact that she used a credit card that her dad pays for. Also, in her first scene, note how Rachel automatically hands the Sweet 'n' Low to Ross . . . and how Ross *automatically* opens it for her and stirs her tea.

Phoebisms: Phoebe tries to cleanse Ross's aura and later tries to calm Rachel by singing her own variation of 'These Are a Few of My Favourite Things', but realises she doesn't actually know the words.

Chandleresque: 'Sometimes I wish I was a lesbian . . . Did I say that out loud?' In one line, Chandler manages to reveal his sexual hang-ups and mixed-up psyche. His dreams, which he insists on sharing, don't help to detract from this: one revolves around a telephone call from his mother via a phone attached to his groin, another sees him appearing in Las Vegas as Liza Minnelli. When Monica says that she's not going on a date with Paul, that it's just two people having dinner and not having sex, Chandler can't help but note that 'it sounds like a date to me'.

The Ballad of Ross & Rachel: Having told the guys that he's afraid he'll never meet another woman again, Ross looks out of his window across the city just as a similar shot of Rachel fades in. A moving and emotional storyline begins with just one shot.

Joey's an Actor?: Joey's appeared in 'regional' productions plus a Reruns Special of *Pinocchio*: 'Look, Geppetto, I'm a real live boy!' chirps Chandler.

Generation X: Rachel compares Barry to 'Mr Potato Head', a really cool toy from the 1970s where you could rearrange the face of a potato (!), recently popularised by his guest appearance in *Toy Story* (John Lassetter, 1995). The gang sits through a really bad Spanish soap opera, cheering when they predict what happens next. Rachel watches *Joanie Loves Chachi*. 'See?' observes Rachel. 'Joanie *loved* Chachi! *That's* the difference!' Ross asks Chandler: 'Do the words "Billy, Don't Be a Hero" mean anything to you?' in reference to the 1974 hit for Paper Lace. Clea Lewis (Monica's co-worker, Franny) is a familiar face to fans of *Ellen*, where she plays Ellen's perky friend Audrey. The song that Phoebe sings to Rachel is a corruption of 'These Are a Few of My Favourite Things' from *The Sound of Music* (Robert Wise, 1965). In his list of alternative flavours of ice cream, Joey mentions 'jimmies', which are similar to hundreds and thousands, apparently. As we see the slow fade from Ross to Rachel, we hear the beautiful 'Sky Blue and Black' by Jackson Browne.

The Story So Far: Monica lives at apartment No. 5 and works at the Iridium restaurant. Monica and Rachel both attended Lincoln High School but lost touch some time since. Ross was a few years above Monica and he once had a crush on Rachel. He is separated from his wife, Carol, who is now living with another woman. Rachel would have been going to Aruba on her honeymoon, had she not left Barry at the altar. Phoebe provides her personal history. She was fourteen when she moved to New York, just after her mother committed suicide (see also 'TO At The Beach' and 'TOW Ross's Wedding' – Part 1) and her stepfather had been sent to prison again. She ended up living with this albino window cleaner until *he* killed himself and she 'found aromatherapy'. Phoebe also once dated a guy named Carl who ate chalk. Well she would, wouldn't she? Cynthia Mann, who appears as a waitress at the Central Perk coffee shop, reappears in Season 3 as Jasmine, Gunther's room-mate and Phoebe's co-worker at the Healing Hands Massage Parlour.

The Last Word: 'Welcome to the real world! It sucks. You're gonna love it!' Monica shares her personal philosophy and gives the series inspiration for its first bumper sticker. Many people have commented on the way it seems Chandler is being established as a gay character, especially considering his 'Liza Minnelli' dream, though later episodes will explain this away. The regular cast (particularly Perry and Schwimmer) might be trying just a little too hard, but generally this is a good, solid start to the series. **Ahhh Rating:** ***

French Title: 'Celui Qui Déménage' (the one who moves house)

German Title: 'Liebe? Nein, Doch Nicht!' (love? No, better not)

102
'The One With The Sonogram At The End'
#456652

Writers: Marta Kauffman & David Crane
Director: James Burrows
First US transmission: 29.09.94
First UK transmission (C4): 05.05.95

Guest Cast: Christopher Miranda (Robbie),
Joan Pringle (Dr Oberman), Merrill Merkoe (Marsha),
Anita Barone (Carol Willick),
and introducing Jessica Hecht (Susan Bunch),
Elliott Gould (Jack Geller), Christina Pickles (Judy Geller),
Mitchell Whitfield (Barry Farber)

Summary: Ross's ex-wife, Carol, tells him that she is pregnant with his child, but that she intends to bring the baby up with Susan, her partner. Meanwhile, Monica is freaking out in preparation for a visit from her overcritical parents. It seems that, while Ross is their 'prince', Monica can do no right in their eyes. The meal goes as badly as she'd suspected it would, so in desperation she asks Ross to tell them his news, but even this rebounds on Monica as their mother blames *her* for not telling them.

Rachel finally gives Barry his engagement ring back (having fished it out of one of Monica's lasagnes first). She's surprised to see him looking tanned; apparently he decided to go on their honeymoon with Mindy, Rachel's maid of honour – and now they're an item.

Ross accompanies Carol and Susan to the obstetrician but ends up bickering with Susan. Realising that maybe this whole situation is going to be too much for him, Ross goes to walk out. Then the Sonogram begins to pick up the heartbeat of his unborn child . . .

Poor Ross: He's not even over discovering his wife is a lesbian before she tells him she's pregnant and that her lover,

Susan, will possibly have more say in the way the child's reared than he will. As Chandler notes, it kind of puts Monica's obsessive pillow-fluffing into perspective.

Freaky Monica: Could those cushions *be* any more fluffed? And don't you just hate the way swallowing when you drink gets in the way of being able to clean the glass? Knowing all this, you'd think Chandler would *know* not to just leave a ball of paper lying where Monica can see it! As Phoebe puts it, Monica's parents have made her all chaotic and twirly, 'and not in a good way!'

Slow Joey: Chandler and Ross's extended metaphor of a Pink Floyd concert being like sex completely loses Joey: 'We still talking about sex?' he asks.

The Ballad of Ross & Rachel: As Ross and Rachel reminisce about when they were at high school, Rachel asks: 'When did it get so complicated . . . didn't you think you were just gonna meet someone, fall in love, and that'd be it?' Ross knows exactly what she means, though not necessarily in the way she means it.

Parents – Who Needs 'Em?: Monica is convinced that her parents held a ceremony inaugurating Ross as 'The Prince' before she was born. Not surprising, really, when we actually see them in action; their mum undermines Monica's confidence while claiming that all the girls fancied Ross when they were younger. Their dad insists on calling his daughter 'Our little Harmonica' and reminding her of how fat and lonely she'd been as a teenager. Even when Ross reveals just exactly why Carol left him, their mother blames Monica for not telling them sooner. No wonder Monica says that if she could change her parents, she'd want Ross's. According to Jack Geller, Rachel's parents spent forty thousand dollars on her non-wedding.

Ugly Naked Guy: Uses a Thigh-Master™. Euw!

Dinosaurs ROCK!: Ross oversees the assembly of an exhibit at the museum which his co-worker, Marsha, insists is a depiction of Stone Age marital 'issues'.

Generation X: The gang watch *Three's Company* (the American remake of *Man About The House*), a sitcom where there's always some 'misunderstanding' with 'hilarious' consequences. Elliott Gould is possibly best known for his roles in the movies *M*A*S*H* (Robert Altman, 1969) and *The Long Goodbye* (Altman, 1973) as well as being Barbra Streisand's ex-husband. Christina Pickles had a long-running stint in *St Elsewhere* as Nurse Helen Rosenthal, played mother to Leonardo Di Caprio's Romeo in *William Shakespeare's Romeo & Juliet* (Baz Luhrmann, 1996) and played 'The Sorceress of Castle Greyskull' in *Masters of the Universe* (Gary Goddard 1987) opposite a young Courteney Cox! When Phoebe says her twin sister is a waitress it's an in-joke referring to Kudrow's character in the sitcom *Mad About You* (see 'TOW Two Parts'). When Rachel begins 'I was in the kitchen with . . .' and Chandler jumps in with 'Dinah?', he's quoting from the traditional banjo tune 'I've Been Working on the Railroad'. Ross's objection to the name Helen is no doubt based on Helen Keller, the deaf, dumb and blind kid who *didn't* play a mean pinball.

The Story So Far: Ross works at the Museum of Prehistoric History. Chandler is an only child. Carol has a relative (brother?) called Marty and we discover that she left Ross for a woman named Susan. Jack Geller lets slip that Monica was a chubby kid who 'had no friends' (see 'TOW The Prom Video').

The Last Word: Our sympathies are firmly with Monica in this episode – her parents are insufferable (though Elliott Gould is inspired casting – David Schwimmer could *be* his son). We can perfectly understand just why she became so much of a kook, though it's nice to see Ross at least *try* to take some of the attention away from Monica's failures. It's just a shame she still ends up getting the blame. **Ahhh Rating:** **

French Title: 'Celui Qui Est Perdu' (the one who is lost)

German Title: 'Familienfreuden' (family pleasures)

103
'The One With The Thumb'
#456651

Writers: Jeffrey Astrof & Mike Sikowitz
Director: James Burrows
First US transmission: 06.10.94
First UK transmission (C4): 12.05.95

Guest Cast: Geoffrey Lower (Alan),
Beth Grant (Lizzy), Jenifer Lewis (Paula),
and introducing James Michael Tyler
(Gunther – uncredited)

Summary: Monica is anxious about the gang meeting her latest boyfriend, Alan. It seems every time she's dated someone the rest of them have hated him. But she's more than a little surprised when they all say they really like him – so much so they begin seeing him more than she does.

Phoebe's bank accidentally credits her account with five hundred dollars. Having reported the mistake, the too-honest-for-her-own-good Pheebs is annoyed when she receives an apology for the mix-up, another five hundred bucks and a football-shaped phone too! In desperation, Phoebe gives the money to a bag lady she knows in return for a soda. On opening the soda can, Phoebe sees a human thumb floating to the top. The soda company compensates Phoebe with a cheque for seven thousand dollars!

Much to the gang's disgust, Chandler begins smoking again after a three-year break. No one can talk any sense into him until Alan phones him and somehow manages to show him the error of his ways. But when Monica finally confesses that she doesn't like Alan as much as her friends do and that she's finished with him, Chandler can't take the pressure any more and resolves to continue smoking. Phoebe's seven-thousand-dollar cheque suddenly comes into use when she bribes him into never smoking again.

Poor Ross: Ross spends most of this episode moping about the sudden discovery that his beloved childhood pet, Chi-Chi, is dead, and not living it up on a farm in Connecticut after all.

Spoilt Rachel: After Phoebe's bank misunderstand her complaint, credit her account with an additional five hundred dollars and send her a phone as an apology, Rachel asks rather too urgently, 'What bank is this?' She gets excited by the fact that she's finally managing to get everyone's orders right at Central Perk – though when she turns round she doesn't see them swapping drinks with each other so they get what they actually ordered.

Phoebisms: Phoebe's delivery of the word 'statement!' in relation to her bank shows just how personally she takes her mail. When Rachel suggests Phoebe just spend the money her bank gave her, Phoebe describes how she'd be able to hear the taps of each footstep telling her the shoes were 'not-mine, not-mine'.

Chandleresque: Chandler tries to describe to Joey the feeling of smoking again after a long time without: 'Think of it as the thing that's been missing from your hand.' Chandler claims he doesn't miss smoking, but we know he's faking it (as the rest of the gang later discover when he's smoking while leaning over the back of Central Perk's couch). Chandler's first attempt at explaining how to cushion the blow (about how when someone tells you you're such a nice guy they're really preparing you for their dating 'leather-wearing alcoholics' and bitching about them to you) could quite conceivably be a reference to an ex-girlfriend . . . or just his dad. The ultimate Chandler line is his rant about the gang's pressure for him to quit smoking again: 'I have had it with you guys and your cancer and your emphysema and your heart disease. The bottom line is, smoking is cool and you know it!'

Just Plain Weird: In addition to Phoebe's bank (we're with Rachel on that one) and the eponymous thumb, there's Phoebe's friend Lizzie, the bag lady, who asks her to remove all the vowels from her alphabet soup.

Joey's an Actor?: Chandler helps Joey rehearse for the part of Damone, a convict on death row about to have his last cigarette – but even a non-smoking actor of Joey's fine talents can't fake the joy of inhaling burning leaves deep into your lungs.

Yo Gunther!: Gunther makes his first appearance, working behind the counter at Central Perk in the very first scene.

Generation X: Ross recalls the Bugs Bunny cartoon *Baseball Bugs* (Friz Freleng, 1946) where Bugs plays all the positions in a baseball game. Lambchop was an old sock-puppet 'owned' by Shari Lewis (and Chandler's verbal attack on it is pretty much what people have been saying for generations). The guys' Laurel and Hardy poster is a still from one of their silent movies, *Leave 'Em Laughing* (Clyde Bruckman, 1928).

The Story So Far: Chandler used to smoke but gave up three years ago (and so sees taking it up again as his 'reward'). Monica used to date a guy called Steve who had a speech impediment (but was 'schexy', apparently). We see the guys' apartment for the first time – they live across the hall from Monica at No. 4.

The Last Word: A good episode for Chandler (again), especially when he's alone in his cubicle at work, trying to cover up the fact that he's smoking at his desk. His summation of the gang's individual flaws is spot-on and much needed in a show that is accused of having a too-perfect cast. However, the two main storylines, Phoebe's predicament with her increasing fortunes and Monica's crisis of conscience over her boyfriend, are not nearly as strong as perhaps we'd like and the other three regulars are hardly used at all. It just shows that, even when part of a minor subplot, Matthew Perry can commit petty larceny and steal the show, a recurring felony that continues throughout the series. **Ahhh Rating: ***

French Title: 'Celui Qui A Un Rôle' (the one who has a role)

German Title: 'Getrennt von Bett und Daumen' (separated from bed and thumb)

104
'The One With George Stephanopoulos'
#456654

Writers: Alexa Junge
Director: James Burrows
First US transmission: 13.10.94
First UK transmission (C4): 19.05.95

Guest Cast: Mary Pat Gleason (Nurse Sizemore),
Marianne Hagan (Joanne), Michele Maika (Kiki),
Leesa Btyte (Leslie), Sean Whalen (Pizza Guy),
Benjamin Caya (Bratty Boy),
James Michael Tyler (Gunther – uncredited)

Summary: Unable to decide who gets to take a date to the hockey game, Chandler and Joey invite a depressed Ross to use their extra ticket. Today marks the anniversary of the first time Ross and his ex-wife consummated their relationship. However, rather than cheering Ross up, the game makes him feel even worse when a puck is whacked straight into his face.

The girls are similarly trying to distract Phoebe. She hasn't been sleeping lately because her grandmother has got a new boyfriend and they're very noisy in bed. They decide to have a slumber party. When the pizza delivery boy brings them the wrong pizza the girls learn that George Stephanopoulos, political adviser to Bill Clinton, is staying in an apartment that can be seen from Monica's balcony. The girls move their party outside in the hope that they might get a peek at what George keeps under his towel . . .

Poor Ross: Beginning with his realisation that it's the anniversary of the first time he slept with Carol (and, he later reveals, the first time he had sex), Ross's day goes from bad to worse. Having spent most of it seeing things that remind him of Carol, he ends up being hit in the face by a hockey puck and left waiting in casualty for over an hour. When Ross is less than enthused when the guys offer him a ticket to the hockey game, Chandler sums up Ross's attitude to life: 'Aren't we Mr "The glass is half empty"?'

Spoilt Rachel: Her credit card company call her up because of unusual activity, i.e. she isn't spending money like it's about to go out of fashion. Rachel is dismayed to discover that 'FICA' has taken a substantial amount of her first cheque: 'Why's he getting all my money?'

Phoebisms: If Phoebe was omnipotent for a day she says she'd want world peace, an end to hunger, good things for the rainforests – and bigger boobs. She also describes Rachel's life as 'floopy', though when Monica suggests she try to get things 'unfloopy' Phoebe points out that there's no such word.

Slow Joey: Joey misunderstands Monica when she asks him what he'd do if he were omnipotent for a day, and as impotence is the worst thing Joey could imagine he says he'd probably kill himself. After Ross says he wants to go home and think about his ex-wife and her lover, Susan, Joey tactlessly crows, 'The hell with hockey, let's all do that!' and later points out that a passing woman has an arse like Carol's in the mistaken belief that Ross is just instigating a game of 'I Spy'.

Just Plain Weird: In all the years Phoebe has had her game of 'Operation', the only piece she's lost appears to be the tweezers.

Boys Will Be Boys: Chandler shows that there's always one person who, if granted a wish, would ask for three more wishes. As Joey accidentally proves, there are some men for whom living is less important than sex.

Generation X: George Stephanopoulos was a senior policy adviser to Bill Clinton and worked as his deputy campaign manager during Clinton's first run for Presidential candidacy. He is now a news analyst on ABC and a tutor at Columbia University. Mr Snuffalopagus was Big Bird's best friend on *Sesame Street*. 'FICA' is the Federal Insurance Contributions Act, similar to National Insurance in the UK.

The Story So Far: Ross claims that he and Carol consummated their relationship on 20 October and that his birthday is seven months before this date (it's actually more than that – see 'TOW Joey's New Girlfriend'). He reminisces about how they ate nectarines, that he walked Carol to the bus stop, how she wore boots that night (and in fact she never took them off), and that there was frost. Phoebe lives with her deaf (and sexually active) grandmother. Joey proves to Chandler that Central Perk is less than a hundred paces from their apartment. Phoebe once worked in a Dairy Queen. Monica once dated a guy called Jason Hurley who Phoebe slept with literally hours after they'd broken up. Monica once received a Valentine card that she'd always believed had been from a guy called Tommy Rollerson, but was actually a prank card from Rachel. When they were in seventh grade, Monica once made Rachel laugh so hard that she wet herself.

The Last Word: Our first real 'boys are different from girls' episode with the hockey match and the slumber party providing a look into how each of the sexes acts when they're apart. Sport, at least superficially, takes precedent over everything else for the guys (note how Chandler and Joey's patience wears thin after spending an evening with Ross moping about after their lost love), but we feel the girls probably have the better time (and don't they always, guys?). **Ahhh Rating:** Depending on whether you feel sorry for Ross or not – * or ****

French Title: 'Celui Avec Georges' (the one with George)

German Title: 'Pizza und Erotik' (pizza and sex)

105
'The One With The East German Laundry Detergent'
#456653

Writers: Jeff Greenstein & Jeff Strauss
Director: Pamela Fryman
First US transmission: 20.10.94
First UK transmission (C4): 26.05.95

Guest Cast: Camille Saviola (The Horrible Woman),
Kim Gillingham (Angela), Jack Armstrong (Bob),
James Michael Tyler (Gunther – uncredited),
and introducing Maggie Wheeler (Janice)

Summary: Chandler is desperate to break up with his girl-friend, Janice, but can't find the right way to do it. Having sought advice from his friends, he agrees to go on a double-dumping date with Phoebe – he'll finish with Janice, she'll finish with her current beau, Tony. But while Phoebe manages to free Tony with a mere hug, Chandler's break-up with Janice doesn't go as well. Luckily, Phoebe manages to diffuse the situation with another hug – much to Chandler's incredulity.

Joey, meanwhile, is desperate to rekindle his relationship with Angela, a stunningly attractive woman he once dated. The only problem is that Angela has a new boyfriend called Bob. Telling Monica that Angela's 'brother' is single, Joey persuades her to join him and Angela on a double date. When she sees Angela and Bob together, Monica is repulsed – until she realises that Joey lied to her.

Ross accompanies Rachel to the launderette to help her continue her quest for independence. But a horrible woman continues to get in Rachel's way, forcing her to confront her in a suds showdown.

Spoilt Rachel: She has evidently never done her own wash-ing before and has major difficulties with confrontation: 'I can't even send back soup,' she confesses.

Phoebisms: Ever the optimist, Phoebe sees Rachel's ruined clothes and thinks she did it on purpose. 'What a neat idea!' she chirps, vowing to do the same with her own clothes.

Slow Joey: Joey is fascinated by the way women can see breasts any time they want to: 'How you get any work done is beyond me.' He gives Chandler advice on how to break up with a woman: 'Be a man, just stop calling!'

The Ballad of Ross & Rachel: What some see as just laundry night is, in Chandler's opinion, Ross and Rachel's first date. Chandler suggests that maybe Ross shouldn't take dirty underwear along. 'This is basically the first time she's gonna see your underwear – do you want it to be dirty?'

Ugly Naked Guy: Monica spies him laying kitchen tiles – euw, *lots* of bending down!

Generation X: As Rachel complains about her father's lack of support, Phoebe breaks into 'That's The Way I Like It' by K.C. and the Sunshine Band. Thanks to Janice, Chandler has two pairs of *Rocky and Bullwinkle* socks, one of each character. Monica refers to the previous year's Thanksgiving parade, when they couldn't inflate the giant 'Underdog' balloon (see 'TOW Underdog Gets Away'). As well as appearing in Woody Allen's *Broadway Danny Rose* (1984), *The Purple Rose of Cairo* (1985) and *Shadows and Fog* (1992), Camille Saviola appeared in a few episodes of *Star Trek: Deep Space Nine* as Kai Opaka.

The Story So Far: Monica once dated a cousin of Joey's who could belch the alphabet. Angela dated Joey for quite some time, but he finished with her (we're guessing this is the legendary Angela Delvecchio – see also 'TOW The Dozen Lasagnes', 'TOW The Dirty Girl'). This is Janice's first appearance, and she seems to work in photography or fashion (she's just been on a 'shoot').

The Last Word: Phoebe's method of getting rid of unwanted lovers might work for her, but the reality, as shown by Chandler and Janice's predicament, is much more painful. Don't worry, Chandler, you'll get many more chances to practise finishing with Janice (notably in 'TOW All The Rugby'). Ross finally gets to spend some quality time with Rachel, and gets to see her underwear. A really sweet moment that really gets **The Ballad of Ross & Rachel** going. **Ahhh Rating:** ***

French Title: 'Celui Qui Lave Plus Blanc' (the one that washes whiter)

German Title: 'Im Schonwaschgang' (on a gentle wash setting)

106
'The One With The Butt'
#456655

Writers: Adam Chase & Ira Ungerleider
Director: Arlene Sanford
First US transmission: 27.10.94
First UK transmission (C4): 02.06.95

Guest Cast: Sofia Milos (Aurora)

Summary: Chandler starts dating an incredibly beautiful woman. Of course, she's married, and she already has another lover, but despite his friends' concern, Chandler's unperturbed by such a tricky situation, boasting that he has all of the fun with none of the responsibilities. However, realising Aurora could never be monogamous like he wants her to be, Chandler begrudgingly ends the relationship.

Joey gets the starring role in a musical based on the life of Freud. Unfortunately, the play stinks. Fortunately, an agent sitting in the audience recognises that he was the best thing in it and offers to represent him. Almost instantly his career reaches new heights as he wins the part of Al Pacino's butt double in a movie. But Joey's enthusiasm for the role (and some cheeky method acting) loses him the job.

Freaky Monica: Rachel discovers just how obsessive her roommate can be. Cleaning up (for, presumably, the first time), Rachel moves Monica's ottoman so it can be an extra seat around the table, but Monica insists she return it to its original position. 'Thank God you didn't try to fan out the magazines,' notes a less-than-helpful Chandler. When Monica defensively claims that she's not *that* picky, Ross reminds her that her 'Raggedy Ann' doll was the only one ever that wasn't raggedy. To prove their point (rather cruelly, we think), the friends present Monica with hypothetical situations guaranteed to freak her out: not paying a bill as soon as it arrives; not buying a detergent with an easy-pour spout; watching as little beads of condensation roll slowly down the side of a glass towards the table top – without a coaster underneath! Unsurprisingly Monica can't take the pressure and cracks straight away.

Slow Joey: Joey is disgusted by Chandler's new girlfriend's promiscuity, claiming that when he's dating a woman, he needs to know he's dating more people than she is.

Joey's an Actor?: Joey's friends are not impressed by the play. Phoebe claims to be scared of the exclamation mark in the title of Joey's play, *Freud!*, while Monica asks the gang if anyone felt like tearing off their skin just for something else to do. Rachel's reaction is short and succinct: 'I feel violated.' Of course, they try to hide their disgust for Joey's sake, focusing on the things they did like – such as the fact he wore a beard and that they didn't know he could dance (quite lame, as support goes). When Joey reveals exactly what he's playing in the Pacino movie, we get the obligatory butt jokes. Chandler congratulates his pal that he's 'finally been able to crack [his] way into show business', while Ross asks if they'll all be invited to 'the big opening'.

Dinosaurs ROCK!: Ross begins to quote a theory about monogamy devised by the renowned palaeoanthropologist Richard Leakey, but everyone manages to shut him up by pretending to fall asleep.

Generation X: Al Pacino is one of the best-regarded actors of his generation and is of Italian-American extraction, so it's no wonder Joey becomes all flustered at the thought of playing his arse lookalike. Joey quotes from Pacino's movies . . . *And Justice for All* (Norman Jewison, 1979) and *The Godfather Part III* (Francis Ford Coppola, 1990). Phoebe explains to Monica just how obsessive she's being by evoking Bernard Hermann's music for Alfred Hitchcock's movie *Psycho* (1960). Joey's song in the play puts Freudian 'penis envy' theory to music. When Ross refers to Richard Leakey, it's likely he would have been quoting from Leakey's study, 'Origins Reconsidered: In Search of What Makes Us Human', published in 1993.

The Story So Far: Rachel has never seen one of Joey's plays before this episode. He once appeared in a production that featured 'trolls' in which his face was covered up. Joey gets signed up by the Estelle Leonard Talent Agency (see 'TOW Russ'). This episode sees the first appearance of a haircut that, across the world, would become known simply as 'the Rachel'.

The Last Word: Monica's obsessions get another outing, and the end-credits sequence reveals just how deeply she thinks about these things – her 'I need help!' is one of the most telling lines she ever gives. Phoebe's optimistic reassurance of Joey's talents, telling him that one day aspiring actors will long to be his butt double, could *only* work on Joey, but it's a sweet gesture that obviously gives him great comfort. **Ahhh Rating: ****

French Title: 'Celui Qui Est Verni' (the lucky one)

German Title: 'Dusch Dich!' (take a shower!)

107
'The One With The Blackout'
#456656

Writers: Jeffrey Astrof & Mike Sikowitz
Director: James Burrows
First US transmission: 03.11.94
First UK transmission (C4): 09.06.95

Guest Cast: Jill Connick (Jill Goodacre),
and introducing Cosimo Fusco (Paolo),
Larry Hankin (Mr Heckles, the weird neighbour)

Summary: New York City is hit by a blackout, and the friends end up holed into Monica's apartment for the evening. The moonlight and candles inspire Ross to finally make a move on Rachel, but when he takes her aside to do so, disaster strikes. Out on the balcony, he is about to ask Rachel out when a cat leaps on to his shoulder, digging its claws into him. Rachel searches for the cat's owner, only to find him in the gorgeous shape of Paolo, an Italian guy living in the same apartment block. As the evening draws on, Rachel gets more and more infatuated with Paolo until, when the lights come back on, they end up in a passionate clinch. All Ross can do is look on, helpless.

Chandler, meanwhile, is trapped in an ATM vestibule with Jill Goodacre, a Victoria's Secret model! He can't believe his good fortune, but neither can he seem to get past his crippling fear and talk to the woman. Maybe if he choked on someone else's chewing gum, that'd help . . .

Phoebisms: We hear Pheebs composing a new song about the blackout in which she claims that she doesn't find it scary '. . . 'cos I stay away from dairy'. When she meets Paolo for the first time, he takes her hand and reels off a long and beautiful-sounding sentence in Italian. When he's finished, she just stares and him and says simply, 'You betcha!'

Chandleresque: This episode, more than any other, gives

us the chance to see exactly how Chandler's mind works. Through a series of scenes where we can 'hear' Chandler's thoughts, we can see his shyness, embarrassment and fear for what it is. When Jill Goodacre offers him some gum, he declines, and almost immediately starts mentally beating himself up about it. A little while later, he tries to open up conversation by backtracking slightly, telling her, 'On second thoughts, gum would be perfection.' Immediately, he thinks of all the other, more naturally phrased, things he could have said, concluding, 'I loathe myself.'

The Ballad of Ross & Rachel: Tonight is the night, as far as Ross is concerned, but Joey warns him that 'It's *never* gonna happen.' It seems Joey believes Ross has waited too long and that now he's 'Major of the Friends Zone'. But Ross is determined to try anyway, and it's such a pity to see his hopes dashed by a cat (especially considering who owns it). From the minute Paolo walks into their lives, Ross is immediately jealous of him, but it's clear that the Italian stallion is going to be around for a while.

Ugly Naked Guy: Phoebe notices that Ugly Naked Guy, caught in the blackout, has lit some candles. The gang gather at the window, and give an intrigued 'Oooh . . .' at the sight, following it immediately with a loud 'Ow!' as, presumably, his wax begins to drip.

Just Plain Weird: On the search for the cat's owners, Phoebe and Rachel come across Mr Heckles. He claims the cat is his, and that it's called Bob Buttons, but the animal is obviously so terrified of him that the girls just walk away. As they depart, he calls quietly after them, 'You owe me a cat.'

Generation X: Larry Hankin played a truck driver who offered a lift to John Cusack and Daphne Zuniga in *The Sure Thing* (1985) and has made a few appearances in *Star Trek: Voyager* as Gaunt Gary. Monica, Joey and Phoebe sing a rendition of 'Top of the World' by the Carpenters.

The Story So Far: Mr Heckles lives at Apartment No. 8 in the same block as Monica and Rachel. Joey reveals that

Chandler's old roommate was Jewish (also 'TOW Russ'). During the discussion about the weirdest place they've ever had sex, Monica claims to have done it on a pool table in her senior year at college. Joey's was the second floor of the New York City Public Library, and Ross remembers him and Carol getting frisky at Disneyland, in the Holland section of the 'It's a Small World After All' ride in 1989. According to Pheebs, Chandler once got bitten by a peacock at the zoo, and Monica had a crush on Joey when he first moved in (see 'TOW The Flashback'). Rachel once spent three weeks in Bermuda with Barry. And finally, Chandler's account number is 7143457.

The Last Word: One of the very best episodes, this tightly scripted, charmingly acted half-hour is pure entertainment from start to finish. Particularly noteworthy are Chandler's internal monologues while he's trapped in the vestibule and his clumsy attempts to appear normal, let alone cool and attractive. Simply fantastic. **Ahhh Rating:** ***

French Title: 'Celui Qui A Du Jus' (the one that has lots of energy)

German Title: 'Dunkle Leidenschaft' (dark passion)

108
'The One Where Nana Dies Twice'
#456657

Writers: Marta Kauffman & David Crane
Director: James Burrows
First US transmission: 10.11.94
First UK transmission (C4): 16.06.95

Guest Cast: Elliott Gould (Jack Geller),
Christina Pickles (Judy Geller),
Elinor Donahue (Aunt Lillian), Nancy Cassaro (Shelley),
Stuart Fratkin (Lowell), Carolyn Lowery (Andrea),
Marilyn Tokuda (Nurse)

Summary: Monica gets a call from her father – her grand-mother is in hospital, seriously ill, and it looks like she hasn't got long to live. Rushing to her bedside, Ross and Monica join their mother and father. Before long, the news is broken to them that Nana has passed on. As Monica and Ross say their final goodbyes, Nana suddenly comes back to life ('This almost never happens,' explains the nurse) only to die for a second time a minute later. At the funeral, Mrs Geller describes to Monica how Nana would always find fault with everything she did. Monica begins to wonder whether she should confront her mother with the fact that she does exactly the same to her.

Chandler is approached by his co-worker Shelley, who wonders whether he's interested in being set up on a date. Of course he is. Shelley starts to tell Chandler about the other guy, Lowell, before she suddenly realises that she's got it wrong – she thought Chandler was gay!

Phoebisms: Talking about death and missing people, Phoebe tells the gang about her friend Debbie, who was struck by lightning on a miniature golf course. Phoebe is convinced that Debbie's spirit now resides inside little stubby pencils, like the ones waitresses use, though not, unfortunately, in the ones that Rachel uses (is this a dig at Rachel's waitressing ability?).

Chandleresque: The lion's share of choice lines goes to Chandler this episode, as he wonders first of all what makes him seem gay, and then why someone like Brian in Payroll is out of his league. When he returns to his friends at the end of the day, he finds out that all the women thought he might well be gay when they first got to know him (which is interesting, considering Rachel's dream in 'The One With The Ick Factor'). He asks his friends to try to pin down what it is that gives this impression, but they can only say that he has 'a quality'. Later, he asks if it's his hair. 'Yeah,' confirms Phoebe, 'you have homosexual hair.' When he enters Monica's apartment on the morning of the funeral, everyone is there in their best sombre outfits. 'Don't we look nice all dressed up?' he asks, a note of jollity to his voice. Then he realises what he's said, and how he's said it. 'It's stuff like that, isn't it?' he concedes. Has he realised that he's just said something stupid and girlie, or has he realised that (as we think the script cues) a daft, inane comment like that in the face of something very serious and bleak is one of the cornerstones of camp?

Parents – Who Needs 'Em?: Judy Geller is on fine form, taking Monica to task over just about everything. As soon as Monica arrives at the hospital, her mother starts commenting on her hair. Ross tries to calm Monica down, especially as they 'still have boyfriends and your career to cover'. After the funeral, Judy Geller explains to Monica how her own mother would pick at and criticise every little thing she did. She says Monica should be thankful she has a mother who is so 'positive [and] life-affirming'! Jack Geller, who is worried about being predictable, asks Monica that she make sure he gets a burial at sea when he dies as he thinks it looks fun and that the family 'could make a day of it'. Monica isn't convinced, but humours him nonetheless.

The Story So Far: Joey claims he never thought Chandler was gay, but see 'TOW The Flashback'. Monica and Ross also had an Aunt Phyllis who died, as well as a pet [?] called Pop-Pop (see also 'TOW The Thumb'). Ross had a retainer when he was younger. For some reason, the boys now live at No. 19 and the girls at No. 20 [the block's apartments were recently renumbered?].

The Last Word: Since this episode features two of our favourite things (Chandler, and Monica's relationship with her mother), what can we say other than: this is classic stuff. **Ahhh Rating:** ***

French Title: 'Celui Qui Hallucine' (the one who hallucines)

German Title: 'Wenn die Oma zweimal stirbt' (when grandma dies twice)

109
'The One Where Underdog Gets Away'
#456659

Writers: Jeff Greenstein & Jeff Strauss
Director: James Burrows
First US transmission: 17.11.94
First UK transmission (C4): 23.06.95

Guest Cast: Max Wright (Terry),
Lara Harris (Obsession Girl), Jessica Hecht (Susan Bunch),
and introducing Jane Sibbett (Carol Willick)

Summary: It's Thanksgiving and Rachel is desperate to join her family for their annual skiing holiday, but after asking in vain for an advance on her wages she realises that her new-found independence has its costs. Monica tells a visibly shocked Ross that they won't be seeing their parents either as they've gone to Puerto Rico with friends. Ross is disappointed, so Monica offers to cook the Thanksgiving meal the way their mom would and invites Phoebe to join them. Chandler won't come as he doesn't celebrate the 'Pilgrim Holidays'. As if things couldn't get more emotional for him, Ross also finds out that Carol and Susan are actually talking to Carol's unborn baby in the belief that it can hear every word. Not wishing to be outdone, Ross begrudgingly joins in but is soon glad he did when his singing prompts the baby to begin kicking for the first time.

Joey gets the chance to be the model for a health promotion, but when he realises that the promotion is a VD awareness campaign his family ban him from their festivities because they think he actually has the disease.

Monica gets the others to chip in for Rachel's plane ticket, but just as she's about to leave, Chandler drags the gang up on to the roof to see the huge inflatable Underdog balloon which has come loose from the Thanksgiving parade and is flying across Central Park. When they return to the apartment they are horrified to discover that they are locked out and that dinner is ruined – much to Chandler's delight!

Poor Ross: The realisation that he's going to be spending Thanksgiving without his mom really hits Ross hard – and we can perfectly understand why Monica rounds on him when he enters the kitchen and starts moaning that 'it's just not the same without Mom'. Still you've gotta feel sorry for him when he learns that his ex-wife's lover tells him that they've told his unborn child that his name is 'Bobo The Sperm Guy'. Typically, Ross doesn't actually believe that unborn children can hear what happens outside of the womb, but he'll speak to his son anyway just to continue his competitive bickering with Susan.

Phoebisms: Pheebs is celebrating Thanksgiving in December because her grandmother's boyfriend is 'lunar'. She suggests Ross stuff his head inside a chicken so he can experience how babies can hear from inside the womb.

Slow Joey: Splitting a cheese toastie with Monica, Joey makes a wish. When he gets the bigger half, Phoebe asks him what he wished for: 'The bigger half,' states Joey, blankly.

Chandleresque: When Joey tells him he's now an 'actor-slash-model', Chandler notes the make-up he's wearing and observes that he looks more like 'man-slash-woman'.

Joey's an Actor/Model?: He once worked at Macy's as an Aramis spritzer (see 'TOW The Breast Milk'). Now that he's between roles he goes after a job as a model for the City Free Clinic's promotions – but they use him on a poster warning all the city's women against venereal disease. Stripping off the buy-line on one of the posters, Joey reveals similar messages for bladder control, a campaign to stop wife-beating, haemorrhoids and finally 'Winner of 3 Tony Awards'. Unsurprisingly he leaves the last message with his face on the poster beaming above it.

Ugly Naked Guy: shares his turkey with Ugly Naked Girl and dances with her.

Dinosaurs ROCK!: Ross tells his unborn son that he had trouble choosing his major when he was preparing to go to college and picked palaeontology on the basis of a dare.

Generation X: Chandler refers to the sickly-sweet teen-angst comedy *Blossom*. Ross performs his own 'unique' rendition of the theme from *The Monkees* TV show. Underdog, by the way, is the big cartoon dog we see in the parade montage. He was a cartoon superhero hound with a big 'U' on his chest in the mid-sixties, and was made by Gamma Productions, creators of *George of the Jungle* and *Rocky and Bullwinkle*. When Joey discovers the effect his VD poster has on women, we hear the Police's song 'Don't Stand So Close To Me'. Max Wright (Terry) played the dad, Willie, in the alien sitcom, *A.L.F.*

The Story So Far: Susan tells Ross that Carol is at a faculty meeting, suggesting she's a teacher of some kind. Rachel's family goes skiing in Vail every Thanksgiving. For some undisclosed reason, Joey and Chandler have a copy of Monica's front-door key. When Chandler was nine years old, his parents informed him during their Thanksgiving meal that they were divorcing. He was immediately sick and has never celebrated Thanksgiving since ('It's very difficult to appreciate a Thanksgiving dinner once you've seen it in reverse' he claims). This episode sees Jane Sibbett take over the role of Carol.

The Last Word: Far too often, Monica is shown as a kook, an obsessive freak who tries too hard. In some ways this episode does little to dissuade the viewer from this view. But when she finally breaks down as her hard work burns away, we see just a glimpse of the fragile and sensitive woman underneath. She spent so much time working to please everyone, to make her first Thanksgiving perfect, and the fact that it couldn't have been less perfect is devastating for her. This is one episode where we get to appreciate just how difficult it is for her to live up to her own impossibly high standards.
Ahhh Rating: ****

French Title: 'Celui Qui Parle Au Ventre De Sa Femme' (the one who speaks to his wife's tummy)

German Title: 'Aufgeblasen!' (puffed up)

110
'The One With The Monkey'
#456661

Writers: Adam Chase & Ira Ungerleider
Director: Peter Bonerz
First US transmission: 15.12.94
First UK transmission (C4): 30.06.95

Guest Cast: Hank Azaria (David), Maggie Wheeler (Janice),
Wayne Pére (Max), Sarah MacDonnell (Sandy),
James Michael Tyler (Gunther – uncredited),
and introducing Vincent Vintresca (Fun Bobby)

Summary: Ross gets a pet monkey called Marcel. They're not getting on that well, and Monica's not too keen on Marcel either. Never mind, it's holiday season, and the gang's New Year party is fast approaching. Chandler, who is depressed about facing the celebration alone, makes everyone agree to a 'no date' pact. But then Phoebe meets David, a sexy scientist; Joey meets a sexy single mum; Paolo's catching a flight back from Rome to see Rachel; Monica's invited Fun Bobby; Ross wants to bring his monkey . . . and anyway, Chandler's cracked and got back in touch with Janice. Phoebe's brief affair with David looks under threat of ending when Max, his fellow scientist, announces that they've been offered the chance of a lifetime – to study with their mentors in Minsk, Russia. Although David initially agrees to stay, Phoebe manages to persuade him to go and follow his dream, breaking her own heart in the process. The rest of the gang are similarly unlucky in love, and as midnight approaches, Chandler becomes increasingly desperate to be kissed . . .

Freaky Monica: She wants the monkey out of her apartment, especially after he pees all over her coffee table. 'He was as embarrassed about that as anyone!' Ross asserts, criticising Monica for not letting bygones be bygones – after all, Marcel has swallowed his pride and shown his face again.

Spoilt Rachel: She brings Joey a big cup of coffee, carrying it very carefully as it's filled right to the brim. When Joey complains that she's not left any room for the milk, Rachel just lifts the cup to her lips, takes a deep slurp, and hands it back to Joey.

Phoebisms: Preparing her set at Central Perk, she says she has twelve songs about her mother's suicide, and one about a snowman. Chandler suggests she open with the snowman song, but unfortunately, this *also* turns out to be about her mother's suicide. We then hear her singing a song called 'My Mother's Ashes'.

Just Plain Weird: The return of Janice's knuckles-through-cheese-grater laugh prompts Chandler to remind Monica 'You remember Janice?' 'Vividly,' she replies coldly. Later, she hands Ross a camera, and flings her arms around Chandler. 'Smile,' she tells him, 'you're on Janice camera!' Ross keeps snapping away, right through the moment of their second break-up. Strangely, there's not a single 'Oh . . . my . . . God!' in this episode. There's just an 'Oh . . .', a long pause, then an anticlimactic 'Nooo'.

Monkey Business: Ross describes the arguments he has been having with Marcel: 'I said some things that I didn't mean, he threw some faeces.' This sets the tone for Marcel's rebellious nature in the rest of his appearances, and only further enforces the lack of control Ross has on the things that affect his life.

Generation X: Hank Azaria is better known as many of the voices on *The Simpsons*. Chandler refers to New Year as a 'Dick Clark' holiday in reference to the man's perennial TV 'Specials'. David, the science guy, and his friend discuss whether Phoebe is better looking than Daryl Hannah, star of *Splash* (Ron Howard, 1984) and *Wall Street* (Oliver

Stone, 1987). Phoebe somehow sees a similarity between her relationship with David and the film *An Officer and a Gentleman* (Taylor Hackford, 1982).

The Story So Far: Marcel was rescued from a lab by Ross's friend Bethel. Chandler tells a fellow partygoer about the time he was bitten by a peacock (see 'TOW The Blackout'). Monica and Fun Bobby used to go out with each other (see also 'TOW Phoebe's Husband' and 'TOW Russ').

The Last Word: A hugely touching storyline for Phoebe and a brief but brilliant appearance by the marvellous Maggie Wheeler as Janice make this episode worthy of a big thumbs-up. Keep a careful eye on the camera work during Janice and Chandler's break-up; the way it cuts whenever the flash goes off is subtle but superb. **Ahhh Rating: ******

French Title: 'Celui Qui Singeait' (the one who monkeys around)

German Title: 'Affen unter sich' (monkeys among each other)

111
'The One With Mrs Bing'
#456660

Writers: Alexa Junge
Director: James Burrows
First US transmission: 05.01.95
First UK transmission (C4): 07.07.95

Guest Cast: Morgan Fairchild (Nora Tyler Bing),
Cosimo Fusco (Paolo), David Sederholm (Coma Guy),
Jay Leno (himself)

Summary: Phoebe and Monica meet a very cute guy at the newsstand, so cute, that Monica shouts 'Woo-hoo!' to attract his attention. When he turns to look back, a truck drives straight into him. Racked with guilt, the girls then proceed to become his bedside companions while he is deep in a coma. They bring him gifts and look after him together, until Phoebe discovers that Monica has been visiting him alone. Phoebe chases Monica to the hospital but, when they get there, they discover that the man has come out of his coma and now seems to want nothing to do with them.

Chandler's mother, the famous author Nora Tyler Bing, comes to New York to visit her son. She is a stunning blonde bombshell of a woman, of whom Chandler is deeply embarrassed: the night before her arrival, she appeared on television and told the world that she was the one who bought her son his first condoms. At dinner with all the gang, Mrs Bing notices that Ross is getting depressed about all the attention Paolo is lavishing on Rachel. When Ross and Mrs Bing meet in a quiet spot in the restaurant, she gives him a peck on the cheek to cheer him up – but the peck turns into a full-blown kiss, which Joey witnesses. Joey tells Ross that he has to admit his indiscretion to Chandler, but Ross is fearful of how his friend will react.

Phoebisms: Phoebe and Monica are wondering what Coma Guy's name might be. Monica suggests Glen, but Phoebe decides that it's not special enough, suggesting Agamemnon instead. She even composes a song for the man, which she performs at Central Perk. 'You don't have to be awake to be my man,' it begins. 'As long as you have brainwaves, I'll be there to hold your hand.'

Slow Joey: After seeing him kissing Chandler's mother, Joey tells Ross that he broke 'the code'. Apparently, in Joey's eyes, sisters are OK (though you should check out 'TOW Chandler Can't Remember Which Sister'), or even a hot-looking aunt, but 'never a mom!' And we're sure Joey would know. Ross tries to explain that Mrs Bing is a sexy mom, which Joey challenges with, 'You don't think *my* mom's sexy?' Ross, convinced they're heading into dangerously strange territory, walks away from the conversation.

The Ballad of Ross & Rachel: More Paolo jealousy here, but Mrs Bing helps to lighten the load. She asserts that, in her books, a man like Paolo is 'a complication you eventually kill off'. 'When?' pleads Ross.

Parents – Who Needs 'Em?: The secret of Nora Tyler Bing's writing style, she admits, is a mix of half a dozen European cities and thirty euphemisms for male genitalia. Morgan Fairchild plays Chandler's mother to perfection: it's obvious that she really does care about him, but equally obvious that she wants to live and love her own life. It's also quite clear how she managed to attract a gay man as a husband – *Falcon Crest* had a huge gay following, after all.

Generation X: Chandler asks the gang if they'd watch *Weekend at Bernie's* instead of his mother's interview (see 'TOW The Embryos'). Jay Leno is one of America's leading chat-show hosts, having inherited *The Tonight Show* from the legendary Johnny Carson. Morgan Fairchild is possibly best known for just being very glamorous, though she did have regular parts in the melodramatic soap operas *Hotel* and *Falcon Crest*. Phoebe and Monica's adventure with the guy in a coma is a nod to *While You Were Sleeping* (John Turtletaub, 1995). As the girls preen the coma guy, we hear 'My Guy' by Mary Wells.

The Story So Far: Joey's mother's first name is Gloria and Joey says she's given birth to seven children (he doesn't count himself – see 'TOW The Baby On The Bus' and 'TOW Chandler Can't Remember Which Sister'). Nora Tyler Bing claimed she bought her son his first condoms, much to Chandler's embarrassment. Her books include *Mistress Bitch*, *Euphoria at Midnight* and her latest, *Euphoria Unbound*. Rachel's middle name is revealed to be Karen.

The Last Word: God bless Morgan Fairchild! She has an amazing rapport with Matthew Perry, and the two of them manage to bring a realism to what is quite a weird relationship. Monica and Phoebe's infatuation with the coma guy is witty: the way they project all their fantasies of the perfect man on to him, only to be inevitably disappointed when he comes round, is terrific stuff. And Rachel's attempt at a Nora

Bing-style book, complete with its comedy typos ('heaving beasts', 'niffle', and 'huge throbbing pens') is great too.
Ahhh Rating: **

French Title: 'Celui Qui Était Comme Tous Les Autres' (the one like all the others)

German Title: 'Der Mutterküsser' (the mother-kisser)

112
'The One With The Dozen Lasagnes'
#456658

Writers: Jeffrey Astrof & Mike Sikowitz and Adam Chase
& Ira Ungerleider
Director: Paul Lazarus
First US transmission: 12.01.95
First UK transmission (C4): 14.07.95

Guest Cast: Jessica Hecht (Susan Bunch),
Jane Sibbett (Carol Willick), Cosimo Fusco (Paolo),
Cynthia Mann (Jasmine, Phoebe's co-worker),
Jo Jean Pagano (customer at Central Perk)

Summary: Rachel prepares to go to Poconos for her first weekend away with Paolo, much to Ross's dismay. Ross considers phoning immigration in one last attempt to get rid of his rival for Rachel's affections. But just before the 'loving' couple leave, Phoebe tells Rachel that Paolo had turned up at her massage parlour and during the session he'd made a pass at her. Exit Paolo. The guys encourage Ross to swoop in and 'usher in the Age of Ross', but when Rachel tells him she's off men for good he settles for a hug instead.

Ross discovers that Susan and Carol have been told what sex the baby will be, but he decides he doesn't want to know until he/she is born. Trying to avoid finding out becomes increasingly difficult as everybody else soon finds out and eventually Rachel lets it slip that Ross is to have a son.

With Special Guest Star . . .

The policy of using guest stars is not something unique to *Friends*: every show from *Cheers* to *Scooby Doo* has resorted to ratings-building 'special appearances' at one time or other. But what makes *Friends* different is the way its guest-star policy seems just that little bit more knowing. It's hard not to use the word 'postmodern', but the production team evidently credits its audience with the ability to recognise that such casting goes beyond PR opportunities and boosts for the mid-season sweeps. For instance, having the soap 'vamp' Morgan Fairchild play Chandler's mother surely goes some way to explaining his tortured, and slightly confused, sexuality. Similarly, Rachel and Monica's excitement at meeting two cute doctors in 'The One With Two Parts' is obviously heightened by the fact that said doctors are played by George Clooney and Noah Wyle, regulars in Warner's medical drama series *ER*. The guest stars themselves understandably relish the chance of sending up their established screen personae in such a popular show.

By the time of 'The One After The Superbowl' in the second season, we have the interesting mix of Chris Isaak, a well-known musician, playing someone who hires Phoebe to sing at a library. In the next episode, Julia Roberts, one-time 'it' girl, plays someone who was emotionally crippled at school because of Chandler's practical joke. Yet we also have Jean-Claude Van Damme playing himself, in a confusing mix of fiction and reality.

But this can sometimes backfire. Realising that *Friends* is hot in the UK, an up-and-coming English actress, Helen Baxendale, was drafted in to be Ross's new girlfriend, Emily for the fourth season. While Baxendale has appeared in two successful shows in the UK (*Cardiac Arrest* and *An Unsuitable Job For A Woman*), she was virtually unknown in the States and reaction to her has been adverse to say the least. An extra-special effort was made to represent British 'talent' at its best for the special 'London episodes' that form the fourth season's finale, with guest appearances by, among others, Sarah 'Fergie' Ferguson and Richard Branson.

Chandler and Joey are forced to find a new kitchen table after the old one collapses under the 'immense' strain of Joey's keys. Considering patio furniture for a brief second, the guys finally settle on something much more suitable – a foosball table. Excited by their new purchase, they invite the Gellers to play their first match, only for Monica to thrash them game after game.

Phoebisms: She tells Rachel that she never lies, and that she bakes the best oatmeal raisin cookies in the world. But she doesn't make them very often because she feels it's unfair on the other cookies.

Slow Joey: Joey mimics the way children ask embarrassing questions in a conversation with Ross: 'How come you don't live with Mommy? How come Mommy lives with that other lady? What's a lesbian?' Monica says she's excited about being an aunt. Trying to hide the sex of the baby from Ross, Joey jumps in with 'or an uncle!'

The Ballad of Ross & Rachel: Realising that Rachel and Paolo are getting closer than he'd like, Ross points out that this was supposed to be just a fling she was having: 'Shouldn't it be . . . flung by now?' After Rachel finishes with Paolo, Ross hugs Rachel to comfort her, but leaves it at that. Ross sums up everyone's hopes for love when he tells Rachel that she deserves to be with someone 'who knows what he has when he has you'.

Generation X: The gang sing the theme tune to the sitcom *The Odd Couple*, but decide against joining Ross in a rousing chorus of the theme from *I Dream of Jeanie*. Ross compares the photo of Carol and Susan's friend to the aging rocker, Huey Lewis, who's biggest hit was 'The Power of Love' (1985). Rachel describes her feelings for Paolo as being like something out of a Danielle Steele book – Steele being synonymous with pulp romantic fiction. Rachel still has a taste for sexploitation novels ('TOW Mrs Bing').

The Story So Far: Ross and Monica have an Aunt Sylvia and an Uncle Freddie (see also 'TOW The Dollhouse'),

Rachel has a sister who lives in Poconos, Susan and Carol have friends called Tanya (who looks like Huey Lewis), Deb and Rona. Chandler reminds Joey about when he and Angela Delvecchio had sex on the late, lamented breakfast table (see also 'TOW The East German Laundry Detergent', 'TOW The Dirty Girl'). Chandler's previous roommate was called Kip, who moved out when he got married and Chandler evidently still sees this as a betrayal. Seeing as Chandler describes Joey as 'my Catholic friend' we can kind of guess his religion.

The Last Word: And so the cat-and-mouse game of Ross and Rachel continues, with Ross's timing as bad as ever. Looking back on this, it does become frustrating when the outcome is so inevitable, but at the time this was as captivating as that other famous 'will they, won't they?' couple, David and Maddie from *Moonlighting*. Fortunately, fans of *Friends* are keener that 'they will' than they were for Mr Addison and Ms Hayes. **Ahhh Rating** (for Ross's comforting chat with Rachel and for his discovery that he's going to have a son): ******

French Title: 'Celui Qui Aimait Les Lasagnes' (the one who liked lasagnes)

German Title: 'Italienische Massage' (Italian massage)

113
'The One With The Boobies'
#456664

Writer: Alexa Junge
Director: Alan Myerson
First US transmission: 19.01.95
First UK transmission (C4): 21.07.95

Guest Cast: Robert Costanzo (Joey Tribbiani Sr),
Brenda Vaccaro (Gloria Tribbiani), Lee Garlington (Ronni),
Fisher Stevens (Roger)

Summary: Phoebe has a new boyfriend, Roger, who is a shrink. Over the course of a few days, Roger performs a number of ad-hoc analysis sessions, causing most of the gang to unwillingly address their own most personal faults and generally making them all decide that they can't stand him.

Joey doesn't need analysis to tell him what's wrong with his life: he suddenly discovers that his father has been having an affair with a taxidermist for the last six years. Joey tries to split them up only to discover that his mother is perfectly happy with the arrangement – Mr Tribbiani Sr has been feeling so guilty about being unfaithful that he's been making the effort to be more attentive and loving to his wife, and now Joey's ruined everything by trying to put things right.

After Chandler accidentally walks in on Rachel in the shower, she becomes determined to get her own back – but she's not necessarily prepared for how far this revenge will go.

Spoilt Rachel: In among everyone's past emotional minefields dragged up by Roger's psychoanalysis, Rachel bemoans the lack of a Weeble Play Palace and Weeble Cruise Ship in her formative years.

Phoebisms: Describing her boyfriend, Roger, she claims that for a shrink he's not too 'shrinky.' When she finally finishes with him, she explains that her friends have a 'liking' problem with him – in that they don't!

Slow Joey: Joey compares the discovery of his father's infidelity to finding out that your father's been leading a double life and that he's actually a spy – before realising that in honesty it's completely different. 'That'd be cool,' he notes to himself. 'This blows!'

Chandleresque: Ross suggests that because Chandler saw Rachel's boobies he should show her his 'pee-pee'. Rachel understandably agrees: 'Tit for tat.' But Chandler refuses to show her his 'tat'. When Ronni tells Chandler that she's a taxidermist, he tells Joey that when he dies he wants to be mounted as if he's looking for his keys. After Joey tells everyone about his family's marital problems, Chandler observes how 'things sure have changed on Waltons' Mountain'.

Parents – Who Needs 'Em?: Rachel sums up Joey's problem: 'Why can't parents just stay parents? Why do they have to become people?'

Generation X: 'Weebles' were egg-shaped people famous for being the toys that wobble but don't fall down. 'Kerplunk' was a game where glass marbles were suspended in a plastic tube, held in place by plastic cocktail sticks; players had to remove one stick at a time, trying to avoid dropping all the marbles. Robert Costanzo (Joey's dad) is maybe more familiar as the voice of Detective Harvey Bullock in *Batman: The Animated Series*. Fisher Stevens has appeared in loads of films (usually playing an irritating, selfish character just like Roger) including *Short Circuit* (John Badham, 1986) and *Hackers* (Iain Softly, 1995). He also appears as the irritating, selfish Chuck in the TV series *Early Edition*.

The Story So Far: Thanks to Roger's analytical skills we are reminded that Chandler is an only child whose parents divorced before he hit puberty (see 'TOW The Sonogram At The End' and 'TOW Underdog Gets Away'). He also reminds Monica that cookies are 'just food, they're not love' (see 'TOW The Prom Video'). Mr Tribbiani remembers an ex of Phoebe's who was a 'puppet guy' and asks Ross how his wife is, suggesting that, true to form, Joey hadn't told his dad about Carol being a lesbian. Joey has a little sister called Tina who has just obtained a restraining order against her husband (see 'TOW Chandler Can't Remember Which Sister'). We learn for the first time of one of the reasons for Chandler's parents' divorce – that his father is an alcoholic (dyed?) blond who chases after young boys.

The Last Word: Could we hate Roger more? His outburst about 'dysfunctional dynamics' and 'stupid big cups'

towards the end of the episode ('oh "*define* me, *love* me"!')
may be good psychoanalysis, but who wants to be analysed
by a psycho. Considering how many 'twenty-something'
shows fall into the trap of turning the parents of characters
into sources of comedy or ridicule, it's nice that we see how
our gang have some form of understanding of the way
things actually are, with Rachel's wry observation that
eventually we all turn into our parents, and Joey's dismay at
his father's adultery. Of course it's none of this that makes
the episode memorable. This is the one that has a nation of
'red-blooded' males going wild at the thought of Jennifer
Aniston's 'nipular area' being visible. Who'd have thought
the phrase 'open weave' could be in any way erotic? **Ahhh
rating:** **

French Title: 'Celui Qui Fait Des Descentes Dans Les
Douches' (literally the one who goes down in the showers – it
means the one who creeps in and looks at people in the
shower)

German Title: 'Der Superbusen-Express' (the big breast
express)

114
'The One With The Candy Hearts'
#456667

Writer: Bill Lawrence
Director: James Burrows
First US transmission: 09.02.95
First UK transmission (C4): 28.07.95

Guest Cast: Maggie Wheeler (Janice),
Jane Sibbett (Carol Willick), Jessica Hecht (Susan Bunch),
Heather Medway (Kristen), Nancy Valen (Lorraine),
Larry Pindexter (Fireman Dave),
Jay Acovone (Fireman Charlie), Joel Gretsch (Fireman Ed),
James Michael Tyler (Gunther – uncredited)

Summary: In preparation for Valentine's Night, Ross manages to get a date with a woman from his apartment block, but manages to screw things up when he takes her to the restaurant that Carol and Susan have chosen for a romantic meal. When Susan is called to work suddenly, Ross invites his ex-wife to join him and a very disgruntled date. Unsurprisingly, the date sneaks out, leaving Carol and Ross alone.

Joey talks Chandler into a double date – with Janice! The night goes well for Joey and progressively worse for Chandler until Joey gives Chandler his credit card as an apology for ducking out with his date. In revenge against their friends, Chandler and Janice order two bottles of the restaurant's 'most overpriced champagne' – and wake up in each other's arms, much to Chandler's horror. The girls, meanwhile, decide to perform a 'bad-boyfriend-cleansing ritual', burning the artefacts left by their exes. Unfortunately, Rachel throws Paolo's Grappa on to the fire, forgetting that it's almost pure alcohol, and causes a near inferno.

Poor Ross: He tries to chat up Kristen by returning an egg he borrowed (lame or what!). As Chandler points out: 'You gotta get back in the game here, OK? The Rachel thing's not happening, your ex-wife is a lesbian . . . I don't think we need a third . . .'

Phoebisms: Despite the fact that Roger was 'creepy and mean and a little frightening', Phoebe still considers dating him again. Is she just able to see the good in everyone or is she just that desperate? She's certain that she is somehow magnetic, which is why she never wears a digital watch.

Slow Joey: This possibly sums up every man in the world: 'C'mon man, she's needy, she's vulnerable, I'm thinking "cha-ching"!' After Lorraine offers to slather his body in chocolate, Joey confides in Chandler: 'I don't even know what "slathering" is, but I definitely want to be a part of it.'

Generation X: Chandler orders a Rob Roy just to find out what it is. It's a cocktail consisting of 2½ tablespoons of Scotch and 1½ tablespoons of vermouth, garnished with lemon.

The Story So Far: Phoebe mentions Abbie, a friend who shaves her head (this might be Bonnie, the friend she introduces to Ross in 'TOW The Ultimate Fighting Champion'). Chandler has dumped Janice twice in the last five months. Phoebe's past boyfriends include Roger (see 'TOW The Boobies') and Nokululu N'K'A-A; Rachel's include Barry (naturally), Pete 'The Weeper' Carney, Adam Ritter and Paolo; while Monica tries to cleanse the memory of the excessively hairy Scotty Jared, plus Howard, the 'I WIN!' guy whom she dated for four months, though she herself never got to 'win' once. Ross tells Kristen that Carol teaches sixth grade.

The Last Word: Whereas in her first appearance Janice was just the Worst Girlfriend in the World . . . Ever™, we almost warm to her here. You can see just how badly Chandler hurt her through the way she almost revels in making Chandler uncomfortable (note her jibes about cutting Chandler's head out of every photo she has of him, so he can use them in his 'Theatre of Cruelty'), yet there's something to admire in her absolute certainty that her and Chandler's story isn't over yet: 'You want me. You need me. You can't live without me. And you know it. You just don't *know* you know it.' Who *could* have known how right she'd be proven to be. **Ahhh Rating** (for Ross's pleading with Carol): ***

French Title: 'Celui Qui Avait Un Coeur D'Artichaut' (the one with the sweet heart)

German Title: 'Feuer und Flamme' (as keen as mustard)

115
'The One With The Stoned Guy'
#456663

Writers: Jeff Greenstein & Jeff Strauss
Director: Alan Myerson
First US transmission: 16.02.95
First UK transmission (C4): 04.08.95

Guest Cast: Jon Lovitz (Steve, the stoned guy),
Melora Hardin (Celia), Fritzi Burr (Ms Tedlock),
James Michael Tyler (Gunther – uncredited)

Summary: When Chandler's boss offers him a promotion, Chandler quits. It seems he'd always thought of his job as being a temporary position and he feels that accepting the position would be an admission that this is what he actually *does*. He decides to undertake career counselling and spends eight hours undergoing numerous tests, only to discover he is already in his 'ideal' job. But when his ex-boss manages to make him an offer he can't refuse, Chandler caves in, and returns to work – and walks straight into his own enormous new office!

Ross manages to get a date with Celia, but Marcel gets in the way. A second date goes slightly better until Celia asks him to talk dirty – he can only think of the word 'vulva'! Joey decides that Ross needs coaching in dirty talk, but while they're practising, Chandler walks in on them, much to his amusement.

Phoebe introduces Monica to one of her new massage clients, Steve, who by a happy coincidence is a restaurateur on the lookout for a new cook. Monica plans an eclectic menu, but Steve arrives at Monica's having smoked a joint and has the munchies. Monica is forced to stand by while her hard work is usurped by gummi-bears and macaroni and cheese.

Poor Ross: Despite Joey's assertion that Marcel is a 'chick magnet', Ross's date with Celia goes less than perfectly when the monkey decides to swing from Celia's hair.

Spoilt Rachel: A confused Rachel accidentally leaves a pencil in Monica's coffee, finding the missing swizzle-stick behind her ear. When Monica hires her co-worker Wendy as a waitress because she's a 'professional', Rachel complains sarcastically that she'd been maintaining her amateur status only to allow her to waitress at the Olympics.

Slow Joey: Joey recommends Tony's restaurant to Ross as a great date place based on the fact that if you can finish a 32-ounce steak there it's free.

Chandleresque: Once again leaning perhaps a little too heavily towards his 'feminine side', he asks Rachel if she can see his nipples through his shirt (See 'TOW Phoebe's Husband'). When Phoebe suggests he might want a job as a chef, Chandler says that he doesn't have the right experience, 'unless it's an all-toast restaurant'.

Chandler's Job: Chandler denies sending prank memos while hiding a rubber chicken. We finally discover what Chandler does here, though processing supervisor doesn't actually mean that much (he's a data processor, if that helps). The company where he works uses WENUS (Weekly Estimated Net Useage System). His boss is called Al Kostlick and his PA is called Helen.

Generation X: When Monica describes Steve's restaurant as being 'not too big, not too small, just right', Chandler asks if it was 'formerly owned by a blonde woman and some bears' in an obvious reference to Goldilocks. When Ross describes Chandler's moaning as the 'lesser-known "I don't have a dream" speech' he's acknowledging the slightly better-known 'I have a dream' speech made by Martin Luther King in 1963. When he finally gets a moment alone with Celia, Ross plays 'Girl, You'll Be A Woman Soon' by Neil Diamond (a song also done by Urge Overkill). Ross compares his dirty talking to James Michener, an author well known for his highly detailed epic novels. Jon Lovitz, a *Saturday Night Live* veteran and voice of *The Critic*, was instrumental in drawing Lisa Kudrow into acting (for which we're all eternally grateful). When Monica says 'I love my life,' Phoebe mistakes it for a quote from *Bryan's Song* (see 'TOW Old Yeller Dies').

The Story So Far: Chandler joined his company five years ago while he was waiting for a better job to come along.

The Last Word: It's a common problem, being stuck in a boring job that we hate. Of course the fact that the job is perfect for Chandler must make the situation so much worse for him. Fortunately, this episode is played strictly for laughs – I doubt the audience would appreciate the cast actually taking such a subject seriously. Of course the high point of this episode is the appearance of Jon Lovitz, who steals the show just by walking through a door. Brilliant. **Ahhh Rating: ****

French Title: 'Celui Qui Pète Les Plombs' (the one who completely loses it)

German Title: 'Aus der Traum . . .' (the dream is over . . .)

116
'The One With Two Parts', Part 1
#456665

Writers: Marta Kauffman & David Crane
Director: Michael Lembeck
First US transmission: 23.02.95
First UK transmission (C4): 11.08.95

Guest Cast: Dorien Wilson (Mr Douglas),
Jane Sibbett (Carol Willick), Jessica Hecht (Susan Bunch),
Larry Hankin (Mr Heckles), Jennifer Grant (Michelle),
Michele Lamar Richards (the Lamaze Teacher),
Helen Hunt (Jamie Buchman),
Leila Kenzle (Fran Devanow), Patty Tiffany (Woman),
James Michael Tyler (Gunther – uncredited),
and introducing Lisa Kudrow (Ursula)

Summary: Chandler and Joey meet a doppelgänger of Phoebe working as a waitress, whom they later discover to be her identical twin sister, Ursula. Joey is completely smitten with her – which causes Phoebe to begin to worry. Since they were children, she and Ursula have not got on. Ursula, she claims, destroyed everything Phoebe loved: like her 'Judy Jetson' thermos flask, and the heart of her boyfriend, Randy

Brown. She's now scared that she will do the same to her friendship with Joey. She decides to confront her friend and tell him how she feels, but, when she knocks on his door, it isn't Joey who answers, it's Ursula, wearing only Joey's shirt.

Chandler finds himself in a compromising position at work. His boss, Mr Douglas, gives him the job of laying off some of the workforce – starting with the vexingly cute Nina Bookbinder. But Chandler is obviously too taken with her looks and charm to do the dirty deed, so asks her out for a date instead. When Mr Douglas asks why Nina hasn't been fired yet, Chandler spins a line explaining that she has a serious mental health problem, meaning that she reacted badly to being fired – her psychiatrist ('Dr Fl–, Dr Flennen–, Dr Flan,' Chandler stumbles, brilliantly) 'mentioned the word "frenzy".' When Nina starts to notice that her workmates are hiding scissors from her, she goes to see Chandler to see if he can offer an explanation. Words finally failing him, Chandler first of all offers her a rise, then a proposal of marriage, before admitting to Nina the situation he has landed them both in – only to receive a staple in the hand as thanks.

Ross, meanwhile, has his own problems as he starts to attend Lamaze classes with Carol and Susan (to prepare for the birth of his son). It is only just beginning to dawn on him how deeply a child is going to affect his life – and he feels he may not be ready for it.

Monica is pestering Rachel to take down the Christmas lights, as she promised she would. When Rachel finally relents and crawls out along the balcony to do so, she slips off the wall, catching her foot in the cable. We see her swinging helplessly outside Mr Heckles's window . . .

Poor Ross: His awkward introduction of Susan at the Lamaze class is wonderfully painful: '. . . and this is Susan Bunch. Susan is Carol's . . . [big pause] Who's next?' When Carol and Susan explain their relationship, Ross merely responds with a feeble, 'You know how women can get.' His realisation of the lifelong commitment of parenthood is quite touching, Schwimmer bringing a great sense of fear and awe to his performance.

Phoebisms: Pheebs is strangely impressed to discover that 'Urkel' in Spanish is ... well, 'Urkel' (see **Generation X** below). Her encounter with Fran and Jamie (who think she is Ursula) is great, though. They mistake her for their usual waitress, and try to place an order with her, but when she responds with a simple (and mystified) 'Good choice', they conclude that it's definitely Ursula.

Slow Joey: Joey claims that he sees a difference between the identical Buffay twins. 'Phoebe's Phoebe. Ursula's ... hot.' This baffling comparison leads Chandler to request, 'You know that thing when you and I talk to each other about things? Let's not do that any more.'

Chandler's Job: There are plenty of snapshots of Chandler's work, including the return of the WENUS (which now apparently stands for 'Weekly Estimated Net Usage *Statistics*' – see 'TOW The Stoned Guy'), and the debut of the ANUS (Annual Net Usage Statistics, obviously). His greatest moments come, though, in his blundering attempts to protect – and seduce – Nina, particularly as his web of lies begins to tighten in around him.

Just Plain Weird: Ursula misunderstands the confused Chandler when he asks her, 'How come you're working here?' ''Cause it's close to where I live, and the aprons are really cute.' Mr Heckles complains that the girls' noise is disturbing his cats. When they point out that he doesn't have cats, he says defensively, 'I could have cats.'

Monkey Business: As stressed out as all our friends are by events of this episode, none of them are prepared for the extra weight put on their shoulders by the mischievous behaviour of Marcel. Marcel steals the TV remote control, forcing everyone to watch television in Spanish. Ross also accuses Marcel of erasing messages from his answering machine, 'supposedly by accident', and of peeing all over the newspaper before Ross can get to the crossword.

Generation X: Phoebe mentions Judy Jetson, from the futuristic *Flintstones* rip-off, *The Jetsons*. Phoebe's erroneous guesses of who Chandler and Joey saw today include the Irish actor Liam Neeson and Morley Safer, journalist, author and presenter of *60 Minutes*. Lisa Kudrow's character Ursula is the ditzy waitress from the sitcom *Mad About You*, which is why the studio audience laugh harder than we did when Helen Hunt and Leila Kenzle (as their *Mad About You* characters) mistake Phoebe for Ursula. Helen Hunt also starred opposite Bill Paxton in *Twister* (Jan DeBont, 1997) and opposite Jack Nicholson in *As Good As It Gets* (James L. Brookes, 1997), for which she won a Best Actress Academy Award. Ross watches a Spanish version of *Laverne and Shirley* and Phoebe watches *Family Matters* (which features the character Steve Urkel – see '**Phoebisms**' above).

The Story So Far: Ursula works at Riffs's, and this is the first time she is mentioned. She's (just) older than Phoebe, started walking (just) before her, and Pheebs claims her sister was always considered the pretty one.

The Last Word: The inclusion of characters from *Mad About You* isn't quite as glaring as the following episode's appearances of George Clooney and Noah Wyle, as there's at least some reason for there to be a crossover with the other series here. Kudrow does a fine job as both a wound-up Phoebe, and her equally ditzy sister (and do we detect a darker, more evil tone to Ursula – or do we just hate her for what she is doing to Phoebe and Joey?). Not enough for Aniston and Cox to get their teeth into, but since the rest of the cast do such great work, we don't really mind. **Ahhh Rating:** ***

French Title: 'Celui Qui Devient Papa' (the one who became a father)

German Title: 'Der Zweiteiler', Teil 1 (the two-parter, Part 1)

117
'The One With Two Parts', Part 2
#456666

Writers: Marta Kauffman & David Crane
Director: Michael Lembeck
First US transmission: 23.02.95
First UK transmission (C4): 18.08.95

Guest Cast: George Clooney (Dr Mitchell),
Noah Wyle (Dr Rosen), Elliott Gould (Jack Geller),
Alaina Reed Hall (the Admissions Woman),
James Michael Tyler (Gunther – uncredited)

Summary: Rachel has been taken to hospital, but panics when she is forced to tell Monica that she doesn't have medical insurance. Since Rachel was sweet enough to nominate Monica as her 'in-case-of-emergency person', Monica reluctantly agrees to commit fraud and let Rachel use her insurance – but to make it convincing, each of them has to pretend to be the other. They are met by Dr Mitchell and Dr Rosen, two 'very cute' doctors. Continuing with their ruse, Monica and Rachel arrange a date with them, but as the girls get more confused and anxious about adopting each other's personality, the gloves come off and the claws come out, frightening the doctors away.

There's trouble in paradise for Joey, as Ursula seems to be ignoring him. Phoebe goes to see Ursula and learns that her sister's affections for Joey have waned. Phoebe decides to dump Joey on Ursula's behalf. In a tender scene, Phoebe (wearing a sweater Joey bought Ursula) pretends to be Ursula and gives Joey a kinder goodbye. They kiss, and it is only when Joey sees 'Ursula' chewing her hair that he realises that it's really Phoebe.

Ross, meanwhile, is continuing to fret about his impending fatherhood – he's really not sure he's ready. As he explains to Joey and Chandler, his stress has been expressed in a dream where he is playing football, using the baby as the ball. He decides to meet with his own father to find out when he first felt like a father. Mr Geller tells Ross about the moment he suddenly realised everything was going to be all right: as a newborn, Ross reached out and clasped his father's finger, and squeezed. 'That's when I knew,' he explains. But Ross gets an early dry run of fatherhood when Marcel, choking on a Scrabble tile, is rushed to hospital. As the gang wait by his bedside, Marcel comes round, reaches out and grabs hold of Ross's finger. Finally, he realises that maybe he is ready for fatherhood after all.

Poor Ross: His football dream is brilliant, especially with the commentary by Joey (who seems unconcerned – Ross is up against Tampa Bay, who've 'got a terrible team') and Chandler (who seems very concerned – when Ross tells them that he hikes the baby down the pitch, Chandler stutters, 'Are you crazy? That's a baby!'). While the scene with his father is touching, it has to be said that the dreadful re-enforcement by the tacked-on Marcel plot is so sweet it is almost enough to make you throw up.

Freaky Monica: When the doctors turn up for their date, Monica and Rachel continue to make a botch of their cover story. Rachel tries to convince Monica that they should just admit their crime, to make the date go more smoothly. But Monica refuses, and an argument ensues. Rachel finally snaps, telling Monica that she's becoming more and more like her mother. That, as far as Monica is concerned, is that. She begins to verbally destroy Rachel in front of the doctors, mentioning that 'she' jilted her husband at the altar (see 'Pilot') – 'I know it's pretty selfish,' she laughs, 'but – hey! That's me!' Rachel, meanwhile, alludes to Monica's bossiness and the fact that she was 'a cow' in high school. The bitching reaches a peak when Rachel, as Monica, claims that she uses her breasts to get people's attention. 'We both do that!' Monica yells. Just then, the phone rings. Dr Mitchell answers and passes the phone to who he thinks is Rachel. In a final act of revenge, Monica tells Mr Green that 'she' and Billy Dreskin (whose father tried to put Mr Green out of business) had sex on his bed – game, set and match to Monica!

Spoilt Rachel: Monica, filling in her admission form at the hospital, asks Rachel for details of her insurance. Rachel just responds with, 'Oh, yeah. Check it. Definitely want some of that.' She has no idea (listen up, you lucky Brits) that medical insurance is a necessity in life.

Phoebisms: Her reaction to her surprise birthday party is wonderful. Everyone has crowded around the mangled cake that Ross has dropped, and so is completely unaware that Phoebe has walked into the room. When she asks, 'Hey, what's going on?', they all respond with a belated 'Surprise!' And, bless her, she is genuinely surprised. Ursula offers Phoebe some chicken, only to be reminded that she doesn't eat 'food with a face'.

Chandleresque: His mouth runs away with itself yet again as he tries to calm Ross's fears about fatherhood. 'Say you never feel like a father. Say your son never feels connected to you as one. Say all of his relationships are affected by this . . .' Ross asks whether he has a point, to which Chandler – in one of Perry's wonderful trademark 'pinched-face' moments – replies, 'You know, you'd think I would.'

Ugly Naked Guy: Over the closing titles, we see a Spanish-dubbed group of friends stare at their nude neighbour as he does . . . something with a hula hoop (see **Just Plain Weird** below for more details).

Just Plain Weird: One of the most perplexing scenes in the entire series is where the end sequence of 'TOW Two Parts', Part 2, is overdubbed in Spanish, just like the programmes Marcel has been watching on Monica's TV. We can finally put you out of your misery by telling you what happens. Ross enters with the takeaway. Monica asks who ordered General Sal's chicken and Chandler laments the fact that General Sal didn't actually turn up. Rachel spies Ugly Naked Guy playing with a hula hoop while Marcel continues to play with the TV remote because he doesn't like what's currently on the TV (i.e. *Friends*?).

Monkey Business: Marcel swallows some letters from a Scrabble game, an 'M', an 'O' and a 'K' – Chandler thinks he was trying to spell 'monkey'.

Generation X: George Clooney is better known for playing Batman in *Batman and Robin* (Joel Schumaker, 1997). Both he and Noah Wyle play doctors Ross and Carter in *ER*, Warner Bros' top-rated show. Dr Rosen claims that his wine is from the vineyards of Ernest and Tova Borgnine (Ernest Borgnine being the crumply-faced actor who appeared in, among many others, *The Dirty Dozen* (Robert Aldrich 1967).

The Story So Far: Rachel tells us that Monica's been living in that apartment for about six years. See also **Freaky Monica** above.

The Last Word: The main reason for this being a two-parter – the Ursula plot – is rather swiftly dealt with. This leaves more room for the 'very cute, cute, cute doctors' plot, which is classic *Friends*. Monica and Rachel's twisted character self-assassinations are brilliantly scripted, and impeccably delivered – especially that line about the boobies. Wyle and Clooney handle the comedy very well, with Clooney getting some great lines, reacting naturally to the madness that ensues. **Ahhh Rating:** **

French Title: 'Celui Qui Devient Papa' (the one who became a father)

German Title: 'Der Zweiteiler', Teil 2 (the two-parter, Part 2)

118
'The One With All The Poker'
#456662

Writers: Jeffrey Astrof & Mike Sikowitz
Director: James Burrows
First US transmission: 02.03.95
First UK transmission (C4): 25.08.95

Guest Cast: Beverly Garland (Aunt Iris)

Summary: The gang are helping Rachel out, stuffing endless envelopes with copies of her résumé – she is finally sick of being a waitress and decides that it's time to move on. Responses begin to pile in, but no one is interested in her. No one, that is, except Ross. As Chandler tries to talk to Ross about his feelings for Rachel, Joey arrives at Central Perk and they are consumed with laughter. It turns out that he broke into tears at their poker game of the previous night, when he confused a three with an eight.

The girls, mystified and offended by their all-male games, manage to persuade them to teach them poker. Things don't go smoothly, though. Rachel, Monica and Phoebe (who has particular difficulty with the ethics of 'bluffing') can't get the hang of the game – they're just too nice – and they lose badly. Tensions rise, as the girls realise that the boys take the game way too seriously, so Monica arranges for the girls to receive poker lessons from her Aunt Iris.

The next day, Rachel arrives at the poker game in a terrific mood. She's just had an interview for a job at Sach's and feels very confident she'll get the job. Her enthusiasm is dampened, though, when she and the other girls fare badly at their second poker game. By the time of their next game, Monica is more competitive than ever, while Rachel – who is still waiting to hear about her job – is even more playfully hostile towards Ross. The playfulness ends, though, when the phone rings and Rachel gets bad news – she didn't get the job. She's sent spinning into a black mood, and she and Ross raise the stakes and face off for the last time . . .

Freaky Monica: After Rachel has taken Ross down a peg (see **The Ballad of Ross & Rachel** below), Monica adds, 'We will play you again. And we will win. And you will lose. And you will beg. And we will laugh. And we will take every last dime you have. And you will hate yourselves for ever.' Which kind of stamps all over Rachel's lecturing Ross about his obsessive manly need to win.

Spoilt Rachel: Tired of being addressed as 'excuse me' by customers, Rachel compiles a CV, presumably for the first time ever. Reading from one of the copies, Ross notes how potential employers will no doubt be impressed with her excellent 'compu*pe*r' skills.

Phoebisms: She really can't get the hang of poker, seemingly more interested in how the eye of a Jack follows her around wherever she holds it (she eventually throws away two Jacks because they look unhappy). When Joey wins by bluffing, an affronted Phoebe points out that bluffing is merely another word for 'lying'. After hearing about Rachel's job interview at Saks, Pheebs comments, 'It's like the mother ship is calling you home.'

Slow Joey: . . . or not. During the Pictionary game over the closing credits, he is the one to guess *The Unbearable Lightness of Being* from Rachel's rather lame drawing of a bean.

Chandleresque: When Phoebe curses the money that Joey wins from her, Chandler offers to take the money instead. Bad things always come his way, he says, but 'this way I can break them up with a movie'.

The Ballad of Ross & Rachel: Ross's need to prove himself to Rachel as a man through playing tough poker is at once brilliant and painful. There are some terrific lines on Ross's part, but Rachel isn't falling for any of it: 'Oh, so typical. Ooh, I'm a man. Ooh, I have a penis. Ooh, I have to win money to exert my power over women.' The final face-off is great – despite the fact he admits he has lost, he doesn't show his hand. Was he just trying to put a smile back on her face after her disappointment over the job? The exchanges between them are excellently sparky. Even the normally wussy Ross shows that he is capable of both anger and genuinely touching compassion.

Just Plain Weird: Aunt Iris is a whirlwind of determination. Her methods to teach the girls bluffing are superb, telling them that 'everything you hear at a poker game is pure 'crap' before praising a momentarily delighted Phoebe on her choice of earrings.

Dinosaurs ROCK!: According to Chandler, Ross finishes with his latest date, Linda, because of a whole '*The Flintstones* could have really happened' issue.

Generation X: The gang whistle 'Colonel Bogey', the theme tune from *The Bridge on the River Kwai* (David Lean, 1957). Marcel's favourite record is 'The Lion Sleeps Tonight', originally sung by the Tokens in 1961, but popularised in the 1980s by Tight Fit. Chandler mentions Dee, Danielle Spencer's character from the seventies sitcom, *What's Happening?* Aunt Iris claims to have just killed the comedian Tony Randall (from the TV series *The Odd Couple*) in an example of good bluffing. And of course, there are the references in Pictionary to the musical *Bye, Bye Birdie* and the film *The Unbearable Lightness of Being* (Philip Kaufman, 1987).

The Story So Far: Becoming increasingly angry about losing, the gang remind Monica of an unfortunate, enraged plate-throwing incident during a previous Pictionary game.

The Last Word: A fantastic war of the sexes episode, with some brilliant friction between Ross and Rachel. This is the episode where the seeds for Ross's resolve are finally sown, as Chandler and Joey finally point out to him that he really should do something about his feelings for Rachel. The poker games that are the set pieces for the vast majority of the episode are blisteringly good – tense in the right places, but funny all the time. Monica's increasing frustration at being rubbish at poker is brilliant, and the pay-off of her tantrum at the closing Pictionary game is perfect. An all-round spiffing episode. **Ahhh rating:** **

French Title: 'Celui Qui Gagnait Au Poker' (the one who won at poker)

German Title: 'Die Pokerbräute' (the poker girlfriend)

119
'The One Where The Monkey Gets Away'
#456668

Writers: Jeffrey Astrof & Mike Sikowitz
Director: Peter Bonerz
First US transmission: 09.03.95
First UK transmission (C4): 01.09.95

Guest Cast: Mitchell Whitfield (Barry Farber),
Larry Hankin (Mr Heckles), Megan Cavanagh
(Luisa Gianetti – the Animal Control Woman),
Angela Visser (Samantha), Elisabeth Sjoli (Tina)

Summary: Rachel's mother callously sends her a magazine that contains an engagement notice for Barry (her ex-fiancé) and Mindy (her ex-maid of honour). Rachel finds this hard to take in, and tells Ross that she suspects she'd be coping better if she had someone of her own to accompany her to the wedding. This sets Ross's hopes at an all-time high. But while he pops out for some wine, Rachel manages to let Marcel escape and a search ensues. When Ross returns he's furious with Rachel, telling her that technically Marcel is an illegal immigrant and that if the authorities catch him he could be deported. Then the authorities turn up in response to Rachel's phone call about a lost monkey.

Ross eventually forgives Rachel and the pair settle down to make a start on the bottle of wine he bought. But just as Ross tries to ask Rachel out, Barry bursts into the apartment declaring his love for Rachel. 'We have *got* to start locking that door!' cries Ross . . .

Spoilt Rachel: Rachel successfully manages to remember all of the different types of tea Central Perk do, only to realise she's telling the wrong customer.

Phoebisms: When she hears that Marcel crapped in Monica's shoes, Pheebs asks which one, because, she claims, the left one is 'lucky'. When Phoebe blows the gaff to the Animal Control woman about Marcel, Monica warns her, 'You remember how we talked about saying things quietly to *yourself* first?'

Slow Joey: Joey claims he doesn't need violence in movies to enjoy them – just a little female nudity. When Joey spoils Chandler's chances with some incredibly hot babes, Chandler tells him that 'from now on, you don't get to talk to other people!'

The Ballad of Ross & Rachel: Still oblivious to Ross's feelings for her, Rachel asks him if he thinks it's possible to have a best friend who can also 'make your toes curl' with passion. Ross is about to tell her just why this is possible when the rest of the gang walk in, spoiling his chances. Despite Ross's optimism, Chandler is still doubtful, noting that if something were going to happen it would have happened by now. Ross declares his intention to 'woo' her, prompting Chandler to advise that maybe he should take her back to the 1890s, 'when that phrase was last used'. After Marcel has been safely returned to Ross, he offers Rachel some wine, asking if she's 'in the mood for, uh, something grape?' But of course Barry gets in the way of things going any further.

Just Plain Weird: Everyone's favourite spooky neighbour, Mr Heckles, claims to have left a Belgian waffle in the hallway because he 'wasn't ready for it'.

Monkey Business: Marcel pleases Ross by finally learning the difference between 'Bring me the rice' and 'Pee in the rice'. However he completely blows it by pooing in Monica's shoe. Heckles dresses him up in a pink frilly tutu.

Generation X: After the gang go to see a film, presumably *Four Weddings and a Funeral* (Mike Newell, 1994), Joey confuses its star, Hugh Grant, with the short, fat and bald Ed Asner, the star of 1980s TV series *Lou Grant*. Heckles claims to have seen the sports TV/radio host Regis Philbin.

The Story So Far: Barry and Mindy announce their engagement in the Country Club newsletter (see 'TOW The Sonogram At The End' and 'TOW Barry And Mindy's Wedding'). According to Rachel, Marcel is a capuchin monkey. Ross is forced to tell his friends that Marcel's an illegal immigrant. The woman from Animal Control, Luisa Gianetti, went to Lincoln High at the same time as Rachel and Monica. Rachel was the Homecoming Queen and the class president. Monica was fat (see 'TOW The Prom Video') and appeared in a production of *The Sound of Music*.

The Last Word: What a strange episode, switching from Ross's continued longing for Rachel to a quest to get to Marcel before a big fat woman with a dart gun! Rachel emerges as the star here, both in her genuine apologies to Ross and in the scene where she pleads with Luisa to do the honourable thing and leave Marcel alone and when this fails she blackmails her for shooting Phoebe in the arse. Despite all this, we'd just as soon have lost Marcel for good if it meant we got more of Mr Heckles – mad as biscuits! **Ahhh Rating:** **

French Title: 'Celui Qui A Perdu Son Singe' (the one who lost his monkey)

German Title: 'Affe auf der Flucht' (fleeing monkey)

120
'The One With The Evil Orthodontist'
#456669

Writer: Doty Abrams
Director: Peter Bonerz
First US transmission: 06.04.95
First UK transmission (C4): 08.09.95

Guest Cast: Mitchell Whitfield (Barry Farber),
Jennifer Grey (Mindy Hunter),
Christopher Miranda (Bobby), Lynn Clark (Danielle)

Summary: Chandler has had a wonderful date with a woman called Danielle, but she hasn't called him back yet. He wants to talk to her, but doesn't want to appear too keen. Eventually, he leaves a message on her answering machine, but still she doesn't ring back. He tries her one last time, and finally gets through – but she's in the middle of a call, so says she'll phone back. But she doesn't, because Chandler has left the phone turned off. Eventually, she comes down to Central Perk to see Chandler – but now he thinks *she* is too needy, so decides not to pursue it any more.

Barry Farber, the man Rachel left at the altar, is back in town, and wants to see Rachel. She finds herself having a great time with him – much to the annoyance of Ross – and the two of them end up having sex again. Mindy (Rachel's one-time maid of honour, and now Barry's bride-to-be) then turns up in the city, wanting to see Rachel. After Rachel has agreed to be Mindy's maid of honour, she tells Rachel that she thinks Barry is seeing someone in the city. Mindy says that he might be doing just what he did when he got engaged to Rachel – and she should know, because she was the one he was sleeping with! Feeling quite justified, Rachel admits that she is the one Barry is having sex with. Both equally disgusted by him, the two decide that they'll break up with him together. But Mindy can't go through with it and confesses that she still loves Barry no matter what.

Freaky Monica: At one point, Chandler rests his feet on a chair while he's using the phone. Monica gets him to lift them up, so that she can drape a tea towel under them to protect the chair.

Phoebisms: She helps Ross out with his crossword. The clue is 'heating device', so she suggests 'radiator'. But it's only five letters, so she amends it to 'rdatr'.

Slow Joey: Rachel tells Joey that Mindy taught her how to kiss at summer camp. Joey's interest is immediately piqued. He asks if Rachel and Mindy were wearing 'any kind of little uniform' during the kissing lesson. Later, he walks into Central Perk to see Rachel and Mindy sharing a supportive hug. 'Oh my,' he mutters to himself. Later still, when he sees Monica and Rachel hugging, he just comments, 'Big day!' It's patently obvious where this man travels in his fantasy life.

Chandleresque: Having spent the entire episode wondering if Danielle will call him, she turns up out of the blue at

Central Perk to check that he's all right. He watches her leave then asks his friends, 'How needy is *that*?'

Ugly Naked Guy: The gang find themselves being spied on by a neighbour with a telescope, which they find unsettling, unnerving and plain rude. As they stare out of the window at the peeping tom, Phoebe suddenly pipes up, having noticed that Ugly Naked Guy has bought gravity boots! Obviously a case of double standards, then.

Cruelty to Animals: From Monica's balcony, Phoebe spies a man kicking a pigeon.

Generation X: Jennifer Grey was Patrick Swayze's co-star in *Dirty Dancing* (Emile Ardolino, 1987). The peeper across from Monica's apartment tells Joey that she thinks Mon looks like the legendary actress Ingrid Bergman. When Chandler refers to 'The Real San Francisco Treat', he's quoting the buy-line from Rice-A-Roni, the easy-cook rice meal (fast-food junkies might also like to know there's a 'Noodle-Roni' alternative). The scene where the gang see someone watching them through a telescope spells out just how far the Ugly Naked Guy idea is inspired by Alfred Hitchcock's *Rear Window* (1954).

The Story So Far: Barry refers to his and Rachel's non-honeymoon in Aruba (see 'Pilot', 'TOW The Sonogram At The End') and Rachel reminds her friends that this was seven months ago.

The Last Word: Chandler's phone-side vigil has to be the stand-out event in this episode. The point where he leaps from one end of the sofa to the other because he thought he heard it ring is brilliant, perfect Chandler. Rachel gets her chance to be strong again, showing how far she's come since leaving Barry: it's just a shame Mindy couldn't do the same. **Ahhh Rating:** *

French Title: 'Celui Qui A Un Dentiste Carié' (the one who has an evil dentist)

German Title: 'Wüstling in Weiß' (lecher in white)

121
'The One With The Fake Monica'
#4566671

Writers: Adam Chase & Ira Ungerleider
Director: Gail Mancuso
First US transmission: 27.04.95
First UK transmission (C4): 15.09.95

Guest Cast: Claudia Shears (Fake Monica),
Harry Shearer (Dr Baldharar),
Karla Tamburrelli (Dance Teacher),
Marta Kauffman, David Crane and Kevin S. Bright
(the casting directors – uncredited)

Summary: Discovering fraudulent payments on her credit-card bill, Monica surprises her friends by not being upset about the loss of money, but by the fact that the bogus Monica is evidently having a better time being Monica than she is. Her jealousy prompts her to root out the fake Monica and challenge her. However, the fake Monica is just too likeable and encourages the real Monica to realise just how much fun she can have by living each day as it comes – until the fake Monica is arrested!

The friends are increasingly disgusted with Marcel's habit of trying to hump everything in sight. Unfortunately, the vet tells Ross that this isn't just a phase he's going through – he's reached sexual maturity and as time goes on he's likely to become aggressive and violent. After searching for a new home for Marcel, Ross finally gives him over to the San Diego Zoo and bids his simian buddy goodbye at the airport . . .

Freaky Monica: As if discovering that someone is using your credit card number weren't enough, Monica has to come to terms with their indulging in 'reckless spending' at her expense. Oh, except for the Wonder Mop, which she actually bought herself. When she's left without a dance partner,

Monica complains, 'Great, it's gym class all over again!' In an attempt to assert her new-found personality, Monica declares that she's not just the person who needs to fluff the pillows and pay the bills straight away: 'When I'm with [the fake Monica] I am so much more than that. I'm – I'm Monana!' When Monica finally confesses to the fake Monica that she's not even Amish, she asks with genuine surprise: 'Really? Then why are you like that?'

Spoilt Rachel: As Monica looks at the life the fake Monica is having she asks, 'Let's compare, shall we?' to which Rachel responds wearily: 'Oh it's so late for "*Shall we . . .*"' The fact that Rachel picks up the dance teacher's steps so quickly might lead one to suspect she's had lessons (according to the Warner Bros press releases, dance was her minor at university). Just watch how Rachel cleans up, by lifting up the magazines, barely wiping the surface underneath, then plonking the magazines back down. She's obviously never polished a table in her entire life.

Phoebisms: Typically 'out-there' reaction to Monica's obsession with the woman who stole her credit card: 'This is madness. It's madness I tell you. For the *love of God, Monica, don't do it!*' followed by a theatrical curtsey and a 'Thank you!' Marvellous!

Chandleresque: After Ross explains Marcel's behaviour as being just a phase, Chandler warns that they said that about Joey. Chandler's suggestions for Joey's new name are the highlight of the episode, with ideas ranging from the silly Joey Pepponi to the more neutral Joey Switzerland, taking advantage of Joey's ignorance (Joey – or Joseph – Stalin) and just taking the piss (Holden McGroin). When Joey asks Ross how he'd go about getting a monkey into a zoo, a distracted Chandler pipes up, 'I know that one! – no, that's popes in a Volkswagen.' (For anyone wondering, the joke he half remembered goes, 'How do you get six popes into a Volkswagen? Take their hats off')

Just Plain Weird: Dr Baldharar from the 'interactive wildlife experience' tries to persuade Ross to let him look after

Marcel, when he's patently trying to gain another victim for his animal gladiator arena.

Joey's an Actor!: When Chandler suggests 'Joseph Stalin' for his new stage name, Joey is later horrified to discover that there already is a Joseph Stalin who was 'this Russian dictator who slaughtered all these people!' God knows what he'll do when he realises the problems inherent in calling himself 'Holden McGroin'. Thankfully, Phoebe's on hand to give him a serious suggestion: 'Flame Boy!'

Generation X: The guys sit in Central Perk in the pose of the Three Wise Monkeys who depicted the edict 'See no evil, hear no evil, speak no evil'. Rachel has a (not so) Curious George doll. Curious George was a monkey created for a series of children's books by Margret and Hans Augusto Rey and first appeared in 1941. The fake Monica suggests that she and Monica audition for Andrew Lloyd Webber's musical *Cats* by singing 'Memories', the touching and highly emotional song made famous by Elaine Page. Harry Shearer voices numerous characters, including Mr Burns, in *The Simpsons* and appeared in the spoof documentary *This Is Spinal Tap* (Rob Reiner, 1983). The musical *Fiddler on the Roof* was written by Joseph Stein, inspired by the plays of Arnold Perl. It tells the story of a poor Russian family at the turn of the century. *Dead Poet's Society* (Peter Weir, 1989) was the tale of a teacher, played by Robin Williams, who inspired a class of unruly pupils and changed their lives. It is much better than the Fake Monica suggests (honest!). *Mrs Doubtfire* (Chris Columbus, 1996) is another film starring Robin Williams. *Bye Bye, Birdie* (written by Michael Stewart, music by Charles Strouse, lyrics by Lee Adams) is a musical about a 1950s rock star, drafted into the army and cajoled into making one final appearance on *The Ed Sullivan Show*. Probably its most famous number is the upbeat 'Put on a Happy Face'. In Joey's audition scene, the shadowy figures the hopefuls perform for are Marta Kauffman, David Crane and Kevin S. Bright, the show's creators.

The Last Word: This is certainly an episode to divide fans. One of us counts this among his favourite episodes of all time, the other hates it. What is notable here is the fact that up until now we've always seen Matthew Perry as the real comic genius and this episode is no exception. Even in the final scene, we as an audience attribute the laughs to Chandler, who isn't even present in the scene, rather than Matt Le Blanc's delivery, which is a tad unfair. Joey's ignorance is played up to the hilt here and Le Blanc has never been so good up to now. And the delivery of the name 'Holden McGroin' is simply priceless. Definitely one of the most memorable scenes of the entire series. **Ahhh Rating:** Inspirational – ****

French Title: 'Celui Qui Avait Un Singe' (the one who had a monkey)

German Title: 'Die Zweite Monica' (the second monica)

122
'The One With The Ick Factor'
#4566670

Writer: Alexa Junge
Director: Robby Benson
First US transmission: 04.05.95
First UK transmission (C4): 22.09.95

Guest Cast: Stan Kirsch (Ethan),
Brian Buckner (Office Worker No. 2),
Darryl Sivad (Office Worker No. 3)

Summary: Monica's got a new boyfriend, Ethan, and he's very young. But it isn't until after they have sex that she realises exactly how young he is – he's seventeen, which means there's a nine-year difference (not to mention the fact that it makes the sex illegal over most of the United States). Unfortunately, Ethan is crazy about Monica, and Monica thinks she could feel the same way too. What is a girl to do?

Phoebe, who's foolishly lost a lot of clients by teaching a 'Massage Yourself At Home' workshop, is filling in for Chandler's secretary while she has a breast reduction operation. Phoebe finds out from her new co-workers that Chandler is no longer the popular guy now he's the boss. In fact, no one likes him any more, and they even make fun of the way he speaks behind his back.

Ross has a beeper, so he can be called the second Carol starts to go into labour. But his number (55-JIMBO) keeps being rung by people who are after someone called André, whose number turns out to be 55-JUMBO. André appears to be a male escort, seeking male customers, and Ross and Carol eventually have to agree that she'll punch in '911' (which is the US equivalent of the UK's 999) as a message to ensure Ross knows it's her.

Freaky Monica: If she already feels like she's about to go over the hill, her relationship with Ethan can't help. When she realises just how young he is, she concludes, 'I'm Joan Collins!' Ethan, mystified, asks, 'Who?'

Phoebisms: Her turn as Chandler's secretary is wonderful, especially as she has no real work to do. Her phone voice is cool and collected – about as far away from the real Phoebe as you can imagine. When Chandler ushers her out of his office so he can get on with his work, seconds later she buzzes him on the intercom to ask, like a bored child, 'Whatcha doin'?' She seems very concerned not to let her new colleagues know that she's a friend of Chandler, suggesting that they don't go to a work party together. While she seems comfortable with siding against Chandler, it obviously seriously gets on his nerves. Her insensitivity to this, as a person who so wholly believes in honesty, is brilliant: when Chandler asks who exactly doesn't like him, she says, 'Everyone. Except for, er . . . No, everyone.' This episode also features a marvellously Phoebe moment: she stands up from a chair to leave and immediately feels dizzy, saying, 'Woah! Head-rush!' She then sits down and says, 'One more, and then I have to go.'

Slow Joey: Looking for a new job, Phoebe finds an ad in the paper and asks, 'Can you see me operating a drill press?' Joey's warped little imagination needs a bit of prompting: 'I don't know. What are you wearing?'

Chandleresque: Chandler discovers that everyone at work enjoys doing impersonations of the way he speaks. When he asks Ross and Joey whether it's that noticeable, they laugh and do their own impressions: 'Could that report *be* any later?' Chandler insists, 'That is so *not* true,' before realising, much to his frustration, that it is.

The Ballad of Ross & Rachel: Throughout this episode, Rachel admits to having erotic dreams, first about Chandler and then about Chandler and Joey. Ross, of course, is terrifically jealous. Right at the end of the episode, Ross is watching television at Monica's, and Rachel is asleep on the sofa next to him. As he gets up to go, he drapes a blanket over her and she starts to moan in her dreams. Immediately, he is disgruntled, but he cheers up when he hears her groan, 'Oh, Ross . . .' He leaps on to the coffee table and does a little dance of triumph, before tripping on the fruit bowl and crashing on to the sofa, waking Rachel. She just stares up at him, confused, and for a second it looks like they just might . . . But then his beeper goes off – and this time, it's for real. This is a brilliant moment, and the first inkling that Rachel could possibly find Ross attractive.

Dinosaurs ROCK!: When the gang discover Ross has a pager, they wonder what someone in his line of work would need it for. '. . . Dinosaur emergencies? Come quick! They're still extinct!'

Generation X: Ross illustrates Chandler's speech patterns by quoting *The Sound of Music*. Monica compares herself to Joan Collins, based presumably on the role she played in *Dynasty* and not on her real-life affairs (avoiding litigation here, leave us alone!). The guys mock Monica by pretending to be *Mighty Morphin Power Rangers*. Chandler apparently sang 'Ebony and Ivory', the old Stevie Wonder/Paul McCartney classic, at a karaoke.

The Story So Far: Monica is 26 by this episode (or 'twenty-five and thirteen months' as she tells Ethan).

The Last Word: A fun little episode, let down slightly by the unconvincing nature of the Ethan plotline. Are we really to believe that Monica could think that someone who behaves (and looks) so young could be as old as he says? Nevertheless, the 55-JUMBO scenes and Chandler's realisation that he really is a boss more than make up for it. **Ahhh Rating:** ***

French Title: 'Celui Qui Rêve Par Procuration' (the one who dreams by proxy)

German Title: 'Junge Triebe' (Jungian desire)

123
'The One With The Birth'
#456672

Writers: David Crane & Marta Kauffman (story), Jeff
Greenstein & Jeff Strauss (teleplay)
Director: James Burrows
First US transmission: 11.05.95
First UK transmission (C4): 29.09.95

Guest Cast: Jonathan Silverman (Dr Franzblau),
Jane Sibbett (Carol Willick), Jessica Hecht (Susan Bunch),
Leah Remini (Lydia), June Gable (Nurse),
Carlo Imperato (Roy), Jackie Bright (Janitor)

Summary: As Carol prepares to give birth, Ross and Susan find that they still can't stand each other. In an attempt to keep Carol calm, Phoebe drags the quarrelsome two into a store cupboard, pointing out that their negativity is not what new-born babies need to be greeted with. Unfortunately, Phoebe then discovers that somehow the door to the store cupboard has locked, trapping them inside.

In the waiting room, Monica becomes broody while Chandler offers his support. Rachel meets a cute doctor and

Joey meets a young, single mother-to-be and stays around to help her through the birth (shame she's a Celtics fan, though). The trapped trio manage to escape and rush to Carol's side just as she begins to give birth. Thanks to a name tag on an overall they found in the storeroom, Ross and Susan finally agree on a name for 'their' son – Ben.

Poor Ross: Ross complains that Carol never threw him out of a room before Susan came along, and Susan rubs it in: 'There's a lot of things Carol never did before I came along!' As he tries to break down the door to the store cupboard, Ross steps in a steel bucket, falls over and delivers the lamest 'Ow' ever. He unwittingly comes up with the ultimate liberal bumper sticker: 'Every day is Lesbian Lover Day!'

Freaky Monica: Monica's persecution complex extends as far as wondering why a woman can have twins when she can't even get a man to help her have just one baby. She even rounds on Chandler when he kindly offers to marry her if, hypothetically, they're both single by the time they're forty: 'OK, hypothetically ... *why* won't I be married when I'm forty?'

Spoilt Rachel: Rachel tries to chat up Carol's obstetrician without much success – she even goes home to *change*! She also drinks the ice chips that were meant for Carol.

Phoebisms: Phoebe brings a guitar to a birth in case 'things get musical'. When they're trapped inside the store cupboard, she composes an inappropriate song that goes, 'They found their bodies the very next day ...' Then she notices Ross and Susan glaring at her.

Slow Joey: As he supports Lydia in her hour of need, Joey is horrified when she 'explodes' and has to be told that it was just her water breaking: 'What's that? Water ... breaking?' It's not surprising that Chandler is spooked by Joey's new-found knowledge of the birthing process when it's Carol's turn.

Chandleresque: As Ross worries that Carol might give birth in a cab, Rachel makes a (quite frankly, hilarious) joke about it costing only two dollars for the first contraction and fifty cents for each additional. When everyone glares at her and she asks why it's OK when Chandler does it, he teaches her a valuable lesson in timing. Rachel can't believe one of them actually has a child: 'I know, I still *am* one of these,' admits Chandler.

Generation X: Jonathan Silverman starred in *Weekend at Bernie's* (Ted Kotcheff, 1989), and appeared in quite a few film adaptations of Neil Simon plays, including *Brighton Beach Memoirs* (Gene Saks, 1986) and *Broadway Bound* (Paul Bogart, 1991).

The Story So Far: Joey is a Knicks fan and at this point is 25 years old. Rachel's father is a doctor, leading Chandler to jump to an oedipal conclusion as to why medical men hold such a primal fascination for Rachel. Susan's first girlfriend was called Jamie, which is why she doesn't want that particular name for 'their' first child.

The Last Word: A story about both the fear of becoming a parent and the fear of maybe never getting the chance to; Ross finally sees his son (and after the whole 'Jessie, Cody, Dylan' fiasco they choose a really nice name for him so that's cool), while Monica's broodiness and closeness to Chandler foreshadow certain episodes from future episodes (see 'TOW The Jam', 'TO At The Beach', 'TOW Ross's Wedding', Part 2'). We defy anyone to watch the end-credits sequence (where Ross tries to explain to his newborn son that he might not be around all the time) without getting a lump in their throat.
Ahhh Rating: ***

French Title: 'Celui Qui a Failli Rater L'accouchementon' (the one who nearly missed the birth)

German Title: 'Wehe, Wenn Die Wehe Kommt!' (watch out for the labour pains)

124
'The One Where Rachel Finds Out'
#456673

Writer: Chris Brown
Director: Kevin Bright
First US transmission: 18.05.95
First UK transmission (C4): 06.10.95

Guest Cast: Tommy Blaise (Carl),
Corinne Bohrer (Melanie, Joey's Girlfriend),
Kerrie Klark (Flight Representative),
and introducing Lauren Tom (Julie)

Summary: Joey's been helping out with a science project at the NYU Med School by donating his sperm in exchange for $700. The only catch is he mustn't undertake any 'personal experiments' for the duration of the project, a bit of a drag considering his new girlfriend, Melanie, is gagging to sleep with him. Monica suggests that he could 'be there for her', a concept Joey finds difficult to grasp – until he sees the rewards this approach reaps.

Ross, meanwhile, has problems of his own. He is once again mulling over his unrequited love for Rachel. During preparations for her birthday barbecue, he talks over his feelings with the guys. Having finally accepted that maybe Rachel will never want him, Ross prepares to leave for a trip to China – it's a 'big bone' thing for the museum. While Ross is en route to the airport, Rachel unwraps her presents and is stunned to discover that Ross has bought her a cameo brooch that she'd once pointed out to him. Overwhelmed, she wonders what provoked such a generous and thoughtful act. Chandler's overactive mouth once again blunders in, reminding Monica of the time Ross was in love with Carol and bought her an expensive crystal duck. Rachel pauses, while Chandler desperately tries to back-pedal. But it's too late – Ross's feelings are out and life can never be the same.

Rachel tries to dismiss this revelation from her mind, but on a date with a boring guy, her mind wanders to thoughts of Ross. Leaving her date behind, she rushes to greet Ross at the airport – unaware that he's brought back a surprise from China . . .

Phoebisms: Weirdness once again rules over propriety. Asked by Ross to show his son Ben a photo of his father every day, Phoebe takes the picture, holds it over her own face and intones in a deep voice, 'Hi, Ben. I'm your father. I am . . . the head! Ahhh!' Chandler's mute-button comment suddenly seems very apposite. And only Phoebe could encourage Joey's work with the fertility study by noting he'll be making money 'hand over fist' and *not* realise what she's said.

Slow Joey: Once again we can only wonder what kind of strange and tortured childhood created the beast we call Joey. Giving Rachel a children's book for her birthday, he explains with undue gravitas, 'That book got me through some tough times.' And you know he means it.

Chandleresque: Who'd have thought a reminiscence about a crystal duck could be so shocking? But of course it's not the 'crystal duck' part that alerts Rachel to Ross's feelings for her and saying 'flah . . . flennin'' won't get Chandler out of a very embarrassing situation. When the obviously smitten Melanie notes how there's a 'little man' inside of Joey, Chandler notes, 'Yes, and the doctors say if they remove it he'll die.' Phoebe's ranting on about the Rachel/Ross situation and how Chandler insensitively blew the gaff provokes Chandler to retort, 'OK, is there a mute button on this woman?' hinting that maybe sometimes Phoebe is more tolerated than actually liked.

The Ballad of Ross & Rachel: Love, when it comes down to it, is about two people and not their friends. As Ross says in the wonderful daydream sequence, what's stopping Rachel going out with him? 'Because it might get weird for everyone else? Who cares about them? This is about us.' Thankfully, Rachel finally gets the message . . .

Dinosaurs ROCK!: His trip to China may be in search of a discovery of amazing significance to the dinosaur world, but if even Ross can reduce it to just a 'big bone thing', then it's no wonder no one else is interested.

Generation X: Joey's gift to Rachel is a book by Dr Seuss. Dr Theodor Seuss Geisel was hailed a pioneer against illiteracy thanks to his children's books, which include the classics *The Cat In The Hat* and *Green Eggs and Ham*. Melanie's company name (the Three Basketeers) is of course inspired by Alexander Dumas's *The Three Musketeers*. As Rachel reaches the airport in search of Ross we hear Madonna's 'Take a Bow'.

The Story So Far: When asked if Ross has shown any interest in her before, a dazed Rachel reminds us of events in the first episode when he broached the subject of the two of them going on a date. And it turns out that Chandler attended the same college as Ross and Carol (where, presumably, the unhappy couple met).

The Last Word: Again, while this episode is ostensibly about Ross and Rachel, it's the peripheral characters that make it what it is. Chandler in particular seems to have more than his fair share of quotable lines, and Joey is showing signs of evolving into the star player he'll become in subsequent seasons. But if ever we doubted just how romantic a person Ross actually is, this is the episode that confirms it, when we finally know that Ross and Rachel *must* get together, making the episode's denouement even more heartbreaking. As we watch Ross seduce Rachel (in what turns out to be a dream sequence) we all know this is a good thing – it just feels *right*. So Rachel races to the airport, not knowing what awaits her just around the corner, and *Friends* fans across the world drown out the end credits with their sniffles and sobs. For many of us, this is the episode where we stopped simply watching the show and realised we'd become fans. One of the defining moments of the series. **Ahhh Rating:** *****

French Title: 'Celui Qui Fait Craquer Rachel' (the one that Rachel fell for)

German Title: 'Die Liebesspender' (the love-giver)

Second Season

1995–1996
24 Episodes

201
'The One With Ross's New Girlfriend'
#457301

Writers: Jeffrey Astrof & Mike Sikowitz
Director: Michael Lembeck
First US transmission: 21.09.95
First UK transmission (C4): 28.06.96

Guest Cast: Cosimo Fusco (Paolo), Lauren Tom (Julie),
Buck Kartalian (Frankie the Tailor)

Summary: Rachel waits at the airport to meet Ross . . . and Julie! Later, at Monica's apartment, a panicked and breathless Rachel bursts in as Monica, Phoebe, Chandler and Joey discuss haircuts. As they try to find out what is bothering Rachel, Ross arrives, introduces Julie and everything becomes clear. After the dust has settled, Monica tries to persuade Phoebe to give her a new look. Although Phoebe initially refuses (citing Monica's obsessiveness as her reason), she eventually caves in and agrees to give Monica a haircut just like Demi Moore's. But Phoebe confuses 'Demi' for 'Dudley', and Monica is distraught.

Chandler has sartorial problems when Joey recommends a tailor to him. Frankie has been making suits for the Tribbiani family for decades, but Joey had never realised that his tailor is 'a very bad man'. It seems that Frankie, while taking

Chandler's measurements, interfered with more than just Chandler's stitching.

Freaky Monica: When she asks Phoebe if she'll cut her hair, Phoebe refuses, claiming to be 'incredibly anal, and an unbelievable control freak'. When a confused Monica disagrees, Phoebe replies, 'I know *I'm* not, but you *are*, and I was trying to spare your feelings.'

Phoebisms: 'You know what I'm thinking?' Monica asks, as a prelude to pestering Phoebe to cut her hair. 'Oh, OK,' chirps Phoebe, excited at the idea of this new game. She sits and thinks for a second, then answers with growing certainty, 'How . . . it's been so long since you had sex, you're wondering if they've changed it?' (Remember that: it's a brilliant way to annoy your friends if they ask the same question.) And, of course, there's her brilliant speech to Monica's hair prior to its being cut: 'Now, some of you are going to get cut, and some of you aren't. But I promise none of you are going to feel a thing.'

Slow Joey: He has a really hard time trying to remember when Frankie made him his first suit. 'I was fifteen,' he says. 'No, wait, sixteen. No, 'scuse me, fifteen.' Finally, he requests some clarification: 'All right – when was 1990?' (at which point, Chandler advises him to 'stop the Q-tip when there's resistance'). Later, when he is trying to console Rachel, he lets slip that he can 'sense when women are depressed and vulnerable. It's one of my gifts.'

Chandleresque: Chandler feels responsible for Rachel's anguish over Ross and Julie – after all, it was he who told Rachel that Ross loved her. When Ross tells him that 'there was always this little voice inside that kept saying "It's never going to happen, move on",' Chandler winces and suggests that it was God's voice, not his (or at the very least, 'maybe it was God doing me'). When he lies to Rachel that the silver lining is that Ross 'made the decision [to give up on her] all by himself without any outside help whatsoever', Rachel asks how that is a silver lining. Chandler, wincing again, says that, 'You have to *really* want to see it.'

The Ballad of Ross & Rachel: After a season where we had Ross pining after Rachel, the tables are suddenly turned. We're left with Rachel missing something she never really had, and never realised she wanted. Her initial reaction to Ross's return arm in arm with Julie is magnificently acted by Aniston, as are her breathless attempts to tell the rest of the gang about it while Ross and Julie are only a few steps behind her on the stairs. (Chandler's reaction to her insensible gibberish – 'Airport. Airport. Ross, not alone. Julie. Arm around her' – as if it was something from *Skippy* or *Lassie* is brilliant: 'OK, I think she's trying to tell us something. Quick, get the verbs!')

It's painful to see how Ross has come to terms with the fact that he should move on from Rachel, and is now enjoying being with Julie. Rachel's discontent with this is hilariously apparent, especially when Ross is on the phone with Julie and neither of them wants to hang up first: 'No, you hang up. You, you, y–' To rightful cheers from the audience, Rachel does it for him.

Whatever happened in China, it's obvious that Ross still cares deeply about Rachel; his reaction to her little indiscretion with Paolo is proof of that. 'I hate him,' he tells her. 'I physically hate him.' But still it's not enough and, just as Rachel is about to tell him how she feels, he begins to tell her how happy he is to be with Julie. While, in the first season, Ross just patiently listened as Rachel would talk about one date after another, Rachel resolves to be a bitch to Julie, making sure she gets a different haircut from Phoebe than she asked for – Roddy, rather than Andie, M(a)cDowell.

Generation X: Chandler compares Phoebe to the celebrated hair stylist, Vidal Sassoon. As Phoebe reminds us, Dudley Moore appeared in the film *10* (Blake Edwards, 1979), amongst many others, whereas Demi Moore, as Monica is at pains to point out, starred in *Disclosure* (Barry Levinson, 1994), *Indecent Proposal* (Adrian Lyne, 1993) and *Ghost* (Jerry Zucker, 1990). Chandler also mocks Monica's new haircut in his comments about being 'caught between the moon and New York City' – this is from 'Arthur's Theme (Best That You Can Do)', which was, funnily enough, the theme to Dudley Moore's film *Arthur*. Monica notes woefully that even a haircut like Mary Tyler Moore's would have been tolerable. Andie MacDowell *is* the girl from *Four Weddings and a Funeral* (Mike Newell, 1994), while Roddy McDowell is, of course, from the *Planet of the Apes* movies. For those that don't know, cotton buds are known as Q-Tips in the States.

The Story So Far: Phoebe gives us a brief recap of the previous episode. There are plenty of references to past events in this episode, particularly those concerning Ross and Rachel (and Paolo, who, we are reminded, once tried to seduce Phoebe – see 'TOW The Dozen Lasagnes'). Ross and Julie, it is revealed, went to grad school together.

The Last Word: 'It's like there's rock bottom, then fifty feet of crap, then me.' An assured start to the second series, which, surprisingly, manages to not sideline anyone, despite the fact that it focuses on the relationship between Ross and Rachel. While Rachel struggles with her disappointment and her surprise that she should feel that way at all, we see the other friends slip into their normal roles. Phoebe and Joey seem a little more ditzy and stupid than before, but if that's the price to pay for the haircut jokes and the retroactive terror over years of sexual abuse from a tailor then so be it. **Ahhh Rating:** ****

(This episode and 'The One With The Breast Milk' were originally shown by Channel 4 in the UK as a double bill.)

French Title: 'Celui Qui A Une Nouvelle Fiancée' (the one who's got a new girlfriend)

German Title: 'Das Mitbringsel' (souvenir)

202
'The One With The Breast Milk'
#457302

Writers: Adam Chase & Ira Ungerleider
Director: Michael Lembeck
First US transmission: 28.09.95
First UK transmission (C4): 28.06.96

Guest Cast: Joel Beeson (Hombre Guy),
Jane Sibbett (Carol Willick), Jessica Hecht (Susan Bunch),
Lauren Tom (Julie), Emily Proctor (Annabel),
Richard Lyons (Man), Stan Sellers (Manager),
Lou Wills (Customer)

Summary: Carol and Susan are visiting Monica's with Ben, when the baby gets hungry. No worry, though: Carol just whips out a breast and starts to feed him. Chandler and Joey are instantly uncomfortable with this, but not as much as Ross is when he sees Phoebe test the temperature of some bottled breast milk a little later. She puts a few drops on to the skin of her arm, and then licks it clean off. The rest of the episode is spent with Ross trying to gather the strength to try Carol's milk for himself. After all, Susan's tried it.

Joey's latest job as a cologne sample guy at Saks is giving him problems. A mysterious cowboy has appeared at the edge of his territory, offering passers-by a new fragrance called Hombre. Soon, he feels that he is being seriously threatened by this cowboy, especially when he is transferred to Hombre duty himself. It seems the only thing left is for him and the cowboy to settle their score the old-fashioned way: using perfume bottles, not pistols, at dawn.

Julie asks Monica to come shopping at Bloomingdales with her. Although it feels like betraying Rachel, she goes along, only to feel incredibly guilt-ridden. But these feelings are as nothing compared with Rachel's wrath when she finds out that her best friend has 'cheated' on her.

Poor Ross: Seeing Phoebe drink the breast milk freaks him out, and Carol wonders why. 'Because it's gross!' he squeals. 'My breast milk is gross?' asks Carol. Susan sits back in the sofa, smiling, and says, 'This should be fun.' The final sequence of Ross sitting at a table gathering strength to try the milk is brilliant. After a long preparation period, he swipes the bottle up and sucks a huge mouthful, swallows it, and then stuffs his face with a pile of cookies – the look on his face is 'hmm, not too bad', but all he can taste are Oreos.

Spoilt Rachel: Her attempts to get on with Julie are fantastic. She makes no secret of the fact that she doesn't like Julie. Julie is nothing but nice to Rachel, and genuinely wants to be her friend. Two-faced, Rachel says that'd be great but, after Julie's gone, she leans back and mutters to herself, 'Manipulative bitch.'

Phoebisms: Phoebe has to excuse herself at one point, saying, 'I have to take my grandmother to the vet.' No explanation is offered and we just have to accept that Phoebe is beyond comprehension.

Slow Joey: When Joey is grossed out by breast feeding, Ross tells him that it's the most natural and beautiful thing in the world. Joey says, 'I know, but there's a baby sucking on it!' When he is asking questions about breast feeding, he wonders, 'If he blows into one, does the other one get bigger?' It's perfectly clear, then, where his interest with breasts lies.

The Last Word: All credit to Aniston and Cox: the confrontation between Rachel and Monica when Monica admits that she has been shopping with Julie is bizarre, being played out as if the two of them were lovers, and Monica had cheated on Rachel with someone else. The scripting is impeccable, and the performances flawless. Quite simply, once seen, it's unforgettable. **Ahhh Rating: ****

(This episode and 'The One With Ross's New Girlfriend' were originally shown by Channel 4 as a double bill.)

French Title: 'Celui Qui Détestait Le Lait Maternel' (the one who hated breast milk)

German Title: 'Harte Drinks und Coole Cowboys' (strong drinks and cool cowboys)

203
'The One Where Heckles Dies'
#457303

Writers: Michael Curtis & Gregory S. Malins
Director: Kevin Bright
First US transmission: 05.10.95
First UK transmission (C4): 05.07.96

Guest Cast: Maggie Wheeler (Janice),
Larry Hankin (Mr Heckles), Danny Dayton (Buddy Boyle),
and introducing Michael G. Hagerty
(Mr Treager – credited as Mr Treeger)

Summary: Mr Heckles, the man who lives below the girls' apartment, complains once again that the girls are making too much noise. When he returns to his own apartment he begins to bang on his ceiling with a broom. In retaliation, the girls stomp on the floor until he gives in. Later, though, they discover that Heckles has died, seemingly in the middle of their thumping match. The next day, Heckles's attorney arrives to tell Monica and Rachel that he's left his entire worldly belongings to 'the noisy girls upstairs'. Although they're initially excited, they discover that Heckles had no money, and has left them an apartment full of garbage and tack in an act of final revenge.

Rachel decides to keep his hideous shell lamp as a memento, against her roommate's wishes. When Monica accidentally breaks it, Rachel jumps to the conclusion that she did it out of spite, that Monica still thinks of the apartment as hers alone, and that Rachel just rents a room from her.

Chandler breaks up with another girlfriend because he feels her nostrils are too big. The girls feel that his selection process is a little extreme, rejecting girls for really insignificant things – though they allow him some slack over Janice. But after reading Heckles's old yearbook, he discovers that, like himself, Heckles had been the class clown at college, and Chandler begins to worry he might end up alone. In desperation he phones Janice, only to find she's not only married, but heavily pregnant.

. . . And Ross tries to enlighten Phoebe on the theory of evolution, a fairytale she's just not willing to accept.

Freaky Monica: Yes, it is a horrible lamp, but Monica really hounds Rachel for bringing it into her home. 'Y'know what we haven't played in a while? "Hide the Lamp".' The little war with Rachel over the lamp, and the 'ownership' of their apartment, is great. It makes perfect sense that she would be unwilling to let go of her dominion over her home, despite the fact that she has been sharing it for over a year.

Spoilt Rachel: To be fair, apart from her asking about whether there's any money in Heckles's will, Rachel's not at all spoilt in this one. But it's fun to see her getting one over on Monica by insisting that they keep the lamp. When Monica claims she's allergic to shellfish, Rachel tells her, 'Well, you'll just have to eat the other lamps.' But Monica was right: it *is* a hideous thing to have in one's apartment.

Slow Joey: Joey's revelation in support of Chandler's habit of dumping women for insignificant reasons shows him to be even more naïve than we thought. He tells the gang that when he first moved to Manhattan, he dated a girl with an enormous Adam's apple. Ross feels compelled to tell him that women don't have Adam's apples but fortunately for Joey he claims he was only joking to spare him from an unpleasant realisation. Oh, and watch out for the way he tries to understand Chandler's problem with women who say 'supposably!': 'Did they go to the zoo? *Supposably!*' When a visibly pregnant Janice turns up at Central Perk, Joey turns to Chandler and says: 'Jeez, look how fat she got!'

Chandleresque: Chandler gets the lion's share of great lines this episode. He has a wonderfully pathetic list of reasons, dotted throughout the episode, for dumping various women. Even after promising to be less selective, Chandler can't help himself – on his date with Alison he tries to think of five things he likes about her: 'Nice smile, good dresser . . . *big head big head big head!*' When he discovers Heckles's similar list of women he's dumped for the lamest of reasons, he begins to fear that he will end up like the weird neighbour. In fact, Chandler has already worked out exactly what kind of weird neighbour he's going to be – Crazy Man with a Snake! 'I'll get more snakes, call them my babies; kids won't walk past my place, they will run. "Run away from Crazy Snake Man!" they'll shout.' Perry's increasingly terrified and manic performance throughout this speech is a wonder to behold.

Just Plain Weird: The man this category was made for, Mr Heckles, complains that the girls' 'stomping' is disturbing his birds. When Rachel points out that he doesn't have any, he says defensively, 'I could have birds.' He then rejoins his imaginary dinner party. We later see his indexed list of women he once dated with comments like 'too tall', 'big gums' and 'makes noise when she eats'.

Dinosaurs ROCK!: Ross tries to prove his argument about evolution by using Heckles's finger puppets to illustrate 'opposable thumbs' (which Phoebe suggests might be because the 'Overlords' needed them to steer their space craft), and by pointing out that all across the world they've found fossils that prove that evolution is a scientific fact, to which Phoebe asks, 'Who put those fossils there, and why?' Eventually their bickering flares up into a full-scale war of attrition – 'Scary Scientist Man' versus ethereal Earth Mother. The way in which Ross is completely unwilling to let his friend keep to her own beliefs (which he believes are totally wrong, of course) is very telling of his own obsessive faith in science. Phoebe, in seemingly angry retaliation, tries to persuade Ross to see that 'there's a teeny, tiny possibility [he] could be wrong' – citing the fact that scientists once believed that 'the atom was the smallest thing, until [they] split it open, and this whole mess of crap came out', and that one time the smartest men in the world believed Earth to be flat. Faced with his own 'unbelievable arrogance', Ross can do nothing but admit that, yes, he might be wrong. An appalled Phoebe just gasps, 'I can't believe you caved,' as a demoralised Ross gathers up his 'briefcase of facts' and leaves. Thank goodness for his sake that he didn't pursue her lack of faith in gravity!

Generation X: Phoebe believes Heckles's spirit is still around and prompts him to 'go into the light' in a brief nod to *Poltergeist* (Tobe Hooper, 1982). Yanni is a Greek pianist-composer who claims his goal is to 'connect with people emotionally'. We think Chandler's hatred of him is entirely justified.

The Story So Far: Chandler was voted 'class clown' and played clarinet in high school (and so did Mr Heckles). The gang play poker at one point (see 'TOW All The Poker). Although the credits always list Treager's name as 'Treeger' we have a very good reason for disagreeing with them – see 'TOW Chandler Crosses The Line'.

The Last Word: Laughing through the pain, we realise that this is one of those shows that make us face up to the reality of an unknown future. Chandler's (and our own) fears come from not knowing if there's a pattern in life, in contrast with Ross and Phoebe's argument, which is basically a conflict of certainties – Ross taking comfort in his belief in scientific facts, Phoebe enjoying her opinion that 'facts' are just elements to be played with, allowing her to imagine many alternative (and generally ludicrous) possibilities. While most of us would side with Ross at the beginning, we soon come to realise that Phoebe's theories are much more fun. **Ahhh Rating** ('Goodbye Mr Heckles . . . we'll try to keep it down'): ****

French Title: 'Celui Qui Est Mort Dans L'Appartement Du Dessous' (the one who died in the apartment downstairs)

German Title: 'Torschlußpanik' (fear of being left on the shelf)

204
'The One With Phoebe's Husband'
#457305

Writer: Alexa Junge
Director: Gail Mancuso
First US transmission: 12.10.95
First UK transmission (C4): 12.07.96

Guest Cast: Lauren Tom (Julie), Steve Zahn (Duncan), Janice Davies (Woman on Bench)

Summary: A man calls at Monica's claiming to be Phoebe's husband! It turns out that Phoebe married Duncan, a gay Canadian friend of hers, so that he could get a Green Card to work as an ice skater in the USA. While the others are simply shocked, Monica is appalled: Phoebe was always secretly in love with Duncan. Now, to complicate things, Duncan wants a divorce. After years of denial, he has realised that he's actually straight and he wants to divorce Phoebe so that he can get married to a woman that he has fallen for.

Ross confides to Rachel that he and Julie have not yet had sex. Rachel is immediately delighted at the news, and tries everything possible to make sure it never happens. Her advice to Ross to put it off even longer almost works, but after Joey tells Ross that he should just get right down to it, Rachel has to watch as Ross moves even further out of her grasp.

Phoebisms: The scene where Duncan tells Pheebs he's straight is very well observed, played as an exact reversal of a gay man 'coming out' – for example Phoebe's summation of the situation: 'You're married to someone for six years, you think you know him, and then, one day, he says, "Oh, I'm not gay".' Her nervous behaviour around Duncan is brilliant, and Kudrow plays the unrequited love of her character very well – check out the way she laughs, embarrassed, at her own 'Olé!' joke.

Chandleresque: The secret's out – Chandler's got a third nipple! When asked if it does anything special, he claims, in a voice dripping with sarcasm, that it 'opens the delivery entrance to the magical land of Narnia'.

Joey's an Actor?: The secret's out – Joey was in a porno movie! Joey explains that he was going to be one of the, shall we say, participants in the movie, but he lost his nerve at the last minute. Instead, he played the photocopier repair man who walks in when a couple are having sex on the copier. His only line in the film is, 'You know, that's bad for the paper tray.' Joey claims that Chandler told him his extra nipple was just a 'nubbin'. When the gang wonder why he believed him, he says, 'I don't know. You see something, you hear a word – I thought that's what it was.'

The Ballad of Ross & Rachel: Telling Ross that women think 'there is *nothing* sexier than a man who does not want to have sex' is unspeakably cruel of Rachel, but brilliantly funny. Her triumphant sashay as she walks away from the conversation, casually throwing a tea towel over her shoulder, makes you want to cheer, despite the fact she's just done something totally evil. When Monica confronts her with the fact that she's just going to have to get over it, Rachel bitingly replies, 'Oh, I'm going to have to get over it. I didn't know *that's* what I had to do!' The sequence outside Ross's apartment, where Rachel describes exactly how she'd like a man to take her the first time they had sex, is very seductive, striking an astonishingly erotic balance between seediness and romance. Once Rachel has finished her steamy descriptions, we all feel like Ross: blown away, and incredibly horny.

Generation X: Chandler mentions Narnia, the magical kingdom from *The Lion, The Witch and The Wardrobe* and six other books by C.S. Lewis. Ross performs a version of the classic dance sequence from *Singin' In The Rain* (Stanley Donen/Gene Kelly, 1952).

The Story So Far: In an episode full of revelations and indiscretions, Phoebe blabs that there's an item of Monica's underwear on the telephone pole below her apartment which somehow got stuck there after she had sex with Fun Bobby (see 'TOW The Monkey' and 'TOW Russ'). Chandler is revealed to have three nipples (see 'TOW Phoebe's Ex-Partner'). Julie is only the second woman Ross has slept with. Ross and Julie have been dating for about two months.

The Last Word: The way Duncan comes out about being straight is innovative, with Phoebe aghast, claiming that he always threw such great Oscar parties, him reassuring Phoebe that his parents already have one straight son, so they were OK about it. But good as it is, it'll never stick in the memory as well as some other things in this episode. Like a Machiavellian Rachel trying to ensure Ross and Julie don't sleep with each other; or the revelation of Chandler's nubbin; or the closing sequence of Ross skipping down the street, as an old woman observes, 'Someone got theirs last night.' 'Twice,' confirms Ross proudly. **Ahhh Rating:** ***

French Title: 'Celui Qui Avait Viré De Bord' (the one who became a turncoat)

German Title: 'Enthüllungen' (revelations)

205
'The One With Five Steaks And An Eggplant'
#457304

Writer: Chris Brown
Director: Ellen Gittelsohn
First US transmission: 19.10.95
First UK transmission (C4): 19.07.96

Guest Cast: Brittney Powell (Jade),
Chris Young (Steven Fisher), Spencer Cherashore (Waiter)

Summary: The fact that Joey, Phoebe and Rachel make less money than Chandler, Monica and Ross threatens to make Ross's birthday a troublesome time for the less well-off members of the gang, and this is compounded by Monica's sudden promotion to chief chef and head of purchasing. When they tell their friends how they feel, it instigates a huge row, and while Chandler, Monica and Ross enjoy a live concert by Hootie and the Blowfish, the two other girls are forced to spend the evening guessing how many fingers Joey is holding up behind his back.

Chandler begins screening his calls through his answerphone and manages to intercept a call from Jade, a beautiful, drunken and naked girl who thinks she's calling Bob, the previous occupant of Chandler's apartment. Chandler pretends to be Bob, arranges a date with Jade, in the hope that when Bob doesn't turn up, he'll be able to sweep her off her feet as the caring and sensitive man on the next table. Chandler's plan goes perfectly and he ends up sleeping with Jade. Unfortunately, when Jade phones and Chandler pretends to be Bob again, she moans to him about the way he stood her up and that she found herself with a man who wasn't very good in bed, much to Chandler's disappointment.

The meat suppliers at Monica's restaurant give her a thank-you gift of an eggplant (aubergine) and some steaks but when her boss hears about it he tells her that she's contravened corporate policy and that he has to fire her.

Spoilt Rachel: When Ross apologises for never thinking of money as an issue, Rachel rightly points out, 'That's because you have it!'

Slow Joey: Joey complains that the wealthier members of the gang are 'always saying "let's go here, let's go there". Like we can afford to go "here" and "there".' When Monica tells them she wants to celebrate her promotion, Joey asks Phoebe, 'How much d'you think I can get for my kidney?'

Chandleresque: Ross calls Chandler 'pure evil'. Chandler visibly weighs up pure evil in his left hand and 'horny and alone' in his right, offering the excuse that he's tried 'horny and alone' already. At the restaurant, the waiter asks Chandler if there'll be anything else, so Chandler asks for a verse of 'Killing Me Softly', then sees the waiter's tired facial expression and says, 'You're gonna sneeze in my fish, aren't you?' (These two lines, if used in conjunction, will always give you a good indication as to the quality of service you can expect in any restaurant.)

Generation X: Jade lies in her first phone message to Bob when she says that her legs appear on the new Bond movie posters (*Goldeneye*'s posters didn't have that kind of design). The guys watch dwarf wrestling on WWF (the World Wrestling Federation). Chandler refers to 'Killing Me Softly With His Song', the 1973 hit for Roberta Flack that was recently covered by the Fugees. Chandler explains to Ross that he's given Jade Ross's telephone number so that she doesn't work out that he's been posing as Bob, which prompts Ross to ask, 'What do I do when Mr Roper Calls?' in reference to the type of confusing situation that might occur in the sitcom *Three's Company*. We hear the Hootie and the Blowfish song 'I Go Blind'.

The Story So Far: Obviously, this is set on and around the date of Ross's birthday (see 'TOW Joey's New Girlfriend'). Chandler has been living in his apartment for less than three years (Jade's phone message reveals that Bob lived there three years ago). At the concert, Monica bumps into Stevie Fisher, whom she used to babysit when he was a kid.

The Last Word: We asked our American friends if they would ever spend $310 on a friend's birthday (which, split five ways, is $62), and they said, 'Are you crazy?', which pretty much sums up Joey, Rachel and Phoebe's point. It's not even as if it were his 25th or 30th, just another birthday. This episode paints itself into a corner on this issue, but as the sacking of Monica distracts the friends from their problem the issue's never really resolved satisfactorily. It's supposed to be a balanced argument but it does end up looking just a little one-sided. **Ahhh rating:** **

French Title: 'Celui Qui Se Faisait Passer Pour Bob' (the one who pretends to be Bob)

German Title: 'Falsch verbunden' (wrong number)

Chandler's appearance in *Caroline In The City*

First US transmission: 02.11.95
First UK transmission: 26.07.96
Writers: Fred Barron & Marco Pennette
Director: James Burrows

Shown on NBC in the slot immediately before *Friends*, *Caroline In The City* centres around the daily lives of a cartoonist (Caroline), her assistant, her boyfriend and her man-mad best friend, Annie. In the episode 'Caroline And The Folks', we see Annie looking around a video store when 'Chandler' (played by Matthew Perry) sidles up to her with a copy of *The Piano* in an attempt to impress her with his sensitivity and complete lack of interest in 'gratuitous nudity in film'. However, when he spies the copy of *Sorority House Massacre II* that Annie's holding, he realises he could have just approached her as himself. Annie suggests, 'So be yourself.' Chandler smiles, fidgets a little, then walks straight out of the store in a panic!

206
'The One With The Baby On The Bus'
#457306

Writer: Betsy Borns
Director: Gail Mancuso
First US transmission: 02.11.95
First UK transmission (C4): 26.07.96

Guest Cast: Max Wright (Terry),
Victor Raider-Wexler (Doctor),
Chrissie Hynde (the New Singer), Catherine Bell (Robin),
Hugh Dane (Jim), Jennifer Sommerfield (Becky),
Giovanni Ribisi (The 'Condom Boy' – uncredited)

Summary: When Ross takes a mouthful of what he thinks is Key Lime Pie, his tongue begins to swell. Monica explains that it's *Kiwi* Lime Pie, forgetting that one of Ross's many allergies is to kiwi fruit, and she and Ross must rush to the hospital so he can get a jab. But who's going to look after Ben? The only available candidates are Joey and Chandler and, worryingly unsuitable as they are, this is an emergency, after all. Deciding to take Ben out with them, the guys meet two women on a bus. When the women say that they're about to get off, Joey and Chandler suggest they all go for a coffee. But on the pavement, Joey and Chandler suddenly realise they've left (oh, you guessed it) the baby on the bus.

While Chandler and Joey race around New York trying to find Ben, Rachel has her own problems at Central Perk. Her boss, Terry, has asked her to break the news to Phoebe that she has been replaced as the café's musician-in-residence by a professional singer, Stephanie Schiffer, with real talent. Even though Terry is prepared to let Phoebe play as well, he is unwilling to pay her the same rate as Stephanie, and so Phoebe storms out and sets up shop as a busker on the street outside.

Freaky Monica: Ben bursts into tears whenever Monica holds him, so she begins to worry: 'What if my own baby hates me?' Somewhat less than helpfully, Chandler tells she's going to have to wait a long time before she has to worry about that – 'You haven't even got a boyfriend,' he reminds her. There's a short pause, in which Monica stares at Chandler, her face like thunder. Chandler quickly reacts to a comment that, curiously, no one else heard: 'Joey, she does not look fat!'

Spoilt Rachel: She's still obviously not got the hang of that 'responsible attitude' thing. When she's trying to bargain with Terry to keep Phoebe on, she tells him that she'll 'even clean the cappuccino machine'. This shocks her boss, so Rachel quickly back-pedals and explains that she means that she'll '*cleeeean* it'.

Phoebisms: There's a slew of songs, including the first celebrity duet of 'Smelly Cat'. Phoebe sings her latest composition to Rachel: a song that reveals that 'tegrin' spelt backward is 'nirget'. Later, when she's busking, she insists in a song that 'I don't need your charity', but chirps a friendly thanks to someone who gives her some money. Then we hear her sing of the strange 'double-double-double-jointed boy'. After all this, we begin to understand Terry's summation of her talent: 'It's not that your friend is bad,' he tells Rachel. 'It's that she's *so* bad, she makes me want to put my finger through my eye, into my brain, and swirl it around.'

Slow Joey: Ross worries that Joey doesn't have much experience of looking after children but he explains that, with his seven Catholic sisters, he's perfectly used to caring for kids. When Ross's tongue swells in reaction to the kiwi, only Joey understands him. He explains that his Uncle Sal has 'a really big tongue'. 'Is he the one with the beautiful wife?' asks Chandler.

Chandleresque: Chandler gets to deliver one of the simplest, and one of the very best, lines of the whole series. Finding that there are two babies at the lost-property office, Joey and Chandler decide to toss a coin to decide which they will choose. But which baby is heads, and which is tails? Well, one has ducks on his shirt and the other has clowns. Since ducks have heads, Joey suggests, heads on the coin should be for the baby with the ducks. 'What kind of scary-ass clowns did you have at your parties?' a frightened Chandler asks. When chasing after the bus that Ben is riding, Joey calls the baby's name. An exasperated Chandler says, 'Maybe he'll hear you, and pull the cord!'

Boys Will Be Boys: Joey sees the baby-sitting gig as simply a chance to pick up women, claiming that 'women love babies'. Of course this backfires first of all when the first woman they meet assumes Joey and Chandler are a gay couple with an adopted child. This leads Chandler to suggest that, the next

ime they want to find women, they should just 'go to the park
nd make out'.

Generation X: Chrissie Hynde was the lead singer of the
ock group the Pretenders. Her set contains a cover of P.P.
Arnold's 1968 single 'Angel of the Morning', recently
ampled by the Fugees for their single 'Rumble In The
Jungle'.

The Story So Far: Ross is allergic to lobster, peanuts and
kiwi (!) and is scared of needles. He once jammed a pencil in
Monica's hand and jammed a broom into the spokes of her
bike. She once hit him in the face with a pumpkin. Joey now
claims to have 'seven Catholic sisters' (see 'TOW Mrs Bing'
and 'TOW Chandler Can't Remember Which Sister'). Joey
says he has an Uncle Sal who has a big tongue. Rachel's boss
Terry (Max Wright) also appears in 'TOW Underdog Gets
Away'. Giovanni Ribisi (series regular, Frank Jr – see 'TOW
The Bullies') makes his first appearance, uncredited, in this
episode as the boy who fishes out the condom from Phoebe's
guitar case. For continuity, we're presuming that this is Frank
Buffay Jr.

The Last Word: One of the best episodes of the series
without a doubt, focusing on the brilliant Perry and Le Blanc
double act. This is more than enough to shoulder the caval-
cade of laughs in this episode. Simply the sight of them
weighed down with all the brightly coloured baby gear is
enough to raise a smile (as is Chandler questioning whether
Joey remembered to 'pack the baby's anvil'). The two actors
have such perfect synergy that the episode just breezes by,
ending long before you want it to. **Ahhh Rating:** **

French Title: 'Celui Qui A Oublié Un Bébé Dans Le Bus'
(the one who loses a baby on the bus)

German Title: 'Baby – Allein in New York' (baby – alone in
New York)

207
'The One Where Ross Finds Out'
#457307

Writer: Michael Borkow
Director: Peter Bonerz
First US transmission: 09.11.95
First UK transmission (C4): 02.08.96

Guest Cast: Lauren Tom (Julie),
Arye Gross (Michael),
Barry Diamond (Phone Guy),
Marcus D. Jacques (Waiter)

Summary: Phoebe convinces Chandler that he's putting on weight, so he agrees to start an exercise regime with Monica – who, after all, has nothing better to do with her time at the moment. Her relentless energy, though, soon begins to grind him down and, before long, he's had enough of their tiring keep-fit. Rachel, meanwhile, is trying to move on from Ross. She goes on a date with a guy called Michael, but proceeds to make a disaster out of it all. Ross and Julie had earlier announced that they were going to get a cat together, which is as good a sign of long-term commitment as any. All Rachel can talk about on the date with Michael is Ross, and Julie, and the cat. As the evening wears on, she gets more and more drunk and depressed about Ross. Michael, a divorcee who's been through a similar thing, suggests that all she needs is closure. Borrowing someone's mobile phone, Rachel leaves a message on Ross's answering machine, saying she's happy that things have worked out for him, and telling him, 'I am over you. And that, my friend, is what they call closure.'

The next day, a hung-over and faintly amnesiac Rachel lets Ross use her phone to check his messages. She, of course, has forgotten all about the message she left – and it isn't until Ross starts listening to it that she remembers what she said . . .

Chandleresque: During one of their exercise sessions, Monica challenges Chandler to do five sit-ups – if he does, she will flash her breasts at him. He manages only two and a half – 'Just show me one of them,' he says. Resenting this invasion of his private life, Chandler complains that Monica's got him doing butt clenches at work 'and now, they won't bring me my mail any more'. At the end of the episode, Chandler has finally had enough of the exercising, so he cleverly compliments Monica on her boundless positive energy, especially considering she has no job, no boyfriend, and she lives in constant fear of disappointing her parents. Deflated, Monica sinks to the sofa, drained of all her energy. As she falls asleep, a gleeful Chandler skips into his own bedroom to do the same. Although this is unspeakably cruel, it's also one of the funniest parts of this episode.

The Ballad of Ross & Rachel: Rachel insists that she's over Ross, and no longer concerned that he's with Julie. When she sees Ross kissing Julie, she claims not to mind that he's passionately pushing her on to the window of Central Perk: 'For all I care, he can throw her through the damn thing.' But, of course, she's not over him, despite her insistence – in the answerphone message – that she is. When Ross hears this, he (and the audience) lapse into a stunned silence. 'Over me?' he stammers. 'When were you under me?' The two try to talk it through, but Ross is too shocked to cope – and Julie's waiting downstairs so that they can go and collect their cat. The most nail-biting moment comes when Ross tries once more to get clarification: 'And now you're over me?' he asks. 'Are you over me?' Rachel says. Neither answers the other's question, and it's left until the end of the episode – featuring that beautifully passionate first kiss – before it's resolved.

Boys Will Be Boys: Throughout this episode, Phoebe is seeing a guy called Scott, who seems nervous of getting physical with her. Although she likes him a lot, she wonders how much longer she's going to have to wait. Finally, he explains that he is worried that sex will complicate things between them, so Phoebe tells him that it's OK and he needn't feel obliged to her just because they'd slept together. Hearing this, Joey points out that Scott got Phoebe to sleep with him and to agree that she would happily never hear from him again, and convinced her that this was 'a good thing'. 'This man is my god,' he says.

Generation X: Arye Gross (Michael) played Adam in the first few seasons of the sitcom *Ellen*. Michael mentions the film *Diner* (Barry Levinson, 1982), claiming he's spent much of the date with Rachel running it through his head. As Chandler prances away from the sleeping Monica we hear an excerpt from 'The Dance of the Hours' by Ponchielli from *La Gioconda*. (a.k.a. 'Hello Mother, Hello Father') .

The Story So Far: Monica once had a cat called Fluffy Meowington. Ross discovers that Chandler blabbed to Rachel about his feelings for her (see 'TOW Rachel Finds Out') and mentions Paolo and Barry.

The Last Word: So it took over a year, but finally Ross and Rachel tickle tonsils! That scene in Central Perk, where he comes to chastise Rachel for complicating his life, is brilliant, no matter how many times you watch it. Although it looks for a second as if nothing will happen – Ross storms off after telling Rachel that he's happy with Julie – Ross, of course, returns, and the pair of them kiss at last. Keep the tissues handy – this is Aniston's finest half-hour. **Ahhh Rating:** ****

French Title: 'Celui Qui Tombe Des Nues' (the one who's flabbergasted)

German Title: 'Geständnis einer Liebenden' (confession of a lover)

208
'The One With The List'
#457308

Writers: Marta Kauffman & David Crane
Director: Mary Kay Place
First US transmission: 16.11.95
First UK transmission (C4): 09.08.96

Guest Cast: Lauren Tom (Julie),
Michael McKean (Mr Ratsetter)

Summary: Despite having wanted Rachel for the last ten years, Ross realises he can't just ditch Julie, because he still loves her. He turns to the guys for help and Chandler suggests they compile a list of the plus and minus points of each girl. He completes the bad list first, but Ross doesn't even need to complete a list of Rachel's good points, because she's always been the girl for him. But then Rachel sees the list of things Ross claims not to have liked about her. Can it really be over before it's begun?

Picky Monica: When Ratsetter, the Mockolate promoter, asks her if she still wants to work with him she says, with a hint of desperation, 'I have no morals and I need the cash.'

Phoebisms: She sings a not quite fictional song called 'Two Of Them Kissed Last Night'. Phoebe takes exception to Chandler's use of the phrase 'karma crap' and says, 'Good luck in your next life as a dung beetle.' After tasting one of Monica's Mockolate concoctions, Phoebe spits, 'Oh sweet Lord! This is what evil must taste like!'

Slow Joey: Joey asks Monica if she's willing to cook naked. When she asks incredulously if there's an ad for a naked chef, he confesses, 'No, but if you're willing to cook naked, then you might be willing to dance naked, and then . . .'

Chandleresque: Chandler is typically unsympathetic with Ross's predicament: 'This must be so hard. "Oh no, two women love me, they're both gorgeous and sexy, my wallet's too small for my fifties and my diamond shoes are too tight".'

The Ballad of Ross & Rachel: Rachel worries that Ross will pick Julie: 'She's gonna be all "Hi, I'm Julie, Ross picked me and we're gonna get married, have lots of kids and dig up stuff together."' Meanwhile Ross's list describes Rachel as being 'too into her looks' and 'a little ditzy'. Despite all this, his main point for Julie is 'she's not Rachel'. Later, Rachel sums up just how hurt she is by Ross's selection process: 'Imagine the worst things you think about yourself. Now, how would you feel if the one person that you trusted the most in the world not only thinks them too, but actually uses them as reasons not to be with you?' Ross tries to get her to see his point of view, saying that there's nothing she could put in a list that would stop him wanting to be with her, but Rachel believes that must be the difference between him and her: 'See, I'd never make a list.'

Just Plain Weird: Mr Ratsetter, creator of Mockolate, a synthetic chocolate. His FDA approval is refused due to 'something about laboratory rats'. His next project is 'fish-tachios', pistachios with reconstituted fish bits. Mmmm, nice!

Boys Will Be Boys: While Rachel is telling the girls about how passionate and intense the kiss was, the guys simply ask Ross one question: 'Tongue?'

Generation X: Chandler asks the guys if they want a game of Doom, the ultra-violent first-person shoot-'em-up computer game that spawned its own genre. The people on the computer helpline that Chandler calls are watching an episode of *Star Trek* in which Spock and his father hug (this *never* happened, by the way, so they are lying). Michael McKean appeared in, and wrote the music for, the spoof documentary *This Is Spinal Tap* (Rob Reiner, 1984). The song that Ross requests the radio station to play is U2's song from 1987, 'With or Without You'.

The Story So Far: Ross reminds us that he's loved Rachel from afar for ten years. Monica says she's allergic to cat hair.

The Last Word: 'That is funny. That is painfully funny. No, wait. Wait, yeah, that's just painful.' Ross and Rachel finally get together, but it lasts for mere seconds thanks to the damaging effect of the eponymous list. It's nice that the writers can still surprise us: when Ross gets the radio station to play U2's emotive ballad, we're all certain this will be enough to melt Rachel's heart and encourage her to forgive

him, so it's great when she tells the DJ what it was he did and
he takes her side. **Ahhh Rating:** ****

French Title: 'Celui Qui A Été Très Maladroit' (the one
who's clumsy)

German Title: 'Die Liste des Grauens' (the list of horror)

209
'The One With Phoebe's Dad'
#457309

Writers: Jeffrey Astrof & Mike Sikowitz
Director: Kevin S. Bright
First US transmission: 14.12.95
First UK transmission (C4): 16.08.96

Guest Cast: Audra Lindley (Frances),
Michael G. Hagerty (Mr Treager, the superintendent),
James Michael Tyler (Gunther)

Summary: Christmas is growing near, and the friends
discuss the ethics of tipping. Monica and Rachel, strapped
for cash, have been giving home-made cookies to everyone,
but they don't seem to be appreciated. The paper delivery
boy has mashed them into the sports section of their paper,
while the postman has shattered a parcel of ornaments from
Monica's mother. Later, the gang are gathered at Central
Perk, where Ross shows them all the presents he has been
buying for people. One of them is a picture frame, containing a sample picture of a model. Phoebe sees it and, excited,
claims that it's her birth father. Monica breaks the news to
her that that's unlikely, so Phoebe confronts her grandmother to find out the truth. As lie after lie about her father
is shattered, Phoebe's grandmother reveals that not only
does she know who he is, but she also knows where he lives.
Enlisting the support of Chandler and Joey, she sets out to
find him. But, when she gets there, she finds she is too

frightened by the prospect of finally meeting her real dad and chickens out.

Monica and Rachel prepare for their Christmas party, but disaster strikes when Ross breaks the knob on their radiator and their apartment begins to get unbearably hot. They call Mr Treager, but he claims that he can't do anything about it until after the weekend. Ross, suspecting that Treager was also less than impressed by Monica's cookies, sees a way of impressing Rachel by 'seizing the day' (something Rachel had told him he never did – see **The Ballad of Ross & Rachel**) and offering to 'tip' him $100 to fix it. But, once again, Ross makes a fool of himself: Treager was telling the truth and, to top it all, he loved the cookies – 'They were so personal, really showed you cared.'

Poor Ross: After he tried so hard to impress Rachel, 'seizing the day' by offering Treager money to fix the radiator, we really feel Ross's embarrassment when he realises that he's making a fool of himself. We can't help smiling at Rachel's smug closing comment, though: 'Nice seizing, gel boy.'

Phoebisms: 'A plate of brownies once told me a limerick . . .' she reveals. When asked if they were 'funny' brownies, a wonderfully blasé Phoebe comments, 'Not especially.'

Slow Joey: 'So I'm trying to get my boss's ex-wife to sleep with me,' Joey tells the gang, just after Phoebe's illusions of her father have been shattered. When the others just gasp at his lack of tact, he retorts, 'Oh, but when Phoebe has a problem, everyone's all ears.' Later, when Phoebe has resolved not to meet her father, a desperate Joey asks, 'Do you think it would be all right if I went in and used his bathroom?' Luckily, the plans for relieving himself change when he looks out of the car's window. 'Cool! Snow! Kinda like a blank canvas.'

Chandleresque: As Christmas looms, Monica is appalled at Chandler and Joey's lack of planning. She squeals, 'You guys haven't gotten your presents yet? Tomorrow's Christmas Eve. What're you gonna do?' Chandler, amazed, asks, 'Don't you have to be Claymation to say stuff like that?' Later, when he returns from the trip to find Phoebe's father, he strides into Monica's sweltering apartment and blurts a wonderfully twisted Christmas greeting. 'Ho! Ho! Ho – holy crap, is it hot in here!'

The Ballad of Ross & Rachel: The list of the pros and cons of seeing Rachel comes up again, as Ross tries to patch things up with her using an impromptu gift of a Slinky. (You remember them – those springs that used to, well, slink downstairs.) Ross suggests that Rachel make a list of her own about him, to try to make her feel better. With clearly apparent relish, she does so: 'You're whiny, you're obsessive, you're insecure, you're gutless . . . you don't just sort of seize the day, you know . . . and you wear too much of that gel in your hair.' This – not unreasonable – précis of his character sends Ross sliding into a bout of extreme paranoia; he spends most of the time at Monica and Rachel's party telling guests that he uses only as much gel as the bottle suggests.

Families – Who Needs 'Em?: We see Phoebe's grandmother updating the phone book, crossing out all the names she finds in the newspaper's obituaries. Chandler reminds us of his father's cross-dressing, recalling a time when he used to dress up in a red suit, with big black boots, and stumble around their house in a drunken state. When Rachel – thinking that Mr Bing was dressing as Santa – comments that it sounds like Christmas in his household must have been pretty horrible, Chandler just says, 'Who said anything about Christmas?'

Ugly Naked Guy: Phoebe spies on him as he puts up his Christmas decorations. 'Oh my God!' she gasps. 'You should see the size of his Christmas balls.' Unsurprisingly, no one rushes to see.

Just Plain Weird: Mr Treager fails to notice the sweltering heat in Monica's apartment. 'My body always stays cool,' he tells them. 'Probably because I have so much skin.' Later, he corners Rachel under what looks like mistletoe. She lies, and tells him it's basil. 'If it was mistletoe,' he says, 'I was gonna kiss you.' Rachel firmly asserts that 'it's still basil'. Phoebe's grandmother gives her a picture of her real father – Einstein!

Boys Will Be Boys: Chandler and Joey end up buying presents from a 24-hour garage. They buy Rachel some windscreen wiper blades and an air freshener that guarantees a 'new-car smell' (despite the fact she hasn't got a car). Phoebe is, bizarrely, grateful for her packet of toilet-seat covers. Ross is given brand-less cola and lemon-and-lime drinks. ('This is too much,' he stutters. 'I feel like I should get you another sweater.') Monica is handed a mysteriously small packet, about which Joey comments, 'They're ribbed, for your pleasure.' Ross and Monica swap presents.

Yo Gunther!: Gunther is finally listed on the end credits for the first time! When Ross's Slinky is turned down by Rachel, he turns to Gunther. When he finds out that Gunther has stairs in his apartment, he hands him the spring and tells him to 'go nuts!'

The Story So Far: We're reminded of Phoebe's tortured family history. Phoebe's father is not a tree surgeon in Burma as she's always believed, but a pharmacist whose last known address is 74 Laurel Drive in Middletown. When he left Phoebe's mother, she couldn't bear having to break the news to her daughters so she just lied to spare them the pain. Phoebe's grandmother still describes him as the 'irresponsible creep who knocked up your mom and stole her Gremlin'.

The Last Word: Sadly, for what should have been quite an emotional storyline, the parts of this episode dealing with Phoebe's father don't quite have the impact they should. The exception, of course, is the scene where she realises that she's not quite ready to face the possible disappointment of her father not living up to her expectations. The accompanying storyline of the party, and Ross's oafish attempts to impress Rachel, are funnier and stick in the memory more. **Ahhh Rating:** ***

French Title: 'Celui Qui Cassait Les Radiateurs' (the one who broke the radiators)

German Title: 'Heiße Weihnacht' (hot Xmas)

210
'The One With Russ'
#457311

Writer: Ira Ungerleider
Director: Tommy Schlamme
First US transmission: 04.01.96
First UK transmission (C4): 23.08.96

Guest Cast: Vincent Vintresca (Fun Bobby),
Snaro (Russ), Scott Stewart (Waiter),
and introducing June Gable
(Estelle Leonard, Joey's agent)

Summary: Rachel's moving on. Or so she says. She announces to everyone that she's got a date with a new guy, to help her get over Ross after the list incident. When he arrives at Central Perk, though, she seems to be the only one to not see what everyone else does. Her date, Russ, bears a striking similarity to a certain palaeontologist they're all familiar with. While everyone else is more than a little freaked out by the similarity, she just carries on as if there were nothing unusual about him. Ross himself also fails to see that he's practically looking into a mirror; he is more concerned with playing little, jealous games of one-upmanship.

Monica, meanwhile, has her own boyfriend problems. She's back together with Fun Bobby, and is only now beginning to realise exactly why he's so much fun. Bobby seems to have a drink problem, so she persuades him to go on the wagon. When he does, though, all the fun drains out of him and he becomes the most boring person on Earth. The only way Monica can cope with going out with him is by getting completely drunk!

Freaky Monica: When the gang decide to celebrate Joey's success in getting the *Days Of Our Lives* audition, Rachel tells them that she's already made plans. An incredulous Monica cries in horror, 'You have other friends?'

Spoilt Rachel: As she's handed a cup of coffee, Monica asks if it's made with nonfat milk. Rachel says she isn't sure and that Monica should try it to find out: she does, and it isn't. Monica offers it back to Rachel, but she explains that she can't take it back as she's already had some. Now that's service.

The Ballad of Ross & Rachel: Of course, it's clear to everyone (even Rachel, in the end) that she's still hung up on Ross. The scenes of Russ and Ross meeting, but completely failing to recognise their similarity, are great. When Ross the palaeontologist discovers that Russ is a periodontist, Monica, trying to look on the bright side, comments that 'they're as different as night and . . . later that night.' Rachel's grossed-out 'ew, ew' when she finally realises that she's dating a Ross-alike is a brilliant overreaction.

Joey's an Actor?: The gang rush to the nearest newsstand to read the reviews of Joey's latest play. Chandler begins, and reads out a review that is quite damning of his performance. Pointing out that it's only one opinion, he asks anyone else to read their review. Phoebe obliges, and begins to read exactly the same one. Ross sheepishly refuses to read his, and just as Joey's about to give up on his dream of being an actor, Monica pipes up that hers says that 'Joey Tribbiani reaches brilliant new levels of . . .' She tails off, as she leafs through the paper to find the continuation of the review. ' . . .Sucking!' she completes. Things begin to take a turn for the better, though, when Joey gets an audition for *Days Of Our Lives* – a part he can get if he sleeps with the casting director. When he goes to the call-back, he refuses to sleep with her – until the stakes are upped and he manages to secure the regular role of Dr Drake Ramoray, neurosurgeon. Joey refers to 'the Little General' – his name for . . . well, you can probably guess. Chandler is sure he used to call it 'the Little Major', and Joey explains that he had to promote it after his time with Denise De Marco.

Just Plain Weird: Finally we meet Estelle Leonard, Joey's agent. This wonderful creation is one of the best recurring characters in the show, ranking right up there with Heckles for out-and-out strangeness. When Joey tells her that he's got a call-back for the *Days Of Our Lives* job, she asks him, 'Have you ever seen me ecstatic?' She then breaks into a horrific grin – like a chain-smoking snarling gerbil. She also has the creakiest little 'Uh-huuuh' when she's speaking on the phone. More please!

Dinosaurs ROCK!: Chandler uses a mug that only Ross could have bought. It is emblazoned with the legend 'I got boned at the Museum of Natural History.'

Generation X: Despite being fairly obvious, the actor who plays Russ, credited as Snaro, is in fact David Schwimmer under not-very-heavy make-up. Phoebe refers to Lorne Greene, veteran (now deceased) star of *Battlestar Galactica* and *Bonanza*.

The Story So Far: We first met 'Fun Bobby' in 'TOW The Monkey'. June Gable (Estelle Leonard) previously appeared in 'TOW The Birth' as a nurse.

The Last Word: A nice little episode, with much to recommend it. Schwimmer's turn as Russ is entertaining, and the difficult sequences of both Ross and Russ having conversations are pulled off very well indeed. Their childish bickerings are great, made all the better by neither of them noticing his similarity to the other. The only criticism that can be levelled at this episode is the way the cop-out ending to the Julie plotline left us feeling somewhat cheated. It would have been better for her to fade into obscurity, rather than be dragged back and have her unconvincingly fall for Russ.
Ahhh Rating: **

French Title: 'Celui Qui Se Dédouble' (the one with his double)

German Title: 'Vorsicht, Sucht!' (attention, addiction)

Days Of Our Lives

Days of our Lives is actually a real daytime soap opera that
runs on the NBC network in the States. Created by Betty
and Ted Corday, it started on 8 November 1965 as a
half-hour melodrama, expanding to an hour later on. It's set
in the fictional town of Salem, in America's Midwest, and
tells of the high-drama and emotional crises in the lives of
two families, the Hortons and the Bradys. Obviously its
references on *Friends* are written as pastiche, but if you've
ever seen the real thing you'll know that Joey's storyline
isn't that far removed from the kind of plots they actually
do.

211
'The One With The Lesbian Wedding'
#457312

Writer: Doty Abrams
Director: Tommy Schlamme
First US transmission: 18.01.96
First UK transmission (C4): 30.08.96

Guest Cast: Jane Sibbett (Carol Willick),
Jessica Hecht (Susan Bunch), Phil Leeds (Mr Adelman),
Candice Gingrich (the Minister),
Symba Smith (Chrissy), Lea DeLaria (Woman),
and introducing Marlo Thomas (Sandra Green)

Summary: Carol and Susan have news for Ross: they're
going to get married, and they'd love him to come along.
Ross, of course, is completely freaked out by this and refuses
to be a part of it. But when Carol's parents bow out the night
before the ceremony and she argues with Susan, it looks as if

they're not going to go through with it. Ross, putting his own feelings aside, persuades Carol that she has to go ahead with it and he eventually walks her up the aisle to give her away.

Rachel's mum comes to visit to see how the younger side lives. She announces that she is planning to divorce Rachel's father. A shocked Rachel has to cope with the idea of her parents breaking up and has great difficulty understanding why her mother wants to do this, until Mrs Green says, 'You didn't marry *your* Barry, honey.' Mrs Green feels she has been trapped for too long in a marriage she was never sure she wanted, and now she's searching for a new life.

Rose Adelman, one of Phoebe's massage clients, dies on her massage table. Although she's quite shaken by this alone, she also has to cope with the spirit of Mrs Adelman, which has decided to take up residence in Phoebe's body. Phoebe meets with Mr Adelman to find out if his wife had any unfinished business on this world. All he can think of is that his wife once said she wanted to see everything before she died . . .

Poor Ross: Trying to come to terms with Carol and Susan's wedding isn't the easiest thing for Ross. Somewhat bitterly, he wonders why he shouldn't go along to the ceremony – after all, he had fun at her *first* wedding!

Freaky Monica: Asked to cater for the wedding, Monica goes into terrifying overdrive. She bullies everyone into helping, barking orders at them from every corner of the kitchen: 'I feel like you should have German subtitles,' says Chandler at one point. As her stress increases, her friends begin to wonder whether she should just calm down and take it easy – 'Do you want to see me cry? Is that what you want?' she asks, with a crack in her voice. When Carol arrives to say that the wedding might be off, the first thing Monica says is, 'You're still going to pay me, right?'

Slow Joey: At the lesbian wedding, Joey gets frightened and agitated by the women's total lack of interest in him: 'I feel like Superman without his powers,' he moans.

Chandleresque: In response to these comments from Joey, Chandler laments that 'the world is my lesbian wedding'.

His final gambit to strike up conversation with a very stern-looking lesbian is sheer embarrassment: 'Look. Penis, schmenis – we're all people!' Not surprisingly, she just walks away.

Parents – Who Needs 'Em?: Rachel's mum is just superb! She practically dances through all her scenes, filled with an obvious glee at the prospect of living a different life for a few days. She asks Rachel if she has any marijuana, then she enquires, 'What's new in sex?' Later, at the wedding reception, she even flirts with lesbians. Her sheer *joie de vivre* is marvellous.

Ugly Naked Guy: Mrs Green spies 'an unattractive nude man' playing a cello. She's told to be thankful that it's not a smaller instrument.

Just Plain Weird: Mr and Mrs Adelman seem to be quite a couple. She's obviously a smart woman who says exactly what's on her mind, even if she does use Phoebe's mouth. The final 'Now I've seen everything' joke is pretty obvious, but funny nonetheless. Mr Adelman is a charming character. When Phoebe asks if his wife still had something to do on Earth, he suggests that she always said she wanted to sleep with him once more. Phoebe just stares at the wizened little man and smiles. 'I'm sorry,' she explains, 'there's laughing in my head.'

Joey's an Actor?: On his first day on *Days Of Our Lives*, Joey is taught about 'Smell the Fart' acting, a method daytime soap actors use when they have a long and complicated line to remember (which is most of the time, with Joey): they take a pause and give a serious, considered look, almost as if they're smelling a fart.

Generation X: Candice Gingrich, who plays the minister at the wedding, is a celebrated author and gay activist. Phoebe's possession by Mrs Adelman is possibly inspired by either the Steve Martin film *All of Me* (Carl Reiner, 1984) or by *Prelude to a Kiss* (Norman René, 1992). Lea DeLaria (the butch woman at the wedding) is a well-known lesbian stand-up comic.

The Last Word: For an episode that focuses around Carol and Susan, it's rather sad that they don't get more screen time than a handful of scenes. They are criminally underused, really, but bearing in mind the lessons *Ellen* has recently learned, maybe that's wise. The wedding itself is very low-key, and almost unromantic. However, the appearance of Candice Gingrich as the minister was apparently a major coup for the production team, adding a 'seal of approval' on the proceedings as she proclaims that there's nothing that pleases God more than to see two people in love – regardless of their sexual orientation. This might not seem that far-reaching to a British audience, but, considering just how conservative American TV sponsors can be, in reality it is an incredibly brave testament, pushing the boundaries of tolerance and love that bit further. **Ahhh Rating:** ***

French Title: 'Celui Qui N'apprécie Pas Certains Mariages' (the one who doesn't appreciate certain marriages)

German Title: 'Die lesbische Hochzeit' (the lesbian wedding)

212
'The One After The Superbowl'
#457313

Writer: Michael Borkow
Director: Michael Lembeck
First US transmission: 28.01.96
First UK transmission (C4): 06.09.96

Guest Cast: Brooke Shields (Erica Ford),
Chris Isaak (Rob Donan),
Dan Castellaneta (the Zoo Keeper),
Roark Critchlow (Doctor), Fred Willard (Mr Lipson),
Tahj Mowry (Little Boy),
Sean Masterson ('Monkeyshine' Guy),
Lawrence A. Mandley (Security Guard),
Elliot Woods (Waiter), Karman Kruschke (Coma Woman)

Summary: Phoebe gets a gig singing for children at the local library. The kids love her because she tells them the truth, but the parents are concerned that her songs are inappropriate and she's fired.

Joey gets his first fan mail, from a woman called Erica, who encloses fourteen of her own eyelashes with the letter as a sign of her love for him. But when Monica sees that the letter was hand-posted to their address rather than the show, Joey realises that he has his own stalker. Erica then comes to their apartment, and Joey is torn between dating a beautiful woman who is infatuated with him and running the risk of being axed to death should she ever realise that he isn't really Dr Drake Ramoray from *Days Of Our Lives*, but just the man who plays him on TV. But this is a concept that Erica just doesn't get. When Erica confronts Joey about his kissing another woman in that day's episode, Ross is compelled to tell her the truth – he is in fact Drake's evil twin!

A monkey appearing in a TV advert for Monkey Shines Beer reminds Ross of Marcel. Eager to see how his old pal is doing, Ross goes to visit him at the zoo in LA, only to be informed by the zoo administrator that Marcel has died. However, one of the zoo janitors manages to let slip that Marcel is working in movies now – he *is* the Monkey Shines monkey! Better still, he's currently filming a movie in New York where Ross is sure he'll be able to meet up with him again!

Phoebisms: Nervous about performing to a child audience, Phoebe suggests to Rob that she might just picture her audience naked, but Rob doesn't think that's such a good idea: 'That's kind of the reason why the last guy got fired.' Phoebe's songs include one about how grandparents die, a cheerful song about things you shouldn't do (such as sleep with people to get them to like you) and a song explaining the origins of hamburgers and one about sexual orientation. 'Not at all inappropriate,' chirps Rachel.

Slow Joey: When he and Chandler are trying to escape his 'stalker', Joey suggests just walking past her on the stairs, as they've never met, so she'll never recognise him (Chandler points out that that's how *radio* stars escape their stalkers). Trying to wriggle out of the fact that, despite Erica's misguided beliefs that he's a doctor, he didn't help a man in a restaurant who was choking, Joey explains that he's a neurosurgeon and that it had clearly been a case of 'foodal chokage'.

Chandleresque: When Joey asks him to guess what he's got, Chandler answers, 'Rhythm?' Later, Joey asks him what he'd like to do for dinner; his response, that they might stay in and cook for themselves, forces them to fall into hysterics. Ross complains that he hasn't seen his monkey in almost a year, prompting Chandler to joke, 'You never look down in the shower?' Ross glares at him, forcing him to ask, 'Oh please! I'm not allowed to make one joke in the "monkey-is-penis" genre?'

Just Plain Weird: Maybe it's something to do with animal people in general (see 'TOW The Fake Monica') but the way the zoo administrator breaks the news of Marcel's 'death' to Ross is either insensitive or just downright cruel. Equally unsettling is the clandestine zoo janitor, who tries to bribe Ross *after* telling him everything he needs to know. And then there's Erica, whom Chandler accurately describes as 'a total whack job'!

Monkey Business: Rachel jokes that thanks to Marcel she has a Malibu Barbie 'that will no longer be wearing white to the wedding'.

Generation X: Chandler describes Erica as being the exact opposite of Kathy Bates in *Misery* (Rob Reiner, 1990). Phoebe inadvertently compares herself to Barney, a big, banal purple dinosaur that passes for edutainment these days. Brooke Shields made a number of films when she was a teenager, including the infamous *Blue Lagoon* (Randal Kleiser, 1980). Chris Isaak starred in *Twin Peaks: Fire Walk With Me* (David Lynch, 1992) and *Little Buddha* (Bernardo Bertolucci, 1993), and played the leader of the SWAT team in *The Silence of the Lambs* (Jonathan Demme, 1990), but is best known as a singer/songwriter whose biggest hit was 'Wicked Game', the theme from David Lynch's *Wild at Heart*

(David Lynch, 1990). Dan Castellaneta is, among others, the voice of Homer Simpson. Tahj Mowry played Teddy in the sitcom *Full House*. Fred Willard played Larry Crockett in *Salem's Lot: The Miniseries* (Tobe Hooper, 1979). Ross gets Marcel's attention by singing 'The Lion Sleeps Tonight' (see 'TOW All The Poker). Chandler refers to George Gershwin's 'I Got Rhythm'. Incidentally, the episode title refers to the fact that it was transmitted the evening of Superbowl XXX (Dallas Cowboys versus Pittsburgh Steelers – final result: Dallas Cowboys 27, Pittsburgh Steelers 17).

The Last Word: There are some lovely moments of slapstick in this episode. Watch out for what Matthew Perry does with the washing-up liquid when he first sees Erica, and the glee with which the gang throw glasses of water into Joey's face for increasingly ludicrous reasons, finishing with Chandler's 'You left the toilet seat up – you bastard!' Chris Isaak is possibly a little too laid back to be paired with Phoebe (in fact he looks positively wooden) but Dan Castellaneta's creepy janitor is fun, if only to see how different Homer Simpson and the man who does his voice really are. **Ahhh Rating** (for Ross's rendition of 'The Lion Sleeps Tonight'): ******

This episode and 'The One After The Superbowl' Part 2 were originally shown as a double bill.

French Title: 'Celui Qui Retrouve Son Singe', Partie 1 (the one who finds his monkey, Part 1)

German Title: 'Affengeil' (1) (supercool 1)

213
'The One After The Superbowl', Part 2
#457314

Writers: Mike Sikowitz & Jeffrey Astrof
Director: Michael Lembeck
First US transmission: 28.01.96
First UK transmission (C4): 06.09.96

Guest Cast: Jean-Claude Van Damme (himself),
Julia Roberts (Susie Moss), Lisa Roberts (Cathy),
Seth Isler (Monkey Trainer),
Steven M. Porter (Security Guard)

Summary: As Ross discovers how 'starry' Marcel has become, Joey tries anything to get a part in Marcel's movie. Chandler bumps into Susie Moss, a girl he once ridiculed back in school, and asks her out on a date. Before they leave his apartment, Susie persuades him to wear her panties (as you do), and then at the restaurant she manoeuvres him into the bathroom and gets him to strip off. But before he can 'enjoy himself', she double-crosses him by running off with his clothes in retribution for his having pulled her dress up when they were in the fourth grade. Revenge for Susie is certainly a dish best served cold.

Rachel tries to ask Jean-Claude Van Damme for a date on behalf of Monica, but the movie star seems only interested in Rachel. This causes friction between the girls and Phoebe is forced to mediate. Rachel agrees to cancel the date and arrange one for Monica instead – by telling Van Damme that Monica is prepared to have a 'threesome' with him and Drew Barrymore . . .

Spoilt Rachel: During their second fight, Rachel hits Monica where it will really hurt: 'You give me back my sweater or it's "Handbag Marinara"!'

Phoebisms: (After breaking up the fight between Monica and Rachel): 'Y'know what? If we were in prison you guys would be, like, my bitches.' And Phoebe provides a cracking punchline to the episode, where she says that one of the strings on her guitar is broken and asks Chandler if she can borrow his 'G string'.

Slow Joey: Joey complains about Ross blowing him out for a monkey. Ross offers to reschedule for later in the week, but Joey says bitterly, 'Yeah, unless you hook up with a bunch of pigeons.' When he discovers Chandler in the cubicle of the gents at the restaurant he sympathetically observes, 'Talk about your bad luck . . . The first time you try panties and someone walks off with your clothes!'

Chandleresque: Speaking to two extras from *Outbreak II*: 'Are you guys in the movie or are you just really paranoid?' To an extra in fatigues: 'Nice camouflage, man. For a minute there I almost didn't see you.' Chandler tells Susie Moss, 'Back then I used to use humour as a defence mechanism. Thank God I don't do that any more.'

Joey's an Actor?: He tries to get the attention of the director as he tells Phoebe about a 'horrible flesh-eating virus!' When he finally gets a part in the film they have to kill him off instantly because of his scenery-chewing overacting.

Generation X: As Ross and Marcel do a tour of the city, we hear Barry Manilow's 'Looks Like We Made It'. Joey and Chandler whistle 'Buffalo Gals, won't you come out tonight?' in the gents, and 'Habenera (L'Amour Est Un Oiseau Rebelle)' from Bizet's *Carmen* is played as Chandler walks out of the restaurant, covered only by his dignity and a toilet cubicle door. The name of Marcel's cuddly elephant (Harry Elephanté) is a play on the name of the singer Harry Belafonte (famous for, among others, 'The Banana Boat Song – Day-O!'). Jean-Claude Van Damme is world-renowned for his action movies (all of them terrible). Julia Roberts was the star of, among other movies, *Pretty Woman* (Garry Marshall, 1990). She claimed she begged the producers for a part because she was such a big *Friends* fan (though this may have had a lot to do with her also being a bigger Matthew Perry fan). Susie describes one of the actresses from the set as having an upper lip so hairy she could be mistaken for Gabe Kaplan, the eponymous star of 1970s sitcom *Welcome Back, Mr Kotter*. The film that Marcel and Jean-Claude are making is a sequel to *Outbreak* (Wolfgang Petersen, 1995), in which a monkey is the source of a lethal virus that threatens to wipe out America. And yes, Marcel played that monkey, too: Greenbay. Susie's revenge on Chandler is inspired by the Italian soft-porn movie *11 Days, 11 Nights* (Aristide Massacchesi – a.k.a. Joe D'Amato, 1988), in which a couple

---

What's with the 'grade' thing in American schools?

The education system in the States is slightly different from the UK's. Their first experience of big scary classes is kindergarten, when they're about five years old. Their equivalent of primary school, sometimes called 'grammar' or 'elementary' in the USA, runs from about the age of six till eleven (first to sixth grade), at which point pupils progress to junior high. High school begins when they're fourteen or fifteen. At the age of sixteen, as in the UK, students can 'drop out' of high school, or else they stay on, and at eighteen they 'graduate' (as opposed to just taking A-levels and leaving school as we do here). Most students therefore leave school at twelfth grade. This system is slowly being introduced into British schools. Except the graduation bit.

---

both strip in a toilet cubicle. She then puts on his clothes but leaves her own, forcing him to walk out in drag, rather than naked as with Chandler.

The Story So Far: Marcel had a toy elephant called Harry Elephanté. His favourite food is bananacake with mealworm. Susie Moss was in fourth grade with Chandler, when he used to wear a denim cap with mirrors all over it. They both knew a guy called Stephen Hurs, who would eat anything for money, and a guy called David Stein, who had no elbows. Susie remembers someone who was caught masturbating at school, but Chandler defensively tells her that 'he' had just been looking for his bus money. Chandler also tells her that he went to an all-boys school (high school).

The Last Word: Well this might be little more than a mid-season ratings boost but the bickering between the girls makes up for it (and Phoebe's 'stop the madness!' outburst is the icing on top). Julia Roberts makes a fine guest star, but Jean-Claude Van Damme is just embarrassing, something that the writers apparently became aware of after they saw how bad his delivery of his lines was. **Ahhh Rating** (Chandler's . . . erm, predicament): ***

French Title: Celui Qui Retrouve Son Singe', Partie 2 (the one who finds his monkey, part 2)

German Title: 'Affengeil' (2) (supercool 2)

214
'The One With The Prom Video'
#457310

Writer: Alexa Junge
Director: James Burrows
First US transmission: 01.02.96
First UK transmission (C4): 13.09.96

Guest Cast: Elliott Gould (Jack Geller),
Christina Pickles (Judy Geller), Patrick Kerr (the Manager),
Michael Ray Bower (Roy Gublick), Lou Thornton (Gail),
Tim Bohn (Jonathan)

Summary: Joey gets his first cheque for *Days Of Our Lives* and decides to pay Chandler back for all of the favours he's done for him over the years. In addition to an envelope of money, he decides to give Chandler an obscenely tacky, engraved bracelet which he insists Chandler wear. Unfortunately, as Chandler discovers, it also doubles as a 'woman repellent'. As Chandler launches into a routine about how much he hates it, Joey walks in and Chandler realises too late how much his ingratitude has hurt his best friend. Chandler begs Joey to forgive him, pointing out that, considering he hated it that much, the fact that he wore it anyway should count for something – but then he loses the bracelet!

After Ross gets in the way of her speaking to a new man, Rachel spells out once and for all that she will never go out with him. That evening, Monica puts on a video of her and Rachel's prom night. But for Rachel at least, the events are shown from a different point of view from how she remembered them . . .

Freaky Monica: After the sleazy interview from Hell, Monica takes five showers just to get herself clean. When Phoebe asks her if she has any other possibilities, she replies, 'There's the possibility that I won't make rent.' Her father does a little trick in pretending to pull a quarter from behind her ear, prompting her to ask, 'Anything larger back there?'

Phoebisms: Pheebs is pleased with her mastery of the male language: 'Dude, eleven o'clock, totally hot babe, checkin' you out,' adding as an afterthought, 'That was really good. I think I'm ready for my penis now.'

Chandleresque: Joey gives Chandler $812 as a payback: 'I don't know what Big Leon told ya,' says Chandler, 'but it's an even thousand if you want me for the whole night.' After an overenthusiastic Joey asks him what he thinks the bracelet will do for his sex life, Chandler says that it'll probably slow it down at first 'but once I get used to the extra weight, I'll be back on track'. When Ross asks what someone called Casey would want with Rachel, culture-junkie Bing can't help himself: 'I'm guessing he wants to do a little dance, y'know, make a little love . . . well, pretty much get down tonight.'

The Ballad of Ross & Rachel: Ross 'saves' Rachel from a conversation with an interesting, attractive man because he thinks she's being pestered. But Rachel takes exception to his constant interference in her life: 'OK, Ross, listen to me, I am not yours to save!' Ross still believes she is, having spoken to Phoebe: 'Well, you're, um, you're my lobster.' But Rachel has run out of patience with Ross, explaining to him that when she fell for him she got 'clobbered', and then when he fell for her, she got clobbered again. 'I'm tired of being clobbered, y'know? It's – it's just not worth it.' But later on, she sees the prom video and discovers that Ross had prepared himself to stand in as her date when it had appeared she'd been stood up, and all her recriminations fall away as she rushes over to kiss the man who has loved her all these years. 'See,' says a smug Phoebe, 'he's her lobster!'

Parents – Who Needs 'Em?: Ross suggests that Monica borrow some money from their parents: 'You feel guilty and tense around them already. You might as well make some money off of them.' Later on, Mr Geller puts his foot in it with Rachel when he talks about her parents' separation, letting slip that Rachel's parents have been unhappy since 'that incident in Hawaii'. Fortunately for Rachel, he doesn't enlarge on that. Unfortunately for Monica, the prom video gives her an insight into parental love that she could well have done without.

Just Plain Weird: The interviewer who seems to get turned on by the thought of Monica making a salad: 'Is it dirty? . . . I like it dirty.' Euch!

Dinosaurs ROCK!: Ross has dinosaur cheques, so he can get his money and learn something at the same time. When he lends Monica some money, she affectionately calls him a 'cheaposaurus'.

Generation X: Chandler paraphrases from K.C. and the Sunshine Band's 1975 single 'Get Down Tonight', as well as mentioning Liberace (the late, camp, flamboyant pianist), Mr T (star of the inane action-adventure series *The A Team*) and the celebrated mime artist Marcel Marceau (of whom Joey does a surprisingly good impression). Ross's mention of 'Casey at the Bat' is a reference to Ernest Thayer's poem of the same name, which was published in the *San Francisco Examiner* on 3 June 1888. It became popular at the turn of the century and is a story of missed opportunity that sank deep into the heart of American culture, so it's ironic that Ross quotes it here. Ross tries to reassure Chandler, saying that his bracelet isn't at all flashy 'for a Goodfella', in reference to The Greatest Gangster Movie Of All Time™, *Goodfellas* (Martin Scorsese, 1990). Chandler chats up a girl by joking with her that he reminds people of Dave Thomas, founder of

Wendy's, one of America's largest burger chains (there are *some* branches in the UK too). Thomas appears as himself in a series of adverts in the States. Jack Geller is apparently an admirer of the German tennis ace, Steffi Graf. Seeing Ross with a moustache and Afro hairdo, Joey is reminded of the 1970s sitcom *Welcome Back Kotter*. We hear Ross playing 'Axel F', Harold Faltermeyer's theme tune to the *Beverley Hills Cop* trilogy.

The Story So Far: The Gellers decide to convert Monica's room into a gym, as Ross's was full of science trophies and plaques and merit badges and they 'didn't want to disturb them' (see 'TOW The Cat'). We knew that Monica was once a little larger than she is today (see 'TOW The Sonogram At The End'), but nothing could have prepared us for quite *how* big she was. As the gang watch her old prom video, she claims that the camera adds ten pounds, and Chandler asks her just how many cameras were on her. We also learn that Rachel has had a nose job, allegedly because of a 'deviated septum'. Rachel's date for the prom was a guy named Chip (see 'TOW The Cat'), and Monica's was Roy Gublick, who saw *Star Wars* 317 times!

The Last Word: What starts as just another episode ends as a watershed in the history of the show. After a couple of false starts, Ross and Rachel are (finally!) together and *Friends* fans across the world cry with tears of joy. It's the sign of a good show that they can switch so effortlessly from comedy to pathos to romance in one short scene. But then this is *Friends*, and would we seriously expect anything less? **Ahhh Rating:** *****

French Title: 'Celui Qui A Failli Aller Au Bal' (the one who nearly got to the ball)

German Title: 'Ein Hummer für Ross' (a lobster for Ross)

215

'The One Where Ross And Rachel . . . You Know'

#457315

Writers: Michael Curtis & Gregory S. Malins
Director: Michael Lembeck
First US transmission: 08.02.96
First UK transmission (C4): 20.09.96

Guest Cast: Introducing Tom Selleck (Richard Burke)

Summary: *Days Of Our Lives* extends Joey's contract, so he treats himself and Chandler to an enormous TV and a pair of reclining leather chairs. But the chairs are so comfortable the boys can't bring themselves to leave them even for a second. Meanwhile, Monica and Phoebe cater a party for Richard Burke, a friend of Monica's father. Richard has recently split from his wife and is trying to get back into socialising, but he finds all of his friends dull and spends most of the party in the kitchen with Monica. Despite the age gap, Monica and Richard are slowly drawn together by their strong mutual attraction.

Ross and Rachel go on their first date and prepare to consummate their relationship, but Rachel gets a fit of the giggles and the moment is lost. They are about to go on a second date when Ross is called to the museum. He finishes work too late for them to get to the restaurant they'd booked, so Ross improvises with some sweet music and a planetarium.

Freaky Monica: Mon is hesitant about dating Richard because he's a 'grown-up'. As Richard points out, he's a 'whole person who can drink' older than she is. She, on the other hand, is worried about dating a guy whose pool she once peed in.

Chandleresque: Joey gets Chandler to cover his eyes to surprise him and Chandler warns him that he'd 'better be wearing clothes when I open my eyes'. Ross asks him if a girl has ever started laughing while they were making out: 'Yeah, but it was 1982 and my Flock of Seagulls haircut was tickling her chin.'

The Ballad of Ross & Rachel: Ross is worried by Rachel's spontaneous hysterics each time he touches her arse. He tells the guys that he's wanted this since he was in 'ninth-grade typing' and that he just wants it to be 'perfect and right' (no pressure from high expectations there, then). The new couple on the block go to see a subtitled movie on their first date and finally consummate their relationship under a rug at the museum on possibly the most romantic date of all time (see 'TOW Chandler In A Box').

Boys Will Be Boys: The guys order pizza and get it delivered to the girls' apartment so they don't have to get out of their chairs: 'Inside – good. Outside – baaad!' When the fire alarm goes off in their building, Chandler checks the floor to see if it's getting hot yet.

Cruelty to Animals: After Phoebe complains about cows having made the ultimate sacrifice just for their chairs, Chandler reassures her by telling her that they were chair-shaped cows: 'They never would have survived in the wild.'

Dinosaurs ROCK!: Ross gets called to the museum because one of the displays has been set out incorrectly (someone got their Australopithecus confused with their *Homo habilus*. Duh!).

Generation X: The guys watch an episode of *The Dick Van Dyke Show*, *Beavis and Butthead*, an infomercial for Miracle Wax and about two days' worth of nonstop TV. Flock of Seagulls were a Liverpool band from the early eighties whose biggest hit was 'Wishing (If I Had A Photograph Of You)' in 1983. *Xanadu* (Robert Greenwald, 1980) is evidently one of Phoebe's favourite films but pretty much any sane person would say it sucks. Ross and Rachel make out to 'Wicked Game' by Chris Isaak (see 'TO After The Superbowl') from the album of the same name. Tom Selleck's most famous role is that of Thomas Magnum in the TV show *Magnum P.I.*

The Story So Far: Richard's ex-wife was called Barbara, he has a daughter called Michelle, a grandson called Henry (with another on the way) and he is 48 years old. Monica is 27. Rachel remembers getting a kiss from Dr Burke when she'd crashed her bike outside his house aged seven. Rachel wears glasses (she didn't want to wear them on her first date with Ross). Ross knows very little about astronomy.

The Last Word: The title says it all, but what really makes this episode stand out is the amount of on-the-edge innuendo – notably Chandler's joke about Australopithecus never being erect because 'maybe he was nervous' and the 'premature ejaculation' setup when Rachel rolls over on to the juice carton and quickly reassures Ross. Possibly the bravest subject an American sitcom can cover. Commendable. **Ahhh Rating** (It's nice to see everyone happy for once): ***

French Title: 'Celui Qui A Fait On Ne Sait Quoi Avec Rachel' (the one who did it with Rachel)

German Title: 'Ross und Rachel – Na endlich!' (Ross and Rachel – finally!)

216
'The One Where Joey Moves Out'
#457316

Writer: Betsy Bornes
Director: Michael Lembeck
First US transmission: 15.02.96
First UK transmission (C4): 27.09.96

Guest Cast: Elliott Gould (Jack Geller),
Christina Pickles (Judy Geller),
Tom Selleck (Dr Richard Burke),
Audrie Neenan (Emily, Judy Geller's friend),
Warren Berliner (Bob), Josie Di Vincenzo (Tattoo Artist),
Stephen Samuels (Arik, Jack Geller's friend)

Summary: Phoebe and Rachel decide to get tattoos. Rachel hasn't told Ross because she wants to surprise him, but when Ross tries to talk Phoebe out of getting hers, she in turn is forced to talk Rachel into doing what she wants to do and to be her own boss. However, after her tattoo is finished, Rachel discovers that Phoebe chickened out. But she is surprised by Ross's reaction to the rose she's had done on her hip – he loves it! Ross and Monica go to their father's birthday party. Everyone is quizzing Richard about his new 'twinkie' girl-friend and eventually Monica feels compelled to tell her parents that she and Richard are dating.

Joey is offered a new apartment by one of his co-stars. He considers taking it, but an argument with Chandler makes his mind up for him, leaving them with one final decision to make – who gets to keep the foosball table?

Phoebisms: While she has decided on a lily, to represent her mother's open, giving spirit, she's equally tempted by the thought of Foghorn Leghorn.

Slow Joey: Joey is surprised to realise that Captain Crunch's eyebrows are on his hat, yet he hasn't worked out that he's been captain of a cereal for the last 40 years. He sees nothing wrong with licking a spoon and putting it straight back in the drawer and he used Chandler's toothbrush to unclog the drain. He's not completely dumb, though, as he points out to Chandler that there's little difference between sharing a toothbrush and sharing soap: 'Think about the last thing I wash and the first thing you wash.' Playing foosball to decide who gets to keep the table, Chandler boasts that Joey's little men are going to 'get scored on more times than your sister'. Joey is understandably appalled: 'Which sister?' And a surprisingly perceptive Joey breaks his best friend's heart when he points out: 'It's not like we agreed to live together for ever. We're not Bert and Ernie.'

Chandleresque: Grossed out about Joey's unsanitary habits, Chandler cries, 'Oh God! Can open – worms *everywhere*!' When Joey expresses concern about leaving Chandler 'high and dry', he says, 'I've never been lower or wetter.'

Parents – Who Needs 'Em?: Joey asks Monica if she's going to tell her parents about Richard, to which she sarcastically says that of course she is, as she's decided to give her father a *stroke* for his birthday (which would be original at least). Ross is only a little more supportive: 'Remember when you were nine and Richard was thirty how Dad used to say "God, I hope they get together"?' After Richard tells Monica that both his parents are dead, Monica cries, 'God, you are *so* lucky!'

Generation X: Phoebe momentarily considers getting a tattoo of Foghorn Leghorn, the Looney Toons rooster. Jack Geller describes Richard's revitalisation (thanks to his 'twinkie in the city') as being like a scene from *Cocoon* (Ron Howard, 1985) – Courteney Cox was a cast member of the sequel, *Cocoon: The Return* (Daniel Petrie, 1988).

The Story So Far: Jack Geller celebrated turning 50 by buying himself a Porsche. Phoebe's Mother's name was Lily. Joey is 28 years old. Monica reminds Ross about the video she once saw of her parents having sex, telling him, 'I just caught the live show' (see 'TOW The Prom Video'). Joey and Chandler once used one of Rachel's bras to fling water balloons down at some junior high kids. According to Judy Geller, Richard has a son (see 'TOW Chandler In A Box').

The Last Word: It must be hard for Jack and Judy Geller to accept that their 'little Harmonica' is dating an older man who just happens to be their best friend, but Monica's heart-warming speech about how much he means to her must have helped in some way to make it easier for them. Courteney Cox is superb in this episode, enjoying a lot of physical comedy (the slapstick squirting of the can of cream and the shocked expression on her face after witnessing her parents make out), as are the two Matt(hew)s. To see Chandler's expression after Joey moves out is just heartbreaking, especially when Joey runs back to give him one last hug. **Ahhh Rating:** ****

French Title: 'Celui Qui Vit Sa Vie' (the one who lives his life)

German Title: 'Ein idealer Schwiegersohn' (the perfect son-in-law)

217
'The One Where Eddie Moves In'
#457317

Writer: Adam Chase
Director: Michael Lembeck
First US transmission: 22.02.96
First UK transmission (C4): 04.10.96

Guest Cast: Dee Dee Rescher (Record Producer),
Barry Heins ('Pie In The Sky' Man),
Linda Lutz (Horrible Woman),
and introducing Adam Goldberg (Eddie Minowick),

Summary: Joey's happily moved into his new apartment, and decked it out with the biggest and weirdest collection of tat anyone's ever seen. Chandler, meanwhile, has decided to get a new roommate, and so Eddie moves in. Joey is surprised and a little hurt that he has been so quickly replaced, but Chandler appears to be getting on very well without him.

Phoebe has good news for the gang: she's been 'discovered' by a record producer who wants to tape a demo of 'Smelly Cat', make a video of the song, and possibly go on to record an album of Phoebe's songs. When everyone eventually sits down to watch the video, though, they realise that Phoebe's voice has been replaced by that of another, better singer.

With Rachel and Ross in the glory days of their new relationship, he is spending most of his free time round at Monica and Rachel's apartment. This is getting on Monica's nerves, and she and her brother soon devolve into the same kind of antics that led Monica to hate Ross as a child. Can the two of them smooth over their differences and, more importantly, can Rachel put up with their squabbling for that much longer?

Spoilt Rachel: Carefully making her way past a customer seated at the bar, she stumbles and drops a slice of apple pie into the hood of his coat. She later implores Ross to rescue the pie from the coat as the man is leaving: to do so, Ross has to put on an act as a complete lunatic, who also plans to fish some coffee out of another man's trousers.

Phoebisms: When she goes into the studio to record 'Smelly Cat', she isn't aware that she'll be singing with backing vocalists. She's not entirely happy about this, though, and has to explain the ethic behind the song to them. But she must do it quickly, as studio time is money: 'The cat stinks, but you love it,' just about sums it up. When she finally sees the video, she initially believes that it's her own voice. 'I'm sorry, but I am so talented,' she asserts.

Slow Joey: He proudly shows off his new apartment, and its tacky *objets d'art*. But, leaving aside the plastic parrot, the porcelain dog, the rain-soaked fake window and the 'Muppetskin' cushions, Joey's proudest novelty in his new home is the phone right by the toilet. Everyone else is a little freaked by this, and Monica makes him promise never to use that phone to speak to her.

Chandleresque: Alone for the first time in his apartment, Chandler sits on a kitchen worktop, wearing a pair of cuddly wolf slippers. He asks them if he should give Joey a call, and then squeezes the right slipper's ear. It makes a tinny barking noise, to which Chandler replies, 'Ask your slippers a question . . . you're going crazy.' Later, Joey and Chandler watch *Baywatch* in their separate apartments, talking all the while on the phone. Seeing Yasmine Bleeth break into a brisk jog, an excited Chandler cries, 'Run, Yasmine! Run like the wind!'

Dinosaurs ROCK!: Ross argues with a work colleague about whether Dino on *The Flintstones* was a velociraptor or not.

Generation X: Adam Goldberg is best known as Mike from *Dazed and Confused* (Richard Linklater, 1993). Joey and Chandler watch Baywatch, admiring both Yasmine Bleeth and the character Lieutenant Stephanie Holden (played by Alexandra Paul). As Chandler and Joey start really missing each other, we hear 'All By Myself' by Neilsson.

The Story So Far: This is the first time we hear the full 'Smelly Cat' lyrics.

The Last Word: With no hint of his insanity to come, Eddie makes a perfectly level impression on his debut. A fine, even episode, whose best parts are the childish arguments between Ross and Monica, and the full video of 'Smelly Cat', but on the whole it's not an episode that sticks in the memory. **Aaah Rating:** **

French Title: 'Celui Qui Remplace Celui Qui Part' (the one who replaces the one who leaves)

German Title: 'Chandler's Neuer' (Chandler's replacement)

218
'The One Where Dr Ramoray Dies'
#457318

Writers: Alexa Junge (story), Michael Borkow (teleplay)
Director: Michael Lembeck
First US transmission: 21.3.96
First UK transmission (C4): 11.10.96

Guest Cast: Tom Selleck (Dr Richard Burke),
Adam Goldburg (Eddie Minowick),
Roark Critchlow (Dr Horton), Mary Gallagher (Tilly),
Vanessa Sandin (Amber, Dr Drake's half-sister),
Brian Posehn (Messanger), Jim Reilly (Writer)

Summary: Joey foolishly claims in an interview that he has an influence over the scripts for *Days Of Our Lives*. When one of the scriptwriters reads this, he writes a little surprise into the script. Suddenly, and unexpectedly, Dr Ramoray is to leave the series in a definitely final way – he falls down an elevator shaft to his death.

Meanwhile, Chandler is beginning to have problems with his new roommate. At first, Eddie just isn't into the same things as Chandler – he doesn't like sports, and won't watch *Baywatch*. When Phoebe forces Chandler and Eddie to get to know each other better, Chandler begins to discover that his roommate has a very big screw loose. The break-up from his girlfriend has left him in an unstable mental state, and when the girlfriend shows up again, he leaps to the wrong conclusion that Chandler has slept with her. *And* killed his fish!

Freaky Monica: After Joey has got the push from *Days Of Our Lives*, the gang gather at his apartment to cheer him up. The only nice thing Monica can think of to say is, 'I straightened out your shower curtain so you won't get mildew . . . To me, that's nice.' We also *don't* discover how many people she's had sex with, although it's 'definitely less than a ballpark'.

Phoebisms: Chandler tries to get Phoebe to play a game of foosball with him, but she vehemently declines, describing the game as a 'human-rights violation'. She is disgusted by the fact that all the little people are forced to do nothing but play foosball for the whole of their lives. When she suggests to Eddie that she, he and Chandler hang out and get to know each other, she slips away with the excuse that she has to go to her *Green Eggs and Ham* discussion group. 'Tonight, it's "Why He Would Not Eat Them on a Train".' We also hear the closing refrain of a new song about a crusty old man and maraca-playing rats.

The Ballad of Ross & Rachel: Rachel makes the fatal error of saying that sex with Paolo was 'meaningless, animal sex'. Ross immediately wonders what's so bad about his technique that means they can't even have 'chipmunk sex'. Rachel desperately tries to claw back the situation, claiming that sex with Ross is different because they 'connect', and saying that it's a great deal better than Paolo sex because of that. Once he's convinced that she's telling the truth, Ross takes the plunge and promises Rachel some animal sex in his own style (complete with hilarious growls and snorts).

Just Plain Weird: The cracks in Eddie's veneer of normality are starting to show. After he becomes convinced that Chandler has slept with Tilly, his ex, Chandler suspects that 'he's stolen all the insoles from my shoes'. He also buys himself a goldfish – although it's only a goldfish-shaped biscuit – and he names it Chandler. Can anyone else hear that violin strain from *Psycho*?

Generation X: Phoebe mentions Dr Seuss's book *Green Eggs and Ham*. Sean Penn is one of Hollywood's maverick actors, having appeared in, among other movies, *Casualties of War* (Brian De Palma, 1989) and *Shanghai Surprise* (Glendon Wasey, 1986), in which he starred alongside his then wife, Madonna.

The Story So Far: According to Eddie's ex-girlfriend, his surname is 'Minowick'. Richard tells Monica that his ex-wife Barbara was his high school sweetheart, and that they were married for 30 years. Rachel tells Ross that the only guys she's ever slept with apart from himself are Billy Dreskin, Pete (the weeper) Carney (see 'TOW The Candy Hearts'), Barry and Paolo. Richard and Ross argue over which 'Nam movie starred John Savage with no legs (it was *The Deer Hunter* – Michael Cimino, 1978) and which starred Jon Voight where he couldn't feel his legs (*Coming Home* – Hal Ashby, 1978) – Richard was right. Dr Drake Ramoray has a half-sister called Amber and a half-brother called Ramon.

The Last Word: The sex farce that takes place in Monica and Rachel's apartment, as they argue over the condom, while Ross and Richard discuss moustaches and the Vietnam War, is excellent; as are Chandler's growing fear of Eddie, and Rachel's desperate attempts to placate a hurt Ross. And poor old Joey. We're sad to see the back of Drake Ramoray, but he more than makes up for it with his final on-screen line. Realising he can't improvise his way out of falling down the lift shaft, he ignores a character's pleas of love for him, saying merely 'Yeah, whatever . . .' before stepping into the black abyss. **Ahhh rating:** ***

French Title: 'Celui Qui Disparait De La Série' (the one who leaves the series)

German Title: 'Fahrstuhl in den Tod' (elevator to instant death)

219
'The One Where Eddie Won't Go'
#457319

Writers: Michael Curtis & Gregory S. Malins
Director: Michael Lembeck
First US transmission: 28.03.96
First UK transmission (C4): 18.10.96

Guest Cast: Adam Goldberg (Eddie Minowick),
June Gable (Estelle Leonard),
James Michael Tyler (Gunther)

Summary: The girls are all fired up by a book called *Be Your Own Windkeeper*, which shows them how men steal their 'wind', preventing them from becoming goddesses. But instead of empowering them, the book just makes the girls bicker and fall out.

Despite having *'Days Of Our Lives'* on his résumé, Joey is finding it hard to get work. After he gets a Visa bill so big it comes in two envelopes, Joey is forced to audition for the small role of a cab driver in another soap opera. Unfortunately he doesn't get the part and is forced to stand by and watch as all of his stuff is reclaimed by the companies.

Back at Joey's old home, Eddie's behaviour is getting worse and Chandler decides he's had enough – he wants him out! But every time he tells him to leave he seems to forget. In the end he resorts to using Eddie's memory problems against him, convincing him that he's never lived there and that Joey never moved out. When a confused Eddie finally leaves, Chandler turns to Joey: 'Welcome home, man.'

Spoilt Rachel: Having read the book, Rachel turns on Ross, demanding why they always have to follow his timetable (Ross points out that it's the movie theatre that has the timetable). She later buys the girls some cakes as an apology for arguing with them. Then, when they accept that she's sorry, she takes them away because otherwise they'd come out of her pay cheque.

Phoebisms: Having introduced the girls to the life-changing book, Pheebs accuses Joey of foistering upon them 'phallic-shaped man cakes'.

Slow Joey: Joey becomes uncharacteristically verbose after Chandler buys him Word-of-the-Day toilet paper. After Ross complains about Rachel's infatuation with the book, Joey notes: 'See, this is why I don't date women who read.'

Just Plain Weird: And Eddie comes in for the third episode on the run. He's started dehydrating fruit and watching Chandler while he sleeps, and later on he turns up with a show dummy's head that he stole from Macy's department store. He also has selective memory loss and cannot seem to grasp that Chandler has thrown him out three times.

Joey's an Actor?: Estelle, his agent, puts him up for cab driver No. 2 in *Another World*, but Joey thinks this is too much of a step backwards: 'How can I go from being a neurosurgeon to driving a cab?' He eventually goes for the interview and tells the casting director that he has a background in medical acting. Estelle ends up giving him the same advice she gave to Al Minser and his Pyramid of dogs: 'Take any job you can get, and don't make on the floor.'

Gunther's an Actor?: He once appeared on *All My Children* as Bryce until they killed him off in an avalanche.

Generation X: Chandler tells Eddie that he'd prefer Hannibal Lecter from *The Silence of the Lambs* (Jonathan

Demme, 1990) as a roommate. Later on he sings 'Ding Dong The Psycho's Gone', in reference to 'Ding Dong The Witch Is Dead' from *The Wizard of Oz* (Victor Fleming, 1938). Rachel compares the book they're all reading to J.R.R. Tolkein's *The Hobbit*. *Another World* is another of NBC's daytime soaps, which tells the ongoing story of four families living in the fictional Bay City in Illinois.

The Story So Far: The girls reassess their past relationships: Monica reminds Phoebe about how she let 'the puppet guy' 'wash his feet in the pool of [her] inner power' (see 'TOW The Boobies'), and Phoebe points out that Monica allowed Paul into her 'forest of righteous truth' on the first date (see 'Pilot'). Monica also accuses Rachel of cheating her out of a chance with Danny Arshak in ninth grade after a 'Spin the Bottle' game, as Monica was convinced the bottle had been pointing at her: 'Only 'cause you took up half the circle,' counters Rachel. Rachel reveals that Phoebe slept with Jason Hurley one hour after he broke up with Monica. Chandler has lost the foosball and replaced it with a dried cantaloupe.

The Last Word: 'How do you expect me to grow if you won't let me blow?' If the girls have learnt one thing from that book it's that they don't need a book to tell them how to run their lives, even one with such interesting metaphors. But thank God Eddie finally goes ('Goodbye, you fruit-drying psychopath'), and Joey comes home where he belongs. The scene where he and Chandler move the porcelain dog into the living room is a treat, finished perfectly by Chandler's reactions to it: 'Is he housetrained or is he gonna leave little bathroom tiles all over the place? *Stay!* Good fake dog.'
Ahhh Rating (Joey comes home): ******

French Title: 'Celui Qui Ne Voulait Pas Partir' (the one who won't go)

German Title: 'Durch den Wind' (through the wind)

220
'The One Where Old Yeller Dies'
#457320

Writers: Michael Curtis & Gregory S. Malins (story),
Adam Chase (teleplay)
Director: Michael Lembeck
First US transmission: 04.04.96
First UK transmission (C4): 25.10.96

Guest Cast: Tom Selleck (Dr Richard Burke),
Jane Sibbett (Carol Willick), Jessica Hecht (Susan Bunch)

Summary: Phoebe discovers just how protective her mother was when she discovers a whole load of films with sad endings that her mother had never allowed her to watch. Acquiring copies of some well-known emotional wrenchers, Phoebe gets a rude awakening as she realises that the world might not be the nice place she's always believed it is.

Monica persuades Joey and Chandler to take Richard along to the Knicks game with them, despite their aversion to spending time with someone that, erm, mature. But she's surprised by the effect her boyfriend has on the guys when Joey starts holding a cigar between his lips and Chandler grows a moustache. They eventually blow it when they accidentally compare Richard to their own 'dads' and Richard realises that maybe they still have a problem with the age gap.

Ross is excited when his son, Ben, manages to pull himself up to stand, but his excitement wanes when he finds out that Carol and Susan saw him do the same thing the previous week. Ross feels that he's missing out on too many 'first-time' things and asks to look after him for a whole weekend. When he sees how badly Rachel handles Ben, he tries to reassure her that she'll be better when it's their own children. This freaks Rachel out a little, especially when she discovers that Ross has got their whole future mapped out in his mind. But after they discuss their thoughts on the future, and after

Rachel has been shown how to change Ben's nappy, they both seem just a little bit happier, especially Rachel, who is the first person to hear Ben's first word!

Poor Ross: Trying to get Ben to say 'Dada', he gets only 'Seh!', which he erroneously hopes will grow into 'Seh-condary care giver'. He later misses out on Ben's first word, but gets to hear his second. Which kind of makes up for everything else.

Freaky Monica: Even though she is hopelessly in love with Richard, she still makes him smoke on the balcony, just like she did with Chandler.

Phoebisms: Her new-found pessimism is just as extremist as her previously rose-tinted optimism: 'You're ultimately just gonna die or get divorced or have to blow your pet's head off.'

Slow Joey: The guys phone Monica to ask what she's wearing. When she claims to have nothing on but rubber gloves, the guys are through her door in a second, only to be disappointed by the sight of a fully clothed Mon: 'One of these times you're gonna really be naked and we're not gonna come over,' Joey warns. Monica is evidently tiring of Joey asking if she sees other women naked at the gym, and of confirming that no, she doesn't ever look.

Chandleresque: Monica tries to divide up the food, saying she has a leg, three breasts and a wing, and Chandler can't resist asking: 'How d'you find clothes that fit?' He then tries to explain why he and Joey don't want to invite Richard to the game, only to dig himself further into a hole: 'He's, y'know, old . . . er, than some people,' adding as an afterthought, 'but, um, younger than some buildings.' When Chandler makes a joke about Richard's age, he retaliates by mocking Chandler's moustache: 'When puberty hits that thing's really gonna kick in.'

The Ballad of Ross & Rachel: Ross asks her to hold Ben for a moment and she grasps him gingerly. When Ross tells her she should hold him like she might hold a football, she snaps,

'This *is* how I would hold a football' (see 'TOW The Football). She apologises, saying she's not very good with babies: 'I haven't been around them, I mean, you know, since I *was* one.' After Ross's preplanning her life makes her run in terror from Central Perk, Rachel tells him that she doesn't want to think that far ahead, and jokes that he's probably already named their children – only to discover that he's been thinking of the name 'Emily', thanks to *The Big Book Of Children's Names* (see 'TOW Joey's Dirty Day'). Rachel explains to him that this was one of the reasons she left Barry – that her whole life had been decided for her. Ross agrees that he'll try to understand that, so long as Rachel accepts that he's the kind of person who does think ahead to their future, simply because he's certain that they'll end up together. In among all this bickering, they suddenly realise that they've just told each other that they love each other for the first time . . .

Cruelty to Animals: Phoebe's pertinent outcry after the end of *Old Yeller*: 'What kind of a sick doggy snuff-film is this?'

Generation X: Poor Phoebe. *Halliwell's Film Guide* describes *Old Yeller* (Robert Stevenson, 1957) as an 'archetypal family movie' and the *Virgin Film Guide* calls it Disney's 'first and best attempt at a boy-and-his-dog film', yet it's famous for emotionally scarring more people for life than any other single childhood experience. Other famous weepies that Phoebe tries are: *Love Story* (Arthur Hiller, 1970, which is described by Halliwell thus: 'Two students marry; she dies'); *Bryan's Song* (Buzz Kulik, 1972, in which James Caan plays an American football player dying of lung cancer); *Terms of Endearment* (James L. Brookes, 1983, in which Debra Winger's character dies); *Alive* (Frank Marshall, 1992, in which a football team's plane crashes and they're forced to eat the flesh of the victims); *E.T. – The Extra Terrestrial* (Steven Spielberg, 1982, in which boy meets alien, alien dies, alien comes back to life and leaves); *Rocky II* (Sylvester Stallone, 1979, where Rocky loses); *Charlotte's Web* (Charles Nichols, 1973, based on the children's book by E.B. White, in which a spider changes everyone's life, and a pig gives birth and dies); *Pride of the Yankees* (Sam Wood, 1942, in which,

Phoebe is shocked to discover, a guy named Lou Gehrig dies of Lou Gehrig's disease, otherwise known as amythropic lateral sclerosis – by doctors); and the classic Christmas flick, *It's a Wonderful Life* (Frank Capra, 1946). Unable to cope with all this emotion, Phoebe ends up watching tapes of *Sesame Street* with Ben, though even this is a little too emotional for her. Ross refers to Joey's roommate as 'the Artist Formerly Known As Chandler', in reference to how the rock 'genius' Prince renamed himself. Phoebe's phrase 'snuff movie' came from the notoriously gory *Snuff* (Michael Findlay, 1976) – the movie that shocked America after allegations that actors in it were killed for real on screen.

The Story So Far: Chandler has a friend called Eric Prower, who has bad breath, and one called Dan, who incessantly pokes people with his finger as he talks. Monica and Ross think that, with the moustache, Chandler looks like their Aunt Sylvia (see 'TOW The Dozen Lasagnes'). Ross and Rachel have been dating for six weeks. Ben's first word is 'Hi!'

The Last Word: We're with Rachel on this one – saying 'poopy diaper' doesn't make the thought of changing a baby's nappy any less unpleasant, but then again, if it's a kid as cute as Ben we'd probably . . . still ask someone else to do it. Tom Selleck continues to solidify his position in the cast, verbally sparring with Chandler and coming off the better for it, but as you've probably guessed, Phoebe is the show-stealer in this episode, especially when she and Ben are left alone to watch *Sesame Street*. It's rare for a grown-up to realise just how scary some supposedly 'family' entertainment actually is (we know one person who finds *Tom and Jerry* absolutely terrifying) and it's just so reassuring to think that Ben will have Phoebe as an 'auntie' when he's growing up, just to keep his mind open and warn him when TV gets just that little bit too unsettling. Charming. **Ahhh Rating:** ***

French Title: 'Celui Qui Se Met Parler' (the one who starts to talk)

German Title: 'Ist Das Leben Nicht Schlecht?' (isn't life bad?)

221
'The One With The Bullies'
#457321

Writers: Sebastian Jones & Brian Buckner
Director: Michael Lembeck
First US transmission: 25.04.96
First UK transmission (C4): 01.11.96

Guest Cast: Peter DeLuise (Carl, the Big Bully),
Nicky Katt (Arthur, the Little Bully),
Laraine Newman (Mrs Buffay),
James Michael Tyler (Gunther),
and introducing Giovanni Ribisi (Frank Jr)

Summary: After a series of typically tenuous 'coincidences', Phoebe becomes convinced that the world is sending her signs telling her to try to find her father again. When she tries to go up to her father's house again, she's attacked by the family's overenthusiastic dog. She takes this as a bad sign and tries to leave, only to accidentally drive over the dog. Having taken the dog to the vet, she returns it to its owners only to discover that her father has left his second family too. A despondent Phoebe gives up on ever meeting her father again, but consoles herself with meeting the half-brother she never knew she had.

Monica has become hooked on stock trading after spending too much time watching the Business Channel. To avoid taking a job in a fifties-themed restaurant, she puts every penny into stock using a highly dubious selection process. But when she ends up losing it all in bad investments, she's forced to take the fifties restaurant job after all.

At Central Perk, Ross and Chandler come into conflict with a pair of bullies after one of them steals Chandler's hat. When the guys are forced to ask Gunther to help, the bullies warn them away from ever setting foot in the coffee house again. Eventually, Ross decides that enough is enough and the pair head down to Central Perk to sort out the situation. Removing their jewellery, watches and keys, the four men prepare for a rumble . . .

Freaky Monica: She gets hooked on stock trading because she sees some stock with her initials: 'Sometimes I have to watch for two or three hours before it comes up again but when it does it's pretty exciting.' According to Joey, she threatens one of the stock traders on the phone by warning him not to make her 'come down there and kick your Wall Street butt!' She ends up buying stock in CHP because she used to fancy Eric Estrada, and ZXY because she thought it sounded 'zexy'. All this because she doesn't want to wear 'flame-retardant boobs'.

Slow Joey: We get a better idea of why the guys are always round at Monica's for food as Joey makes himself an olive-loaf-and-ham-spread sandwich (no mayo). Rachel comments, 'The dog will lick himself but he will not touch your sandwich – what does that tell you?' When Monica claims her new motto to be 'Get out before they go down', Joey boasts, 'That is *so* not my motto.' He later phones the owners of the dog for Phoebe. When Rachel asks him why he put on a strange voice for the call, Joey just shrugs: 'Hard to say.' Seems he just can't help but act.

Chandleresque: Joey volunteers to go down to Central Perk and get Chandler's cap back: 'Nah, forget it,' says a defeated Chandler. 'It's probably stripped and sold for parts by now.' When the bullies lay claim to the couch in Central Perk, Chandler unadvisedly suggests, 'I'll tell you what – you call the couch and then . . . and then we'll call the couch, and we'll see who it comes to.' In preference to confronting the bullies, he suggests to Ross that they might just try to lose their virginities again, 'because I think actually mine's growing back'. Before the rumble can begin, a robber runs off with the cap containing all their valuables. As the four men chase him, Chandler trips on a little girl's skipping rope.

Just Plain Weird: Phoebe's idea of a sign is just out there! OK, so the buffet and franks references are understandable, but rotisseries with spinning chicken, which cannot, as

Monica suggests, refer to her father's Indian name, remind her of how she 'chickened out' from seeing her father last time, and somehow Phoebe gets from hamburger to pharmacist with fewer degrees of separation than Kevin Bacon. Later on, we see that she carries round a small box of Kibbles dog food just in case . . . she finds a dog or something. But now at least we can see it does run in the family, as Frank Buffay sounds weird (he liked stilts), and Frank Jr's definitely weird (see 'TOW Frank Jr').

Gunther's a Hero!: Gunther briefly intervenes in the War of the Couch.

Cruelty to Animals: Schnoodle, the Buffays' dog, immediately attacks Phoebe: 'All right, get the hell off my leg, you yippity piece of crap!' After waiting till nightfall for it to go away, Phoebe accidentally knocks over the dog, which was hiding in front of her cab. The doctor tells her that he'll need stitches and that 'only once in a blue moon does a dog's ear grow back'.

Generation X: One of the dishes at the diner is the Laverne and Curly Fries, in tribute to the criminally underappreciated 1970s sitcom, *Laverne and Shirley*, which was a spin-off from *Happy Days*. Monica's first 'performance' there is the 1978 anthem 'YMCA' by the Village People. Eric Estrada was the co-star of the long-running highway patrol series *CHiPS*. After Ross insists they go down to the coffee house to sort out the bullies, Chandler calls him 'Custer' in reference to the General famous for his 'last stand'. Peter DeLuise is the son of the actor Dom Deluise (the little round guy in all those seventies Burt Reynolds movies). Giovanni Ribisi appeared in *The X Files* as Darren Peter Oswald in the episode 'DPO'.

The Story So Far: Monica now works at a fifties-themed diner where the staff are forced to dress in fifties costumes and sing. Although this episode introduces Giovanni Ribisi as Frank Jr, Ribisi first appeared back in 'TOW The Baby On The Bus'. For the purposes of continuity, we're presuming that the character he played then was also Frank Buffay.

The Last Word: This is possibly the most disappointing episode of the season. It's OK, but it does kind of feel like everyone else has been given storylines just to give them something to do while Phoebe goes in search of her father again. Rachel and Joey are pretty much sidelined while the Gellers and Chandler deal with their problems, which aren't really that interesting, and while the climax to the episode is hilarious (Monica's ensemble dance routine to 'YMCA') it's maybe just a little too late to save this episode from veering towards the quality threshold of *Who's the Boss*. **Ahhh Rating:** *

French Title: 'Celui Qui Affronte Les Voyous' (the one who confronts the bullies)

German Title: 'Im Namen Der Männlichkeit (in the name of manliness)

222
'The One With Two Parties'
#457322

Writer: Alexa Junge
Director: Michael Lembeck
First US transmission: 02.05.96
First UK transmission (C4): 08.11.96

Guest Cast: Marlo Thomas (Sandra Green),
James Michael Tyler (Gunther),
Nancy Rubin (Guest), Lewis Dix (Man),
and introducing Rob Leibman (Dr Leonard Green)

Summary: The gang are planning a surprise birthday party for Rachel. After much deliberation, it is decided not to invite her parents: their impending divorce is getting Rachel down, and her mother and father are incapable of being in the same room without arguing. But Monica admits that she has already invited Mrs Green, and then Dr Green turns up out of the blue to wish his daughter a happy birthday.

In an effort to make sure the parents don't meet, a second party is set up in Chandler and Joey's apartment. Here, Dr Green is kept in the dark, while Mrs Green is entertained in Monica's apartment. As the evening goes on, people desperately try to slip away to Joey and Chandler's party, since Monica's consists of no-fun party games, which she rules with an obsessive iron fist. With the night drawing to a close, Rachel is once again depressed, as she has had to listen to her mother and father independently moan about each other's foibles. Could this be the worst birthday she's ever had?

Poor Ross: Throughout the episode, to cover for the fact that he's running errands for her husband, Ross has to pretend to Mrs Green that he drinks the same drinks as Dr Green, wears the same glasses, and smokes the same cigarettes. This leads Mrs Green to suggest to Rachel that she see a therapist – she's obviously hooked up with Ross just because he reminds her of her father.

Freaky Monica: While planning the party, she outlines exactly how things are going to work. The others ask why they can't just get a gang of people round, to have some drinks and some fun: 'Why do we always have parties with committees?' they ask her. At her party later on, she is getting people to write their most embarrassing memories on pieces of paper. She gives everyone a marker pen, and then makes a little speech about making sure that they put the caps back on – firmly, so they click. It's no wonder that Phoebe has to run a secret railroad of escapee party-people, helping them across the hallway to freedom at Joey and Chandler's. At one point, Phoebe makes a distraction so that some people can get away: she looks at one of Monica's tables and gasps, 'Did someone forget to use a coaster?'

Spoilt Rachel: She tells Ross that she loves the earrings he bought her. When he says that she can exchange them if she wants, she says, 'Now I love you even more' (see 'TOW The Embryos').

Slow Joey: When the gang are trying to decide who to invite, Joey vetoes Shannon Cooper, saying 'she steals stuff'. This is shorthand for the real reason – that he slept with her, then never called her again. When Stacy Roth is suggested, he says, 'She also steals.' It's quite clear, though, that he's fooling no one.

Chandleresque: When he sees Rachel is upset by her bickering parents, he calls her 'Tiger', explaining, 'When my parents were getting divorced, I got a lot of "Tigers" ...' Rachel asks him how he coped when his mother and father split up, and he confesses that he relied on a 'carefully regimented programme of denial and bed-wetting.'

Yo Gunther!: He lives in mortal terror of Monica's obsessiveness, and is grateful to Phoebe when she says that she can get him out of her dull party. The guilty look on his face when he is eventually discovered by Monica at Joey and Chandler's party is unique.

Generation X: As the party begins to get farcical, Chandler ponders what 'Jack and Chrissy' would do – another reference to the sitcom *Three's Company* (see his comments in 'Pilot'). Ross mentions Neil Sedaka, the pianist/singer with the permanently upbeat persona. According to Dr Green, one of Rachel's mother's favourite films is *The Bridges of Madison County* (Clint Eastwood, 1995).

The Story So Far: The place where Monica works is called the Moondance Diner.

The Last Word: This is a fantastic episode, a good, confident attempt at a farce. Throughout the whole thing, the tension rises as we wonder exactly when Mrs and Dr Green are going to see each other. It seems such an inevitability, that the fact that they never do comes as a surprise. When the two of them are in the hallway outside the apartments at the same time, the lengths to which the gang go to ensure they don't meet are phenomenal. First, Joey, Chandler and Ross dance Dr Green across the hallway, then Joey has to passionately kiss Mrs

Green to hide her from her husband. Terrific stuff. **Ahhh Rating:** **

French Title: 'Celui Qui Faisait Le Lien' (the one who made the connection)

German Title: 'Zwei Parties für Rachel' (two parties for Rachel)

223
'The One With The Chicken Pox'
#457324

Writer: Brown Mandell
Director: Michael Lembeck
First US transmission: 09.05.96
First UK transmission (C4): 15.11.96

Guest Cast: Tom Selleck (Dr Richard Burke),
Charlie Sheen (Ryan), Dorien Wilson (Mr Kogen),
Mary-Pat Green (Jeannie), Steve Park (Scott)

Summary: Phoebe's excited as Ryan, her on-off boyfriend in the navy, is coming into dock. He spends months at a time in a submarine, visiting Phoebe on those few days he has free. This time, he's coming for two weeks, and Phoebe's delighted to be able to spend so much time with him. But her plans run aground when she discovers that she's got chicken pox, and that Ryan has never had it: in theory, he should stay well clear of her. Romance and sheer physical attraction take over, though, and soon they both have 'the pox'.

Monica is beginning to have trouble with Richard, because he doesn't 'have a thing'. While she is crazily obsessive about almost everything, Richard is quite easygoing. He frantically tries to think of something, anything, kooky about himself, to make Monica feel less like a freak.

Joey, now out of work, accepts a job as a temporary processor at Chandler's company. He treats this work as an acting job, slipping into the role of 'Joseph the Processing Guy', making up a wife and children to fill out his character's background. While Chandler thinks this is bad enough, things take a turn for the worse when Joey starts to point the finger at Chandler over lax working practices. Eventually, Chandler realises he has to get rid of 'Joseph the Processing Guy', or his job could be in danger.

Freaky Monica: She enters her bedroom to see that Richard has made the bed, but he's got it all wrong: the duvet tag should be at the bottom right corner, and the flowers in the pattern should point towards the headboard, 'because . . . the head of the bed is where the sun would be'. Monica then sets about trying to organise Richard's life by her own mad rules. First of all, she makes sure everything on his desk is perpendicular ('If it's not a right angle, it's a wrong angle,' Richard intones), then she says she's going to set all his clocks 'to my time' (which differs, depending on which room of the house you're in). All this adds up to make this one of the definitive Freaky Monica episodes.

Phoebisms: She finds the fact that she has chicken pox 'so ironic', considering she's a vegetarian. When she's bidding a final goodbye to Ryan as they stand outside the gang's favourite haunt, she says that she's sorry they couldn't do everything she'd planned, 'like a picnic in Central Park, a coffee at Central Perk – oh, I just got that!' There's also a mention of a song of hers called 'Salt-Water Taffy Man', which the gang mistakenly presume she wrote about Ryan.

Chandleresque: The episode opens with Chandler and Monica arguing over ownership of a muffin. He solves the problem by licking right down one side of it. As he begins to eat it, Phoebe arrives to tell everyone about Ryan. 'This guy goes down for, like, two years at a time?' says Rachel. Chandler, desperate to make the obvious joke, can only give a muffled scream, as his mouth is gummed up with cake. 'That'll teach you to lick my muffin,' says Monica. More muffled protests ensue.

The Ballad of Ross & Rachel: Rachel is a very big fan of the naval uniform, it turns out, and Ross stops at nothing to hire his own for the night. When he appears to collect her from work, he swoops her into his arms and begins to carry her out of Central Perk. Rachel ruins the spontaneity of the moment, though. First, she realises that she's left the cappuccino machine on, then she forgets her handbag ... Eventually, Ross just dumps her on the sofa, and says he'll meet her upstairs.

Generation X: Charlie Sheen is the star of such films as *Platoon* (Oliver Stone, 1986), *Wall Street*, (Stone again, 1987) and the *Hot Shots* comedies (Jim Abrahams, 1991–3) as well as being the brother of Emilio Esteves and son of Martin Sheen. When Ross walks into Central Perk dressed as a sailor we hear a rendition of 'Up Where We Belong', a nod to the ending of *An Officer And A Gentleman* (Taylor Hackford, 1982).

The Story So Far: All of the gang have had chicken pox, apart from Phoebe – until now. Richard mentions Jim Croce's song 'Bad, Bad, Leroy Brown', who was the baddest, not the fattest, man in town. As Ross leaves Rachel in Central Perk, telling her he'll see her 'upstairs', we can presume that the coffee house is on the same block as the friends' apartments (but round the corner from the views we usually see when the camera shifts up from the street to a window).

The Last Word: Not one of the best episodes, but it has a few things to recommend it. Phoebe and Ryan's constantly lost battle to avoid scratching is hugely entertaining, as is Monica's fussiness overdrive. The big letdown, though, is the Chandler and Joey plotline: Joey seems a little bit too clever here, being devious in the way he gets people to like him. It's frankly wrong that Joey should get one over Chandler in anything other than chasing women. **Ahhh Rating:** *

French Title: 'Celui Qui Attrape La Varicelle' (the one who caught chicken pox)

German Title: 'Pocken statt Liebe' (pox instead of love)

224
'The One With Barry And Mindy's Wedding'
#457323

Writers: Ira Ungerleider (story), Brown Mandell (teleplay)
Director: Michael Lembeck
First US transmission: 16.05.96
First UK transmission (C4): 22.11.96

Guest Cast: Tom Selleck (Dr Richard Burke),
Mitchell Whitfield (Barry Farber),
Marie Hupp (Mindy Hunter-Farber), Peter Spears (Joel),
Jackie Bright (Mr Weinberg), Fritzi Burr (Mrs Weinberg),
Mindy Sterling (Wedding Planner), Maggie Wheeler (Janice)

Summary: Joey auditions for Warren Beatty for a part that demands he convincingly kiss another man, and, apparently, Beatty feels that he's a good actor but a lousy kisser. Phoebe agrees to let him practise on her (having already kissed him once), but Monica suggests that maybe Joey's problem is that he's just not used to kissing men. Unfortunately for Joey, none of his male friends are willing to go that far to help him in his career – despite many attempts on Joey's part to persuade them otherwise. Eventually Ross kisses Joey – only to hear that he'd already been turned down for the part.

Asked to be Mindy's matron of honour, Rachel prepares herself to face all of the guests who'd turned up for her non-wedding to Barry. Her lack of confidence isn't helped by her having to wear a dress that makes her look like the pink-fondant version of Little Bo Peep. It's made worse when she ends up walking down the aisle with her dress tucked into her knickers, and worse still when she finds out that all of the wedding guests had been told that she ran out on Barry because she'd gone mad with syphilis.

Monica and Richard are prompted by the wedding to assess their own future together. Monica is desperate to have children, so she's understandably disappointed to discover that Richard is not that keen on going through the parent thing again so late in life. Such a problem is too great for the relationship to withstand and the couple realise that it'd be for the best if they separated.

And Chandler begins a relationship via the Internet with a married woman. Realising he's falling for her, he agrees to meet up with her. She finally arrives at Central Perk – it's Janice, and the couple fall instantly into a passionate kiss.

Phoebisms: She tries to persuade Chandler to give his cyber-girlfriend a chance, despite the fact that she's married: 'If you don't meet her now, you're gonna be kicking yourself when you're eighty – which is hard to do and that's how you break a hip!' Yeah, Pheebs, we just about understand you there.

Slow Joey: He complains that saying he's not a good kisser is like someone accusing Mother Teresa of not being a good mother.

Chandleresque: He admits to sometimes getting a little 'defended and quippy'. He visits the website for the Guggenheim Museum because his cyber-chick likes museums and he likes funny words. He asks Joey, 'How come you don't fall down more?' after he makes a daft suggestion.

Cruelty to Animals: Monica reads an article that advises against throwing rice at weddings because rice can kill pigeons. Richard observes that this is why so few pigeons eat at sushi bars.

Generation X: Warren Beatty is a respected actor/director, having starred in films such as *Bonnie and Clyde* (Arthur Penn, 1967) and directed *Heaven Can Wait* (1978), *Reds* (1981), and *Dick Tracy* (1990). He's also managed to acquire a reputation as a bit of a Lothario, hence the comedy in Phoebe's question, 'What does Warren Beatty know about kissing?' When Monica tries to reassure Richard over her desires for children, she says that she's thinking way into the future, a time when 'apes [are] taking over the planet', in a reference (unsurprisingly) to *Planet of the Apes* (Franklin Schaffner, 1968). 'Copa Cobana' has become a bit of an anthem for its writer/singer, the legendary Barry Manilow.

The website for the Guggenheim Museum can be found at www.guggenheim.org and is really informative. Honest!

The Story So Far: In eighth grade, Rachel was forced to sing 'Copa Cobana' in front of the whole school but she 'freaked out' and ran off-stage. Mindy takes Barry's surname to create a new hyphenated name for herself – Mindy Hunter-Farber

The Last Word: Ross really is the perfect partner here, standing by his girlfriend and making her confront her fears – and being there for her afterwards. His speech at the wedding is really sweet, acknowledging just how much courage it took for Rachel to turn up, though he might have wanted to leave out the reference to syphilis. Rachel's impromptu performance of 'Copa Cobana' is just painful, yet she manages to finish with at least some of the dignity she had been striving for. It's sad, though, to see a couple as good as Richard and Monica splitting up, especially as Tom Selleck has been such a welcome addition to the regular cast. And, of course, Chandler's one chance of love comes round again, and the cast's reaction to Janice's appearance is spectacular (all together now, '*Oh – My – Gohhhddd!*'). On reflection, maybe the episode should have ended here, because the payoff with Ross finally agreeing to kiss Joey isn't really as good. But Joey is, for once, absolutely right: 'Rachel is a very lucky girl.' **Ahhh Rating:** * for Rachel, ** for Monica and Richard, and * each for Chandler and Janice. Which, erm, rather surprisingly makes *****

French Title: 'Celui Qui Embrassait Mal' (the one who kisses badly)

German Title: 'Rosarote Träume' (pink dreams)

Third Season

1996–1997

25 Episodes

301

'The One With The Princess Leia Fantasy'
#465251

Writers: Michael Curtis & Gregory S. Malins
Director: Gail Mancuso
First US transmission: 16.09.96
First UK transmission (C4): 04.07.97

Guest Cast: Maggie Wheeler (Janice), Christina Pickles
(Judy Geller), Elliott Gould (Jack Geller)

Summary: Since Monica broke off the relationship with Richard, she's done nothing but mooch around the house and everyone is beginning to suspect that she's not slept at all. Every little thing reminds her of Richard – even a clump of hair she finds in the bathroom drain. Phoebe decides to step in with some meditative techniques designed to take her to a Happy Place, but even these won't work.

Chandler and Janice run into problems when Joey makes it clear that he still can't stand the woman. Chandler, a little hurt by this, tells Janice about Joey's feelings – she then sets about arranging 'Joey and Janice's Day of Fun'. ('Does it have to be a whole day?' Joey asks. 'Yes,' Janice replies, 'because that's how long it takes to love me.') The whole thing is to little avail, though, as Joey returns hating Janice just as much.

Rachel, a little peeved that Ross is spending so much time in bed working on dinosaurs instead of working on her, tries to find out how she can spice up their love life. With a little cajoling, Ross admits to having a fantasy about Princess Leia's gold bikini outfit in *Return of the Jedi*. When Rachel, a little shocked by this, shares this information with Phoebe, she tells Rachel that it's not that surprising a fantasy at all. So she kits up and plays the part for Ross – but Ross has the moment shattered for him by the memory of Chandler's frightening confession (see **Chandleresque** opposite).

Poor Ross: When he discovers that the women tell each other 'pretty much' everything, Ross – proud and excited – asks Rachel if she tells people about the night of five times only to be reminded that was with Carol. Both Phoebe and Monica take their opportunities to have a dig at his Leia fantasy. Early on, Phoebe holds two Danish pastries to the side of her head and wonders where her brave 'Ross Skywalker' is – before noticing that he's right in front of her. Later, Rachel asks a distraught Monica if she wants to be taken home. 'Uh-huh,' she replies, 'or maybe to a galaxy far, far away.'

Freaky Monica: Monica is desperately hoping that Richard is feeling as bad as she is and refuses to rest easy until she knows that this is the case. When she plaintively cries, 'Why hasn't he called?', Phoebe suggests it's 'because you told him not to'. 'What are you?' she snaps. 'The Memory Woman?'

Phoebisms: When she is told that Monica is taking the break-up with Richard badly, Phoebe says that this would explain a call at two in the morning, where all she could hear was a 'high squeaky sound'. She'd presumed it was a mouse or a possum, but soon realised that it couldn't have been, because 'where would a mouse or a possum get the money to make the phone call?' Phoebe tells Rachel that she had also dated a man with a Princess Leia fantasy. When Rachel asks if it was fun, Phoebe replies, 'Oh, yeah. Mmm-mmm. Oh!' Rachel begins to think this Leia thing is a good idea, but Phoebe points out that the response had more to do with her new pager – she had it in her pocket, set to vibrate. Her attempts to calm Monica are lovely, sitting by her bedside, telling her to 'listen to the plinky, plunky music' to take her to the Happy Place. But Monica doesn't seem to be able to concentrate totally on relaxing: when Phoebe tells her to think about 'the lovely waterfalls, and the trickling fountains, and the calming sounds of the babbling brook', all Monica wants to do is pee. When Monica accidentally drops the wad of 'drain hair' into Ross's breakfast, Pheebs claims it looks like a tiny little person drowning in his cereal.

Slow Joey: Joey, when Ross tells him about Chandler's sick admission, goes to Chandler to reassure him that he suffers from exactly the same affliction: 'I always picture your mom when I'm having sex.' Earlier in the episode, he is watching *Wheel of Fortune*. The legend _OUN_ _USHMORE is on the screen, to which he screams, 'It's Count Rushmore!' Chandler later points out that there was no such person as Count Rushmore; Joey responds, 'Yeah? Then who's the guy that painted the faces on the mountain?' It's revealed in this episode that Joey has dated a prostitute and had sex on the Staten Island Ferry.

Chandleresque: When Ross tells Chandler that the women share everything, he suggests that they should do the same. Ross admits to his Princess Leia fantasy, while Chandler offers up the fact that he sometimes pictures his mother while he is having sex. Ross, deeply appalled, cries, 'I said "share" not "scare"!' Later, when he tells Joey how much he loves Janice, he declares, 'I think this could be the real thing. Capital "R"! Capital "T"!' adding for Joey's benefit 'Don't worry, those *are* the right letters.'

Parents – Who Needs 'Em?: It's a visit from her father, seeking 'a little Monicuddle', that finally enables her to sleep soundly and relax about the break-up. Ross, meanwhile, has problems with his mother. Thanks to Chandler's confession, an image of his mother in the gold bikini replaces the beautiful sight of Rachel in the same outfit and we see Mrs Geller say to Ross, 'Come on, sweetie, you're, like, freaking me out here.'

Just Plain Weird: It's not that weird, but it goes to show how familiar the producers expect their audience to be with the show. In the opening scene, they make a joke out of the way the gang walk into Central Perk, see strangers sitting at the couch, and dejectedly walk straight out again.

Boys Will Be Boys: There's one thing they won't discuss when Ross and Chandler embark upon their failed attempt at sharing. Ross says that the girls talk about everything: 'stuff you like, stuff she likes, technique, stamina, girth . . .' Panicked, Chandler checks, 'We're not going to talk about girth, are we?'

Generation X: The 'Most Romantic Song Ever' debate includes votes for 'Tupolo Honey' by Van Morrison (Ross) and 'The Way We Were' by Barbra Streisand (Rachel). Phoebe votes for 'that one that Elton John wrote for, um, that guy on *Who's The Boss*', which turns out to be 'Hold me close, young Tony Dan-za'. Oh, and a little-known trilogy called *Star Wars* (notably *Return of the Jedi*) is referenced . . . a lot.

The Story So Far: Ross mentions the naval uniform he hired in 'TOW The Chicken Pox'.

The Last Word: A pretty low-key beginning to the season, especially when compared with the frenetic, harrowing events of the second season's opener, 'The One With Ross's New Girlfriend', but pretty entertaining nevertheless. If anything, everything's a little too normal: everything's fine between Ross and Rachel (that will change, of course), everything's fine between Chandler and Joey (excepting the Janice thing), Chandler's happy (for the moment), Monica's down (which is about the only interesting thing on a dramatic level), and Phoebe's . . . well, Phoebe's Phoebe. If this is too stable, then it only serves to highlight how the weakness of the rest of the season is its soap-opera fluctuation. All in all, a merely ho-hum outing. **Ahhh rating:** **

French Title: 'Celui Qui Rêvait De La Princesse Leia' (the one who dreamt of Princess Leia)

German Title: 'Phantasien' (fantasy)

302
'The One Where No One's Ready'
#465252

Writer: Ira Ungerleider
Director: Gail Mancuso
First US transmission: 26.09.96
First UK transmission (C4): 11.07.97

Guest Cast: Peter Dennis (Sherman Whitfield), Tom Selleck
(the voice of Dr Richard Burke)

Summary: Ross has an important speech to make at a dinner
at the museum, and he wants everyone to come with him. The
only problem is, it starts in half an hour and, well, no one's
ready. Ross has to contend with all sorts of things before they
can leave: Joey and Chandler fighting over sovereignty of
an armchair, Phoebe getting hummus down her dress, and
Monica obsessing over a message she's heard on Richard's
answering machine. Worst of all, he loses his temper at
Rachel and she then refuses to go. Will he be able to save his
relationship *and* get to dinner on time?

Poor Ross: Of course, the whole episode is about 'Poor
Ross', but one particularly good put-down comes when
Monica sees him all dressed up in his bow tie and suit, and
asks if he's going to 'do magic'.

Freaky Monica: Playing back her messages, Monica hears
one from Richard and panics when she can't work out
whether it's old or new. Eventually she phones him, leaving
what she describes as a 'breezy' message on his machine.
When she plays it back to everyone (of course, she still knows
the code to 'break into' his machine), she realises that it's not
as breezy as she'd hoped. This leads to a riotous series of
calls, her neurosis increasing with every one. The final
indignity comes when she leaves a message to Richard
excusing her behaviour, saying that her period may be to
blame – what she's actually done is left it as his *outgoing*

message, letting anyone who calls him hear it. This brilliant sequence of events is the best thing about this otherwise tired and tiring episode, and Monica's trademark '*No!*' (used here twice, with little pause) possibly explains why Cox ended up in a film called *Scream*.

Phoebisms: During a fight between Joey and Chandler, some hummus is spilt on her dress. After calling them 'rotten boys', the only thing she can do – given the time constraints, and the fact Ross is getting freaky – is to cover the stain with a Christmas decoration. She explains that she thought, 'All right, fine. I'll be political.' When Chandler asks, 'What are you supporting?', she just replies, 'Duh! Christmas!'

Slow Joey: Joey explains that he wants to wear underwear when he puts on the hired tuxedo: 'I'm not going to go commando in another man's fatigues.' When he puts on all of Chandler's clothes in revenge for his flatmate hiding his underwear ('Look at me! I'm Chandler!' he mocks. 'Could I *be* wearing any more clothes?'), Joey is still going commando. Chandler's horror is perfectly justified when Joey starts to lunge.

Chandleresque: Having completed the Cosmopolitan quiz while in the bathroom, Chandler concludes, 'It turns out I *do* put career before men.' His verbal sparring with Joey over ownership of the chair is good, with Chandler claiming he wrote a song today called 'Get Up!', and finally resorting to quoting 'the words of A.A. Milne: "Get out of my chair, dillhole!"' It's also revealed that he once borrowed some inflatable sheep that went with Rachel's Little Bo Peep outfit, although he claims, 'We used them as pillows when we went camping.' When Chandler tells his roommate to taste what he thinks is cider, Joey discovers the 'cider' is actually fat. Chandler calmly tells him, 'Yeah, I know, I did that two minutes ago.'

The Ballad of Ross & Rachel: Having seriously upset Rachel by shouting at her when she took too long to get ready, Ross has to find a way to paper over the cracks so that he can persuade her to come to the dinner. Joey suggests that he drink a glass of fat that Monica has been keeping in the refrigerator, to prove just how sorry he is. Rachel supports the suggestion, and he's about to do it when she stops him, amazed that he might have drank something so gross out of love for her. In return for this weird display of love, Rachel quickly gets dressed in a stunning gown, revealing to Ross as they leave that she's going 'commando' too.

Dinosaurs ROCK!: When Rachel asks whether one of her many outfits looks like 'something the girlfriend of a palaeontologist would wear', Phoebe says, 'I don't know. You might be the first one.' Ross also has a dinosaur watch.

Generation X: Chandler refers to A.A. Milne, the author of the Winnie the Pooh stories.

The Story So Far: We're reminded that Joey often wears no underwear (see 'TOW The Boobies').

The Last Word: Well, if the last episode was a bit lame, this one is trying to walk without any legs at all. While the setup seems promising – the six of them spend the entire episode in Monica and Rachel's apartment – the execution is frankly poor. The script is dull and the performers seem to know it, with none of them trying particularly hard to make it work. The scenes focusing on Monica's answering-machine exploits are by far the best, and Cox does a great job with them. But it's not enough to save this episode from a forgettable fate. **Ahhh rating:** *

French Title: 'Celui Qui A Du Mal À Se Préparer' (the one who has trouble getting ready)

German Title: 'Eile mit Weile!' (literally 'rushing with time-taking', which we suppose is similar to 'more haste, less speed')

303
'The One With The Jam'
#465253

Writer: Wil Calhoun
Director: Kevin S. Bright
First US transmission: 03.10.96
First UK transmission (C4): 18.07.97

Guest Cast: David Arquette (Malcolm), Maggie Wheeler
(Janice), James Michael Tyler (Gunther), Lisa Kudrow
(Ursula Buffay)

Summary: Monica, trying to fill the hole in her life left by
Richard, has become a one-woman jam factory, churning out
jar after jar of the stuff. While Joey is in heaven – he loves the
stuff – she soon realises that it's something she can't do for
ever. Instead, she decides to make a visit to the nearest sperm
bank and get herself pregnant!

Phoebe notices that she's beginning to get unwanted attention: she is being stalked by a man called Malcolm. When she
confronts him on the street, it becomes clear that he thought
that she was Ursula, Phoebe's twin sister, who apparently
dumped him. Somewhat taken by Malcolm, Phoebe suggests
that they go for a coffee and, over time, she begins to fall for
him. Little does she know, however, that he's still stalking
Ursula . . .

Freaky Monica: Yet again, Monica is the best thing in this
episode. Her aching need to find some way to make her life
valid is touching. Her final solution, getting pregnant by an
anonymous donor, is, on the one hand, just another example
of her desperation and, on the other, terribly, terribly sad.
Joey, for once being clever and cunning, manages to talk her
out of it by playing up to her fantasies of a proper family life:
in this fantasy, she's married to a guy called Hoyt ('It's a
name,' confirms Joey). This is a deeply emotional scene,
played beautifully by Cox and Le Blanc. Monica also gets the

best line of the episode, and one to remember when an overhelpful friend is trying to talk over you. When Ross tries to interrupt her explanation of wanting to become pregnant, Monica snaps, 'Lips moving! Still talking!' It is also revealed that Monica signs little notes to Rachel using her *full* name.

Spoilt Rachel: Although she has lived in New York for over two years, there are still a couple of things Rachel doesn't know. When Monica explains that she bought all her jam-bound fruit at the docks and boasts, 'Bet you didn't know you could get it wholesale,' Rachel says, 'I didn't know there were docks.' Later, when Monica says she knows where she can get some sperm, Rachel suggests, 'Down at the docks again?'

Phoebisms: Her efforts to 'de-Ursula-ise' Malcolm fail miserably when she discovers that he is still stalking her sister. She suggests instead that he stalk her for a while: 'I'll be like an Ursula patch.' It is revealed that Phoebe, when she was in school, thought she was a witch. She tells of how her guidance counsellor gave her these words of wisdom: 'OK, you're not a witch, you're just an average student.' She apparently took all their hidden meanings to heart, summarising the advice as, 'Get over it.'

Slow Joey: As Chandler sits alone in the living room of their apartment, a rhythmic bed-spring squeak starts up from Joey's room. A yelp follows, and Chandler bursts in on him to point out that this is why his parents warned him not to jump on the bed. His love of jam is revealed in this episode: he explains to Rachel how, when he was younger, his mother would drop him off at the cinema, leaving him a pot of jam and a little spoon. Rachel, smiling, looks at him and says, 'You're so pretty.' Later, Chandler holds out a hand, representing 'the girl from the Xerox place, buck naked'. He then holds out his other hand and adds, '. . . or a big tub of jam'. Joey just grins and says, seedily, 'Put your hands *together*.' When he has to go to hospital following the bed jumping incident, he considers claiming that his arm just 'fell out of its socket' until Chandler warns him that the doctor is unlikely to believe him.

Chandleresque: Ross explains to Chandler how to fool a girlfriend into thinking she's being cuddled while asleep. 'Hug for her, roll for you,' he demonstrates, hugging a cushion to him before carefully rolling away from it. Later, when Chandler is in bed, his mind drifts to the amount of space on Janice's side: 'You could fit a giant penguin over there!' he thinks to himself. 'That'd be weird, though.' He attempts the hug-roll manoeuvre, but his arm remains trapped under Janice, and trying to tug it out he sends her crashing to the floor. After Monica tells everyone she's ditched the jam-making for baby-making, Chandler advises that she's 'gonna need much bigger jars'.

The Ballad of Ross & Rachel: The lovers give Chandler advice on how to handle a girlfriend's asking if she looks fat. Immediate response is the key, and Rachel adequately demonstrates how that works both ways. As an example, Ross asks, 'Does size matter?', to which she snappily responds, 'No!' But, when Chandler tells them of the cuddling-in-bed problem, Rachel says, 'I'm sorry, we can't help you there, because we're cuddly sleepers.' Ross playfully agrees, but, the minute she leaves, he begins to explain his hug-roll technique.

Generation X: Ursula's stalker is played by David Arquette (brother of the actor Alexis and the actresses Patricia and Rosanna), who also stars opposite Courteney Cox in *Scream* and *Scream 2* (Wes Craven, 1997–8). Monica's ideal sperm donor describes himself as a male Geena Davis, star of, among others, *Thelma and Louise* (Ridley Scott, 1991).

The Story So Far: Shortly after his fertility experiment for the NYU, Joey made a 'donation' to a sperm bank (see 'TOW Rachel Finds Out'). Monica finds his details in her list of prospective donors (when Joey checks with the bank, he discovers that no one has taken any of his donations and considers adding his work on *Days of Our Lives* (see 'TOW Russ') to attract more potential buyers). This episode is the first time we hear of 'the girl from the Xerox place' (see 'TOW Ross And Rachel Take A Break'). In

Joey's sperm-donor description we learn that Joey was born in Queens.

The Last Word: Another decidedly average episode, made better by Monica's moving plotline. It seems that whenever Phoebe is given a sizeable piece of the action, her dizziness has to take second place, making her less interesting and far less funny. While there are enough laughs to keep you entertained, this is a fairly run-of-the-mill outing. We're just grateful that everyone is too polite to see the irony in Matthew Perry asking Ross and Rachel if he looks fat. **Ahhh Rating:** ***

French Title: 'Celui Qui Avait La Technique Du Câlin' (the one with the hugging technique)

German Title: 'Süße Gelüste' (sweet lust)

304
'The One With The Metaphorical Tunnel'
#465254

Writer: Alexa Junge
Director: Steve Zuckerman
First US transmission: 10.10.96
First UK transmission (C4): 25.07.97

Guest Cast: Jane Sibbett (Carol Willick), Jessica Hecht (Susan Bunch), Maggie Wheeler (Janice), Charlie & Jack Allen (Ben), Edo Azran (Young Ross), Sierra Dawn Hill (Young Monica)

Summary: Chandler is reaching crisis point in his relationship with Janice. Now that he's fearing that they're becoming 'a couple', all sorts of alarm bells are ringing and he's beginning to want to run a mile. When Monica and Rachel persuade him that commitment is no bad thing, he overcompensates and, over dinner with his girlfriend, makes the mistake of saying that he might be ready for them to live together. To Chandler's surprise, she freaks out and he must embark on some serious damage limitation if he is to save his relationship.

Phoebe gets herself in trouble with Joey when she forgets to remind him about an audition, and as an apology offers to pretend to be his agent, phone the casting director and get the audition rescheduled. Joey immediately starts to ask Phoebe to arrange more auditions for him. But, although it's fun to begin with, Phoebe soon has a problem finding ways to tell Joey that people think he sucks without breaking his heart.

Poor Ross: Carol and Susan bring Ben round to visit his dad, and Ben brings with him his new favourite toy – a Barbie doll. Ross spends the rest of the episode trying to persuade Ben to part with the Barbie in favour of something more manly, like monster trucks, Dinosoldiers, and GI Joe. His efforts are finally successful, but Monica still doesn't see what the big deal is. She recalls a time when, as a child, Ross used to dress up in his mother's clothes, including 'the big hat, the pearls, the little pink handbag'. Ross called himself Bea, and he sang a song: 'I am Bea, I like tea, Won't you dance around with me?' Susan's glee at this is barely disguised: 'I've literally never been this happy.' Over the closing titles, we see film of a younger Ross at a table in the garden, dressed as Bea and singing his song. It's a marvellous touch.

Freaky Monica: She explains that she always keeps notepads around, so that notes can be taken in any emergency – like when you're panicked and in the middle of a game of hide and seek, as Phoebe was. She suggests that, if Phoebe had done the same, she wouldn't have had to write the message from the casting director on her hand – Phoebe confesses that that's why they don't invite her to play.

Phoebisms: Her wonderful methods of fooling people into thinking she's an agent, while she calls from the phone in Central Perk, are breathtaking. Putting on two voices (the agent and her secretary), she's soon arranged a multitude of auditions for Joey. But trouble starts when she has to tell him he's being rejected by all of them. When she breaks the first bit of bad news to him, she says, 'Oh God, I don't want to be the person who makes your face look like that.' Joey, though, relies on her honesty, and bravely sticks it out when Phoebe reports that people have said that he isn't 'believable as a human being', and that he's 'pretty but dumb' – sorry, that's 'pretty dumb'!

Chandleresque: Joey suggests he should confront his fears and enter the metaphorical tunnel: 'Jump off the high dive, stare down the barrel of the gun, pee into the wind!' Chandler replies, 'I assure you, if I'm staring down the barrel of a gun, I'm pretty much peeing every which way.' When Janice finally calls him back after he freaked her out, Monica and Rachel suggest he should act sleepy and grumpy: 'Stop naming dwarves!' he cries.

Joey's an Actor?: Joey appears in an infomercial for the Milk Master 2000, a device designed to stop you covering yourself in milk when you try to open the carton. When he finally persuades Phoebe to tell him exactly what the casting directors thought of him, she's forced to tell him they claimed to have never met an Italian with a worse Italian accent (and they're right, too!).

Girl Power: We learn the secrets of ice cream usage in emotional emergencies. Monica and Rachel use the 'low-cal, non-dairy, soy-milk junk' for everyday crises, because 'when you start to get screwed over all the time, you gotta switch to low-fat'. They bring out the full-fat ice cream for Chandler when his obsessive need to express his feelings for Janice has seemingly driven her away.

Generation X: When Monica asks if anyone has seen her left boob, Joey confuses it with the movie *My Left Foot* (Jim Sheridan, 1989) and claims he has.

The Story So Far: Joey's arm is still in a sling from the previous episode. We are reminded that Joey's real agent is Estelle (see 'TOW The Butt', and 'TOW Russ').

The Last Word: The troubles between Chandler and Janice give Matthew Perry the perfect chance to play Chandler

touched with a sadness and desperation that's truly touching.
The scene in the supermarket, when he is faux-casually trying
to coax Janice back, is both side-splittingly funny and almost
tear-jerking. Meanwhile, Ross and Phoebe get a couple of
decent scenes. While there are duds in the third season, this is
pretty much standard – and it's a good standard too.

    . . . And are any of you beginning to actually *like* Janice
yet? 'I gotta buy a vowel, because . . . oh – my – Gahhhd!!'
Ahhh Rating: ***

French Title: 'Celui Qui Ne Supportait Pas Les Poupées'
(the one who couldn't stand dolls)

German Title: 'Die andere Seite des Tunnels' (the other side
of the tunnel)

305
'The One With Frank Jr'
#465255

Writers: Scott Silveri & Shana Goldberg-Meehan
Director: Steve Zuckerman
First US transmission: 17.10.96
First UK transmission (C4): 01.08.97

Guest Cast: Isabella Rossellini (herself), Giovanni Ribisi
(Frank Jr), **and introducing** Cynthia Mann (Jasmine)

Summary: Phoebe's half-brother Frank Jr is spending the
weekend in the city with his sister. While he is excited about
how he could go down to Times Square and pick up some
'ninja stars', Phoebe soon begins to worry that the two of
them aren't connecting. Phoebe tries to engage Frank in all
sorts of conversations, but he seems far more interested in
melting things. When she takes him to see where she works,
she offers him a free massage, but his ideas of the seedy city
land him in trouble: he thinks this is a different kind of

'massage parlour' altogether, and he tries it on with one of the other workers.

Chaos reigns at Chandler and Joey's: to Chandler's extreme annoyance, Joey is building an 'entertainment unit', and their apartment is full of pieces of wood and a plethora of power tools. Rachel and Ross, meanwhile, work out their 'freebie lists': the lists of those five celebrities they are allowed to have sex with, should they meet them. Ross, being Ross, takes a lot of time and care over his, pulling Isabella Rossellini from the list just a little while before she walks into Central Perk.

Poor Ross: While considering his freebie list, he names Isabella Rossellini as a possible candidate. Chandler points out that she's too 'international' and is never around. 'Yeah,' laughs Rachel, 'that's why you won't get Isabella Rossellini – geography.' When he reveals his final decisions, he pulls a little credit-card-sized list from his pocket – typeset and laminated! The final list includes Uma Thurman, Winona Ryder, Elizabeth Hurley, Michelle Pfieffer and Dorothy Hamill. When, ironically, he gets the chance to meet Isabella Rossellini, Rachel decides to let him have her as 'an alternate'. Making an embarrassing botch of it, as everyone else looks on, he is eventually forced into showing her the list. 'That's not the final draft,' he explains. 'It's laminated!' she says. Once he has explained that she was 'bumped' in favour of Winona Ryder, Isabella claims that she has a list of five 'goofy coffee house guys', and that (pointing to another customer) 'yesterday I bumped *you* for that guy over there'. She leaves, and Ross tells the others, 'We're just going to be friends.'

Freaky Monica: Joey tells her that her bathroom floor is 'old and dingy', but Monica won't believe him until he moves her laundry basket to show her the original colour of the floor underneath. Seeing it, she gasps, 'I can't live like this! What are we going to do? What are we going to do?'

Spoilt Rachel: When asked who might appear on her freebie list, Rachel *instantly* lists Chris O'Donnell, John F. Kennedy

Jr, Daniel Day Lewis, Sting and Parker Stevenson (the Hardy Boy). At Central Perk, she brings a customer his order: 'Let's see if I got this right. So, this is a half-caf, double tall, easy hazelnut, non-fat, no foam, with whip, extra-hot latte, right?' Amazingly, she *has* got it right, but as she walks away, she whispers to herself, 'Freak!'

Phoebisms: Waiting outside Central Perk for Frank Jr to arrive, she tells Rachel that he's always late. When Rachel gets Phoebe to confirm that she's only met her half-brother once, Phoebe says, 'I think it sounds big-sistery, you know? "Frank's always late".' Exhibiting unusually quick wits, Phoebe manages to win the shadow game with Monica. After Monica starts to copy everything Pheebs says, she eventually tells her that she doesn't have the time to waste. 'No, that is what the game is,' Monica explains. 'Which you gave up really quickly!' Phoebe explains, victoriously. When the entertainment unit is finally finished and erected, it blocks half of Chandler's bedroom door and half of Joey's. Joey wonders whether his ruler is wrong. 'Maybe,' adds Phoebe, '*all* the rulers are wrong.'

Chandleresque: Joey reminds him that they're always saying they need somewhere to put the mail, but he got carried away and decided to take it to the next step. Seeing all the wood around him, Chandler asks, 'You're building a post office?' When Frank Jr says that his friend Larry wants him to bring a photo of a prostitute back from Manhattan, Chandler muses, 'You know, we don't really take advantage of living in the city.' His freebie list, by the way, comprises Kim Basinger, Cindy Crawford, Halle Berry, Yasmine Bleeth and Jessica Rabbit (who, Rachel feels compelled to mention, is a cartoon, and therefore way out of his league).

Just Plain Weird: On meeting Rachel and Monica, Frank Jr asks the boys, 'How do you guys get anything done?' (To which Chandler replies, 'We don't, really.') Trying to get to know him a little better, Phoebe asks, 'What kind of things do you like to do at home?' 'Melt stuff,' Frank replies, blankly. Later, Phoebe watches while Frank melts a plastic spoon. She asks him if his hobby is art, and Frank says, 'Yeah, you can melt art.' Saying that she's going to bed (the fumes are giving her a headache), she leaves him a fire extinguisher – 'Just in case.' 'Cool!' says Frank, trying to melt its nozzle. After clearing up the misunderstanding with Phoebe's co-worker, Frank starts to list all the things he enjoyed about the weekend. 'I almost got my arm broken by a hooker,' he says. 'She wasn't a hooker,' Phoebe corrects him, once again. 'Well,' explains Frank, 'when I tell my friends about her, she will be.'

Generation X: Isabella Rossellini is the daughter of Ingrid Bergman and Roberto Rossellini, and the star of David Lynch's *Blue Velvet* (1986) and *Wild at Heart* (1990). One of Ross's 'freebie list' women is Dorothy Hamill, a celebrated American ice skater.

The Story So Far: Phoebe's birthday is 16 February (she *is* a typical Aquarian), and Frank Jr's is 25 October (Scorpio). Frank can fold his tongue in half (!) and Phoebe can't. Although this episode introduces Cynthia Mann, as Phoebe's co-worker, Jasmine, she did make an appearance as a waitress in the very first episode.

The Last Word: Giovanni Ribisi (Frank Jr) is the star turn of this episode, and we're ecstatic that he's become a series regular. It's quite sweet to see Phoebe trying so hard to get on with Frank, trying to build herself a family. This must be the first time that a serious Phoebe subplot doesn't become the most boring thing in the episode. The appearance of Rossellini, while so obviously gratuitous, is brilliantly funny; although she sticks out like a sore thumb at Central Perk, that only serves to highlight the fact that Ross doesn't have a snowball's chance in hell. **Ahhh Rating: ****

French Title: 'Celui Qui Bricolait' (the one who does DIY)

German Title: 'Erotische Pläne' (sexy plans)

306
'The One With The Flashback'
#465256

Writers: Marta Kauffman & David Crane
Director: Peter Bonerz
First US transmission: 31.10.96
First UK transmission (C4): 08.08.97

Guest Cast: Maggie Wheeler (Janice), John Lehr (Eric, the photographer), Larry Hankin (Mr Heckles), Michele Maika (Kiki), Marissa Ribisi (Betsy), Christy L. Medrano (Waitress)

Summary: It all starts when Janice innocuously asks whether any of the friends have ever slept with each other. When an emphatic 'no' comes back, she asks if they've ever come close . . . What follows is a tale of the gang exactly a year before Rachel moved to the city, before anyone had met Joey, before Ross and Carol broke up, and before Phoebe moved out of Monica's. At least, before Monica *found out* she'd moved. We discover that Joey nearly didn't move in – but Mr Heckles's intervention saw that he did. Rachel was doubtful about marrying Barry well before the wedding itself – and she used to have a horrible perm.

As this slice of history draws to a close, Janice has her question answered. Phoebe and Ross were very close to making out shortly after Carol told him she was a lesbian; Monica had the hots for Joey the minute they met, and Joey mistook her offer of a lemonade for an offer of sex; Chandler and Monica shared a tender moment in each other's arms; and Rachel fantasised about having a fling with some weird bloke she met in a bar – who is later introduced to her as Chandler!

Poor Ross: Ross is over the moon when Carol meets a woman at the gym called Susan. 'I think it's going to make a difference,' he smiles naïvely, pleased she finally has a friend of her own. In the bar later, he explains to Phoebe that he suspects his marriage might be over, because his wife's a lesbian and he's not: '. . . and apparently it's not a mix-and-match situation.' Commenting on it later, he criticises himself, saying, 'Maybe this wouldn't have happened if I'd been more nurturing, or I'd paid more attention, or I . . . had a uterus.'

Freaky Monica: When Phoebe finally admits that she has moved out of the apartment, she confesses that Monica's tidiness drove her away: 'I need to live in a land where people can spill!' 'You can spill,' Monica asserts, '. . . in the sink.' Answering a question most of us have pondered, we discover that Monica's apartment actually belongs to her grandmother, who let her have it when she moved to Florida – 'otherwise I could never afford a place like this,' she explains to Joey.

Spoilt Rachel: Meeting Monica in the bar that will become Central Perk, Rachel shows off her engagement ring ('You can't even see where the *Titanic* hit it,' gasps Monica), explaining that her husband-to-be is 'a doctor, thank you very much'. 'Just like you always wanted,' coos Monica. Rach admonishes the waitress for getting her order wrong. As the waitress walks away, she turns to her friends. 'I mean, how hard is it to get a couple of drinks right, huh?'

Phoebisms: When Janice asks, 'Who, of the six of you, has slept with the six of you?' Phoebe, dazed, replies, 'Wow, it's like a dirty math problem.' During the flashback, we see how Phoebe tried to hide that she'd moved out of Monica's. Ross and Chandler know, but Monica has no idea. When Monica notices that Phoebe's bed is missing, she asks her where it's gone. 'It's not in the apartment?' Pheebs asks lamely. After the gang almost catch Ross and Phoebe making out on the pool table, Phoebe diffuses the situation by stroking the green felt on the table and declaring that Ross was right. 'I don't know why I always thought this was real grass!'

Slow Joey: Joey alludes to one time when Monica and Rachel got together. When they strongly protest that there was no such event, Joey smiles and says, 'OK, but let's say there was. How might that go?' (See 'TOW All The Haste' to find out.) During the flashback, we see Monica invite Joey, who's busy moving his stuff into Chandler's, in for a lemonade. As she pours, she tells him to make himself comfortable, which Joey does by stripping quite naked. Monica, shocked, asks, 'When someone asks you in for lemonade, and to you that means they want to have sex?' Joey, putting his clothes back on, replies, 'Well, usually, yeah! Well, not just lemonade: iced tea, sometimes juice . . .' At the close of the episode, Ross tells the gang, 'My wife's a lesbian.' Joey – who hasn't even been introduced to Ross, let alone his marriage problems – grins. 'Cool!'

Chandleresque: Joey, being shown around Chandler's flat, tells his prospective new flatmate that he's 'totally OK with the gay thing'. Chandler blankly stares at him, asking, 'What gay thing?' Monica is practically begging Chandler to let Joey move in, as she fancies him. Chandler replies, sarcastically, that he's always wanted a roommate who enables him to be referred to as 'the *funny* one'.

Ugly Naked Guy: 'Oh, that is so unfortunate,' says Phoebe at the start of the flashback, staring out of the window. 'Cute naked guy is really starting to put on weight.'

Just Plain Weird: 'You're disturbing my oboe practice,' Mr Heckles (resurrected thanks to the flashback) tells Phoebe. In an inspired moment of quick thinking, Phoebe replies, 'Then I'm going to have to ask you to keep it down.' Later, Heckles scares off Eric, the photographer with the porn-star sister who's due to move into Chandler's, by introducing himself as 'Chandler's new roommate'.

Generation X: As Rachel fantasises about Chandler, we hear the Zombies' 'Time of the Season' from 1968. Chandler didn't start watching *Baywatch* until 1993 (the year Joey moved in), meaning he missed the first four seasons (it kind of went downhill after then).

The Story So Far: On top of everything else, we learn that Central Perk used to be a bar.

The Last Word: A blessed relief from the plot-heavy

episodes that surround it, 'TOW The Flashback' is a welcome burst of pure *Friends*, something both new and wonderfully familiar. We get to see how the gang got together, and what life was like before Rachel and Joey came along. On the flip side, there's dramatic irony-a-gogo, particularly in the way we're just waiting for Ross's marriage to fall apart. The most surprising moment is also the most funny: having seen a couple of years of Ross not thinking much of Phoebe, to see that the two of them came so close to making mad, passionate love is a complete shock. The sequence itself ('I can't get it out'; 'That's not something a girl wants to hear') is blinding – a masterpiece! **Ahhh Rating:** **

French Title: 'Celui Qui Se Souvient' (the one who remembered)

German Title: 'Zurück in die Vergangenheit' (back to the past)

307
'The One With The Race Car Bed'
#465257

Writer: Seth Kurland
Director: Gail Mancuso
First US transmission: 07.11.96
First UK transmission (C4): 15.08.97

Guest Cast: Ron Leibman (Dr Green), Khalil Kain (Cal), Maggie Wheeler (Janice), Mark Cohen (the Mattress King), Rosey Brown (Delivery Man), James Michael Tyler (Gunther), Simon Harvey (Jester), Shashi Bhatia (Acting Student No. 1), Steven Harad (Acting Student No. 2)

Summary: The gang are at Monica and Rachel's watching television, when they see Janice's estranged husband, the Mattress King, advertising his latest sale. He uses his depression over his upcoming divorce as the reason for slashing his prices, which Janice finds abhorrent: Monica, though, points out, 'At four hundred and ninety-nine dollars for a pillow-top queen set, who cares about the divorce? Those babies will sell themselves!' She adds to Janice, after an uncomfortable pause, 'And I'm appalled for you, by the way.' Appalled or not, she's still taken enough by the idea of the sale to head down to the showroom and pick up a bed for herself. When it's delivered, though, Phoebe signs on her behalf and, as she is distracted by Joey's nose bleed, fails to notice that the delivery men are dragging in a child's race-car bed instead of the one Monica ordered. When she and Joey return to the showroom to complain, Joey catches a glimpse of the Mattress King kissing a woman in his office – it's Janice!

Rachel has invited her father down for dinner, and Ross is dreading the prospect of spending an evening with the man: he always goes out of his way to be rude and unpleasant to him. He agrees to go along, but Dr Green is his usual self and Ross's hackles rise and rise. Ross then causes an argument by adding to Dr Green's miserly tip. It looks like the two of them are destined never to get along, but when he and Dr Green begin to discuss Rachel's way of living her life, at brunch the following day (seeing a two-bit chiropractor, and failing to get renters' insurance), the two men finally find some common ground.

Joey finally has some work, teaching a class on soap opera acting. He seems to have found a niche, and things get even better when he receives a call to an audition for *All Our Children*. The only problem is, one of his students is up for the role too – and Joey knows he's better than him . . .

Freaky Monica: When the bed is delivered, Phoebe tells the men to carry it into 'the compulsively neat [room] by the window'.

Spoilt Rachel: She admits to Ross that if she received a tip as low as the kind her father normally gives out, she'd be giving that customer 'sneezers'. We're not a hundred per cent sure what they are, but we can guess she wouldn't just be snotty with them.

Phoebisms: Just how psychic and mad is she? When everyone else is thinking of other things, as Ross tells his dinosaur story, Joey's thoughts are taken up entirely with him singing. Phoebe, distracted, silently wonders, 'Who's singing?' When she is accompanying Monica to the Mattress King's showroom, she comes across a young boy driving the race-car bed that will later cause her so much trouble. 'You know,' she confides in him, 'in England, this car would be on the other side of the store.' The kid, though, doesn't find her joke funny at all: Phoebe, brilliantly, just supposes that it has gone over his head. When she is signing for Monica's bed – pretending to be Monica – she asks Joey, 'Do I have a middle name?' before making one up: 'Falula!'

Chandleresque: The image of him playing on the race-car bed, making car noises and pretending to shout at and chat up other drivers, is brilliantly childlike. This innocence, of course, is all the more poignant when you consider that the audience has just seen Janice and her husband kissing – the poor kid doesn't know what's going to hit him.

Joey's a Teacher?: His acting classes are a delight. At the start of the first one, he writes his name on the blackboard, turning to face his students *as he does so*. The resultant 'Tribbiani'-slide (brilliantly highlighted by a line that should pass under his name, but instead passes *through* it) is one of the funniest moments in the episode. His first lesson to the class is teaching them how to react. This does not, he tells them, mean 'acting again', perhaps remembering a mistake he himself once made. The insight into Joey's acting methods afforded by these classes is terrific: pulling out pubic hair with tweezers to elicit tears, pretending to enjoy having a fish hook through your eyebrow to evoke nastiness, and attempting long division to simulate shock and confusion. As far as studying Joey's bizarre choice of career goes, this episode is a big hit.

The Ballad of Ross & Rachel: 'I just want him to love you like I do,' Rachel tells Ross of her father's impending visit. 'All right, well not exactly like I do ... But if you do come to dinner, I'll love you like I do in the black thing that you like.'

Ross mulls over the quandary. 'I'll go,' offers an overeager Chandler. Throughout the episode, poor Rachel is desperately trying to make Ross and her father get on, and it's quite touching when she explains that it's bad enough that her parents can't stand to be in the same room as each other. 'I don't want to have to have a separate room for you too.'

Gunther's There For You, Rachel: We finally get an affirmation of what we've always suspected as we hear Gunther longing for Rachel: 'I wish she was my wife,' he laments. Later on, as Rachel asks Ross to join her and her father for dinner we can see Gunther glaring at Ross. As Ross says hello, Gunther warns him 'We'll see . . .'

Dinosaurs ROCK!: Ross is talking about work, but we soon hear the sound of his voice fade away to be replaced by the thoughts of the other gathered friends. 'I love how he cares so much about stuff,' Rachel thinks. 'If I squint, I can pretend he's Alan Alda.' Monica, though, is less impressed. 'Oh good,' she thinks, 'another dinosaur story. When are *those* going to become extinct?'

Generation X: As we hear everybody's thoughts, Joey hums 'Baby Elephant Walk'.

The Story So Far: Ross tells Dr Green that he can't eat lobster (see 'TOW The Baby On The Bus'). Phoebe learnt to box when she spent some time at the YMCA. 'Some of the young men weren't acting Christian enough,' she explains.

The Last Word: A nice little episode which, like all the best, has plenty going on. The only casualty, really, is Chandler, who doesn't get the chance to do much at all; but, since he's the hook for the whole of the next episode, we'll let it pass. A typically funny script with a couple of blisteringly smart moments, this makes for some good viewing. **Ahhh Rating: ****

French Title: 'Celui Qui Était Prof Et Élève' (the one who's both teacher and pupil)

German Title: 'Rasende Träume' (racing dreams)

308
'The One With The Giant Poking Device'
#465258

Writer: Adam Chase
Director: Gail Mancuso
First US transmission: 14.11.96
First UK transmission (C4): 22.08.97

Guest Cast: James Michael Tyler (Gunther),
Maggie Wheeler (Janice), Charlie & Jack Allen (Ben)

Summary: Racked with guilt and driven by loyalty, Joey tells Chandler that Janice is cheating on him. Chandler confronts Janice with this but comes to realise that he should stand aside and let her go back to her husband and child – however hard he finds it to let go.

Ross is called into the museum at short notice, so Rachel looks after Ben. During the afternoon, though, Monica knocks Ben's head against a wooden beam and panic ensues. Will he be all right, and how on Earth are they going to tell Ross? Of course, they decide not to. And they would have got away with it, too, had Ross not noticed the bump on Ben's head, and Rachel hadn't cracked and snitched on Monica.

Phoebe is suffering from agonising toothache, but refuses to seek help because every time she goes to the dentist someone dies. Eventually, she realises she has no other choice and is relieved to find her weird curse broken. Until, that is, Joey notices that Ugly Naked Guy is 'awfully still'. Together, the gang fashion a 'giant poking device' from old chopsticks and feed it over through his apartment window to see if he's still alive.

Freaky Monica: Her panic over Ben's bump is superb: 'Push it in! Push it in!' she screams at Rachel, as if the child were a cartoon character. When Ben starts to repeat 'Monica bang!' over and over, she says, 'We all do it all the time. See, watch this . . .' She then proceeds to hit her head repeatedly against the wooden beam, before entreating Rachel to join her. When they decide to hide the bump using the hat from Rachel's Rainy Day Bear, Rachel is dismayed to find that the hat is sown on to the soft toy's head. Monica snatches it from her and tugs hard at the hat, pulling the bear's head off in the process and sending stuffing flying everywhere. 'Oh,' moans a distraught Rachel, 'it's just like a bloodbath in here today!'

Spoilt Rachel: When she offers to babysit Ben, Ross is obviously wary of leaving him alone with her. But, behind Rachel's back, Monica clearly mouths, 'I'll be here the whole time,' so Ross feels safer about the whole thing. Later, Rachel is holding Ben and showing him a spoon: 'Look, Benny. Spoon! Spoon! I think he's bored.' Meaning, of course, that *she* is.

Phoebisms: Her fear of killing someone by visiting the dentist is pure Phoebe. Her fond farewells to everyone before she leaves are brilliant: 'Be on the lookout for anything that you can fall *into*, or that can fall *on* you, or . . . All right, just look out!' It all becomes too much for her, though, so she bursts into tears and runs out. After the visit to the dentist, she frantically phones everyone she knows to check that they're still alive. When she tries Chandler, she doesn't realise that he's in the middle of a deeply serious conversation with Janice. She runs across the hallway, bursts in on them, and yells, 'If you're alive, you answer your phone!'

Slow Joey: He has some difficulty coming to terms with the idea of *Homo sapiens*. He asks Ross if the reason *Homo sapiens* became extinct was because they '*were* "homo" *sapiens*'. Ross corrects him, telling him, '*Homo sapiens are people.*' 'Hey,' says Joey, 'I'm not judging!' Later, Rachel is listing a number of reasons why Monica can't bribe Ben into not telling Ross about the 'bonking incident'. 'Number one, I don't think Ben understands the concept of bribery, and number two –' She is interrupted by a snigger from Joey: 'You said "number two".' Rachel points out that she also said 'number one', to which Joey just laughs again, saying, 'I know!'

Chandleresque: Chandler's desperation at the thought of losing Janice is played out wonderfully by Perry. Their final scene together, in Central Perk, where Chandler is telling Janice that she must go back to her husband, that it's for the best, is heart-rending. When Janice says that their love is like 'movie love', that he is her 'soulmate', and that she 'can't believe we're not going to be spending the rest of our lives together', Chandler just responds with a hysterical, 'Then don't leave me!' But, of course, it has to end, and watching Perry give Chandler the same kind of desolate terror of loneliness we saw in 'The One Where Heckles Dies' is a bitter pleasure.

Ugly Naked Guy: Joey watches him sleep in a new hammock, remarking that it looks like a 'Play-Doh Fat Factory'. When Phoebe thinks that her dental curse has killed Ugly Naked Guy, she laments that the curse is getting stronger too, to bring down something that big! When they've poked him and got him riled, he comes to his window, prompting Rachel to say, 'Now he's showing us *his* poking device.' Joey takes one look and shouts, 'That's never gonna make it all the way over here, buddy!'

Gunther's There For You, Rachel: More Rachel obsessing. Ross asks him for a napkin, and he just snaps, 'Like you don't already have everything?' When Chandler stands in front of him holding Janice's shoe – the only thing of hers he was able to cling on to – Gunther stares at it and sighs that Rachel has similar shoes in burgundy. Ahh, bless.

Generation X: Phoebe and Chandler sing Lionel Ritchie's classic ballad, 'Endless Love'.

The Last Word: Fabulous Phoebe and cracking Chandler make this a must-see episode for them alone, especially their final scene where they try (and fail) to harmonise on 'Endless Love'. Unfortunately, the poking-device plot is a little dull, and proves why Ugly Naked Guy is funny: because he's never normally responsible for more that just a throwaway line in an episode. Drag a character like that in more, and the laughs become forced. **Ahhh Rating:** ****

French Title: 'Celui Qui Avait Pris Un Coup Sur La Tête' (the one who takes a bang to the head)

German Title: 'Hurra, sie leben noch!' (hurray, he's still alive!)

309
'The One With The Football'
#465259

Writer: Ira Ungerleider
Director: Kevin S. Bright
First US transmission: 21.11.96
First UK transmission (C4): 29.08.97

Guest Cast: Susanna Voltaire (Margha)

Summary: The gang prepare for another Thanksgiving dinner. Well, the girls are preparing while the boys lounge on the sofa watching a football match. Having never played the game before, an intrigued Phoebe suggests that they should all play a quick game of football before dinner is ready. Joey and Rachel agree, but there is dissent from the others. Chandler is still depressed about breaking up with Janice, and Monica and Ross reveal that their mother won't let them play football any more because they get too competitive. They explain to the gang that they always used to play football, holding an annual tournament called the Gellerbowl. But the final Gellerbowl ended in tragedy, when Monica broke Ross's nose and their family forbade them to play ever again, lest any more injuries be sustained. It's obvious that they're still unsure about letting themselves play again, but the gang eventually manage to bring them round. But little do they know how deeply Monica and Ross's competitiveness runs.

As the game goes on, the rivalry between the brother and sister reaches ridiculous heights, while Joey and Chandler develop a rivalry of their own. A beautiful young Dutch woman, Margha, appears at the side of the pitch, and they invite her to watch. The game soon develops into a Ross-versus-Monica–Joey-versus-Chandler match, with poor Phoebe and Rachel being pushed (literally, in Rachel's case) to the sidelines. Eventually, Monica offers to make the game girls versus boys, and then the fun really begins . . .

Freaky Monica: As Rachel prepares the dessert for the meal, Monica complains that she should be putting 'the marshmallows in concentric circles'. Rachel just responds by stuffing a marshmallow up Monica's nose – which she promptly 'sniffs' out into the bowl (see also **Gellerbowl VII** on page 187).

Spoilt Rachel: The poor woman doesn't get much of a look-in on the game, as everyone is convinced that she's going to be no good. First, neither Monica nor Ross picks her for their team: when she is the last choice, Ross invites her on to his team, saying, 'Sweetie, now I pick you.' She just grumbles, 'You don't pick me – you're *stuck* with me.' During the game, she is always told to 'go long' (at one point, Ross tells her to go so long that 'we start to look very small'). Eventually, she turns up in the middle of the field eating a pretzel. When Ross asks where she got it from, she explains that she 'went really long'. When she is switched to Monica's team, she finally gets to have a go at running with the ball, only to end up panicking, screaming 'Catch!' and thwacking Monica in the face with it. Of course, it is Rachel who scores the final, winning touchdown – or at least she *thinks* she's won. As Chandler explains, she was about five yards short of the line. Later, when she and Phoebe are seriously considering joining some sort of league so they can play more football, she is told of the National Football League, who, Chandler claims, play on Sundays and Mondays. 'Oh, shoot!' she says. 'I work Monday nights.'

Phoebisms: When Monica, discussing their football tactics, complains that she thought Phoebe knew what she was doing, a confused Pheebs says, 'I thought you meant in *life*.' When she catches the ball for the first time, she takes it full on the chest, squealing, 'Ooh! Broken boobs!' And, of course, it's her boobs that are responsible for the funniest moment in the episode. When the game becomes girls versus boys, as Chandler tries to run for a touchdown, Phoebe lifts up her top and flashes her boobs at him. Mesmerised, Chandler is unable to resist when Phoebe snatches the ball from him and makes a run for it. The second time she uses this tactic Chandler is ready for it, covering his eyes to protect himself. Of course, this means he doesn't notice the big shrub he is about to stumble into.

Slow Joey: A quick lesson in 'geography for the insane', as Joey fumbles with his ignorance of the world when meeting Margha. 'You're, like, from a whole other country!' he states, amazed, when he hears her accent for the first time. Later, when Chandler is trying to impress the Dutch Margha, he asks Joey – in front of the woman – where Dutch people come from. He is stumped, so Chandler gives him a clue. He says they come from 'somewhere near the Netherlands'. Joey's not going to be fooled, though, because he *knows* that the Netherlands is the where Peter Pan lives.

Chandleresque: Smarting over the break-up with Janice, Chandler is accused of not wanting to do anything any more. He snaps that he does – he wants to loaf around the house, and he's even started to want to drink in the mornings. 'Don't say that I don't have goals!' he cries. When he takes the ball for the first time at the beginning of the game, he mutters a little mantra to himself: 'The ball is Janice. The ball is Janice.' And when he 'beats' Joey by being the chosen beau of Margha, he gleefully tells his friend, 'From now on *I* get the dates, and *you* have to stay home on Saturday nights watching *Ready, Set, Cook!*'

Generation X: During the ballgame we hear 2Unlimited's 'Get Ready For This' and 'Misirlou' by Dirk Dale & His Del Tones, a.k.a. the theme from Quentin Tarantino's *Pulp Fiction* (1995).

The Story So Far: Ross, rather cruelly, invokes what seems to be a childhood chant when, in the middle of the game, he accuses Monica of being a 'cheater, cheater, compulsive eater!' Ross's nose was broken by Monica at the last 'Gellerbowl', twelve years ago (see also **Gellerbowl VII** below). Phoebe once dated a guy with a glass eye.

Gellerbowl VII

We always knew that Ross and Monica had a pretty competitive, spiteful relationship as children, but this episode really shows the depths it went to. As punishment for the violence of Gellerbowl VI, along with banning Ross and Monica from playing the game ever again, their father took the prized Geller Cup and threw it into the middle of a lake. (Chandler, terrified by the story so far, asks 'Was the curse lifted?') Even the story of the loss of the Geller Cup is nearly enough to bring Ross to tears, which is why it's even more amazing when the Cup is revealed to be still in Monica's possession. She explains that while Ross was at the hospital, she swam into the middle of the lake to save the prized trophy. The Cup itself, the source of so much anguish, is revealed to be just a plastic troll (the sort with the ugly face and wild hair) nailed to a bit of wood. With the spirit of the Gellerbowl thus invoked, this latest match between them should, we suppose, be termed Gellerbowl VII.

The Last Word: The jewel in the third season's crown, 'The One With The Football' brings Monica and Ross to centre stage once more, with their twisted childhood rivalry back with a vengeance. We're used to Monica's extreme competitiveness by now, so it seems more like Ross is being the petty one. The love rivals, Joey and Chandler, counterbalance this well, though it's distressing to note how Perry's clothes are now literally hanging off him, and how the physical comedy at which he's usually so adept seems to be draining him. Regardless, the pace and direction of this episode make it a strong challenger to the positions of 'The One With The Flashback' and 'The One With A Chick. And A Duck' as best episode of the season. **Ahhh Rating:** *

French Title: 'Celui Pour Qui Le Foot C'est Le Pied' (the one who thinks football is bliss)

German Title: 'Die mit dem Ball spielen' (the ones who play ball)

310
'The One Where Rachel Quits'
#465260

Writers: Michael Curtis & Gregory S. Malins
Director: Terry Hughes
First US transmission: 12.12.96
First UK transmission (C4): 05.09.97

Guest Cast: Mae Whitman (Sarah Tuttle), Shelley Berman
(Mr Kaplan, Jr), James Michael Tyler (Gunther), Kyla Pratta
(Charla Nichols, 'Scrud'), Romy Rosemont (Troop Leader),
Sandra Gould (Old Woman), Gene Crane
(Christmas Tree Customer)

Summary: Gunther takes Rachel aside at Central Perk and tells her that the boss has said that she must be retrained for her job. Grudgingly, she enters the training programme normally designed for first-timers, and it soon begins to drag her down. Joey and Chandler suggest that maybe she should leave, and search for a job she really wants. As the demeaning retraining continues, she does what they suggest, but the Fear sets in when she realises that she has no job to go to.

Ross, while demonstrating the fine art of racquetball, knocks Sarah, a little Brown Bird (the US version of a Brownie in the UK), down a flight of stairs, breaking her leg. Overcome with guilt, he goes to visit her and discovers that she can no longer sell cookies for the Brown Birds. Sarah wanted to sell the most, so she could win her dream trip to Space Camp, and stand aboard a real space shuttle. Out of remorse, Ross takes her box of cookies and sets out to sell them himself.

Joey has a seasonal job selling Christmas trees, which Phoebe finds reprehensible. When she is told, though, that the poor, hacked-down trees are actually fulfilling their 'Christmas destiny', she is somewhat appeased. Trouble strikes when she visits Joey at work only to discover what they do to the aged and dying trees . . .

Poor Ross: After the Sarah incident, Ross's friends enjoy making a joke out of his growing reputation as a batterer of small, helpless beings. Chandler, reading from a paper, tells him, 'Says here that a Muppet got whacked on Sesame Street last night . . . Where exactly were you around ten-ish?'

Freaky Monica: The roots of her compulsive eating as a teenager are probed here as we learn that she was once a Brown Bird, but that she used to eat all her own cookies, forcing her father to pay for them all. When Ross's cookie sales rekindle Monica's passion for the demon biscuit, she ends up becoming hooked again, finding it difficult to go 'cold turkey' when they finally run out: 'Just a couple more boxes,' she pleads. 'It's no big deal, all right? You gotta help me out with a couple more boxes!'

Spoilt Rachel: Rachel's retraining is made all the better by Gunther's having to help her with it. With every line, you can see his discomfort at having to demean the object of his affections. Highlights include: Rachel being told about the Tray Spot, which she'd heard other waiting staff talk about but had just assumed it was a club they went to; Gunther promising to tell Rachel why she shouldn't just trap spiders under coffee mugs and leave them there; and Rachel's distress at the talents of her replacement. 'Last night,' she tells her friends, 'she was teaching everybody how to make napkin . . .' And that's as far as she gets before emotion takes over and she begins to whine and shed tears. 'That word was "swans",' Ross completes on her behalf. When she finally quits, she tells a shocked Gunther that she just doesn't care which is decaf and which is regular. Once again, she's dropped everything and stepped out on her own, without any promise of something to go to. As much as we know Rachel's done the right thing, the scene where she serves her final coffee (and still gets it wrong) is almost enough to bring a tear to the eye. Great stuff.

Phoebisms: This is an exceptional episode for Kudrow as Phoebe tries to accept Joey's claim that Christmas trees are actually happy to die in the name of the holiday they celebrate. Once she has got over this, with a fair degree of discomfort, she is then confronted with the horrible truth about the trees that aren't (excuse the pun) spruce enough to be sold. When she discovers that old, unwanted trees get thrown in 'the chipper', she asks Joey, 'Why do I have a feeling that's not as happy as it sounds?' Her screams of terror (accompanied by well-chosen horror-movie music) as she sees a tree being fed into the chipper are superb.

Slow Joey: Joey arrives with 'great news'. He then tells Rachel that he's heard about an opening in a fashion house, and his father might be able to get Rachel an interview. Then he says, 'And now for the great news ...' He rummages around in his pocket, pulling out an aerosol: 'Snow-in-a-can!'

Chandleresque: Walking into the girls' apartment and seeing all the trees they rescued for Phoebe, Chandler claims it looks like 'Night of the Living Dead Christmas Trees'. Seconds after Rachel quits her job, on his advice, he wonders whether this means they'll now have to pay for their coffee. Helping Ross count up his box sales, Chandler sniggers to himself, having just worked out how to write 'BOOBIES' on the calculator.

Gunther's There For You, Rachel: His anguish at being the one who has to get Rachel to be a better worker is brilliant. At one point, as she walks away disconsolate, he tells her, 'It's all right.' After she's gone, he adds, 'Sweetheart.' His barely held-back tears at her departure is a wonderful touch.

Generation X: Phoebe's exclamation 'God bless us, every-one!' evokes the spirit of Christmas as laid out by Tiny Tim in Dickens' *A Christmas Carol*. The gang hum 'Land of Hope and Glory' as Rachel serves her last ever coffee.

The Story So Far: Rachel leaves Central Perk to work at Fortunata Fashions.

The Last Word: Another excellent episode puts paid to the myth that the third season isn't much cop. Everyone is on top form and there are tons of great lines. Highlights, without a doubt, include Phoebe's campaign to save the older Christmas trees (particularly the well-directed chipper scene), and Rachel biting the bullet and leaving her job. **Ahhh Rating:** ***

French Title: 'Celui Qui Fait Démissionner Rachel' (the one who sacked Rachel)

German Title: 'Knabbereien' (things to nibble)

311

'The One Where Chandler Can't Remember Which Sister'

#465261

Writer: Alexa Junge
Director: Terry Hughes
First US transmission: 09.01.97
First UK transmission (C4): 12.09.97

Guest Cast: Mimi Lieber (Mary Theresa), Alex Meneses (Cookie), Penny Santon (Nonna), K. J. Steinberg (Gina), Lisa Melilli (Dina), James Michael Tyler (Gunther), Shelley Berman (Mr Kaplan, Jr), **and introducing** Steven Eckholdt (Mark)

Summary: Rachel doesn't seem to be particularly enjoying her job at Fortunata Fashions; ironically for someone who was sick of making coffee, her biggest responsibility at this new job seems to be just that. When Mark, a handsome customer at the Moondance Diner, overhears her moaning to Monica about her crappy new job, he pipes up and tells her that he works as an assistant buyer at Bloomingdales and that there's a job vacancy. When Rachel tells Ross the exciting news, he is immediately concerned that Mark's intentions are less than altruistic, suggesting to Rachel that all he wants is sex. Rachel won't listen, though, and is eventually proven right when she gets an interview and is hired. Through it all, Ross's jealousy of Mark steadily increases.

Phoebe takes on Monica and Rachel's noisy neighbour upstairs, but only ends up having the socks (and a lot more) charmed off her. Just as she begins to fall for him, the gang overhear him having sex with another woman. But when the guys head upstairs to sort him out, they too are charmed to meet him.

Chandler, depressed at losing Janice, gets hammered on vodka Jell-O and, during Joey's birthday party, gets amorous with one of Joey's sisters in a storage cupboard. The next day, he remembers that he fooled around with 'a sister', but he can't remember which one – after all, all seven of them are very similar. Mary Angela – for it is she – phones Joey to tell him what happened, and he confronts Chandler. Was he just taking advantage of Mary Angela, or is he serious about her? Chandler, faced with the wrath of his friend, claims he was serious – much to Joey's delight. Chandler knows he must come clean, but, when he calls round at the sisters' house, he is met by Joey and his entire family. He still can't remember which sister is Mary Angela and desperately hopes to extricate himself from the relationship without causing himself pain, embarrassment, humiliation or serious bodily harm from the Tribbiani family . . .

Slow Joey: The episode opens with Joey's brilliantly bad demonstration of how his hand is quicker than the eye. He shows off his new card trick, asking Monica to pick a card and look at it. As he puts it back in the pack, he quite clearly takes a look at it. He thinks he's got everyone fooled, and they humour him. Brilliant stuff. Later he talks about his bad feelings after breaking up with a woman called Katherine: he claims to remember how cut up he felt when he saw her walking down the street with her friend Donna. 'Yes,' says Chandler, 'but you ended up having sex with both of them that afternoon.' Joey smiles: 'Any excuse to tell that story.'

Chandleresque: Chandler drunk is a wonder to behold. He

lollops around Joey's party, desperately trying to be sensible. Erasing Janice's number from his speed-dial list, he ponders, 'Why must we dial so speedily?' just before he tells one of Joey's sisters that she has 'huge breasts'. For an episode focused around what is usually Perry's forte – a mixture of angst, desperation and excitement – it's when he's incapable of feeling any of these that he's at his best. The morning after, he tells everyone that 'when I've been drinking, sometimes I tend to get overly friendly, and I'm sorry', in reference to the fact that he kissed Monica. 'That's OK,' she replies. As does Rachel. And Ross.

Parents – Who Needs 'Em?: When Chandler is told that the Jell-O he's just wolfed down is composed of pure vodka, he says that it's 'just like Mom used to make'.

Just Plain Weird: Joey's sisters have among them a fair crop of nutters. Cookie, in particular, seems slightly deranged. When Phoebe tells her that she's drinking vodka and cranberry juice, Cookie replies that it's 'the exact same drink I made myself right after I shot my husband'. Joey's grandma, too, is a force to be reckoned with. According to Joey she was 'the sixth person to spit on Mussolini's hanging body'.

Generation X: The Moonlight Diner's corny film-related menu includes a 'Yentl soup' (presumably a lentil soup named after Barbra Streisand's 1983 movie *Yentl*), a 'James Beans' inspired by, we guess, James Dean, and a 'Howdy hold the Dowdy', named after a clown.

The Story So Far: Rachel's interview for the Bloomingdales job is conducted by an unnamed woman, but it's a safe bet to assume this was Joanna (see 'TOW The Dollhouse').

The Last Word: Unfortunately, this episode really shows how off form Matthew Perry was at this time. Although it's a good script, with plenty of typical Chandler hilarity, there are times when it doesn't quite work. At this stage, the Ross-and-Rachel friction is merely refreshing, although it gets annoying as this plotline unfolds: all it achieves is drawing our sympathies away from Ross. As he's one of the central characters, that's not necessarily a wise thing to do. **Ahhh Rating:** *

French Title: 'Celui Qui Ne S'y Retrouvait Plus' (the one who can't remember any more)

German Title: 'Welche Schwester war's doch gleich?' (which sister was it?)

312
'The One With All The Jealousy'
#465262

Writer: Doty Abrams
Director: Robby Benson
First US transmission: 16.01.97
First UK transmission (C4): 19.09.97

Guest Cast: Steven Eckholdt (Mark), Obba Babatunde (the Director), Carlos Gomez (Julio), James Michael Tyler (Gunther), Wendy Schall (Jeannine), Hillary Matthews (Nancy)

Summary: Monica, whose love life has been less than busy since splitting up with Richard, gets to date Julio, a cute waiter from the Moondance Diner. As well as being handsome, he turns out to be creative too: he has aspirations to be a poet, and writes a poem just for Monica called 'The Empty Vase'. Her excitement at this romantic gesture wanes when Phoebe explains the meaning of the poem to her: he seems to be suggesting that Monica is something of an airhead.

Joey is auditioning for a role in a musical version of *A Tale of Two Cities*. The liberal untruths on his CV, though, backfire. He claims to be an accomplished and well-practised dancer, and is horrified to learn that the role requires a *lot* of dancing. When he turns up for the call-back dance audition, the casting director announces that the person who was originally going to go through the routines with everyone at the audition can't make it. He asks Joey to step in, since he is so experienced, but poor Joey hasn't a clue about anything except his own 'special' style of dancing.

Rachel is blissfully happy learning the ropes at her new job at Bloomingdales. Mark is teaching her everything, which is giving Ross deep, jealous concerns. He begins to shower Rachel with gifts at work, the final one being an embarrassing barbershop quartet who ram home the point about her having a boyfriend. All this overzealous attention begins to get on Rachel's nerves . . .

Slow Joey: Chandler tries to patiently explain what Joey's letting himself in for in his *A Tale of Two Cities* audition, but Joey is completely unfamiliar with Charles Dickens, Cliff Notes, and the concept of abridgement. This is a brilliant little exchange – especially the clear belief that Le Blanc gives Joey that there is such a person as 'Mr Dickens' still alive today. When Monica tells him that she and Julio stopped during sex, so he could write a poem, Joey brags that he couldn't stop if a meteor hit him. When told that the stripper at the bachelor party of one of Chandler's friends is called Crystal Chandelier, he says, 'You name a kid that, what do you expect them to grow up to be?'

Chandleresque: When Ross is desperately seeking advice on how to cope with his jealousy over Mark, Chandler – equally desperate, and displaying his typically twisted emotions – tells him, 'Don't do anything. Keep it inside. Learn how to hide your feelings!' He realises his gaffe, though, and follows it up with a sheepish, 'Don't cry out loud.' At the bachelor party, he's given a pen which shows a picture of a woman whose clothes all fall off when the button is pressed – his obvious delight at this little gadget is both sweet and seedy.

The Ballad of Ross & Rachel: And so, as the title suggests, Ross's jealousy increases. His tirade of flowers and gifts to Rachel's workplace is desperately obsessive, and makes for worrying viewing. The final barbershop-quartet gambit is a strange sight: it's as embarrassing as it's meant to be, in context, but is without doubt the creepiest, stalker-level thing

Ross has ever done. Finally, Rachel tries to convince Ross that he has nothing to worry about, giving him a huge romantic kiss. All fired up, Ross then heads out to a 'play date' with the stripper from the bachelor party and her kid. Although she's proud of how she handled Ross's feelings, Chandler points out to Rachel that she could have 'just turned him on and sent him to a stripper'.

Gunther's There For You, Rachel!: Ross laments that he is worried that he could lose Rachel to another man. 'Let it be me, let it be me,' mutters Gunther to himself.

Dinosaurs ROCK!: Ross is invited to the bachelor party. He doesn't even know the guy and wonders why he's been asked along. Chandler explains that the groom doesn't have many friends – he's a botanist. Understanding, Ross says that 'botanists are such geeks', right before showing off his dinosaur tie (making the relevant embarrassing sound effects).

Generation X: Considering what songs to sing at his *A Tale of Two Cities* audition, Joey decides to plump for 'New York, New York' and 'I Left My Heart in San Francisco'. Though 'New York, New York' became something of an anthem for Frank Sinatra, it was actually written for Liza Minnelli for the film of the same name (Martin Scorsese, 1977).

The Story So Far: Phoebe's unique handbag leads us to discover that Rachel is scared of turtles.

The Last Word: Joey is the stand-out turn in this episode, demonstrating his amazing stupidity in almost every scene. Of all the Ross/Rachel/Mark episodes, this one remains the best, if only because there seems to be some sort of resolution to it – Rachel convincing Ross, by kissing him, that he has nothing to worry about. But, as we know, this plot carries on, and will become more irritating before it is finished. **Ahhh Rating:** *

French Title: 'Celui Qui Était Très Jaloux' (the one who was very jealous)

German Title: 'Lästige Eifersucht' (annoying jealousy)

313
'The One Where Monica And Richard Are Just Friends'
#465265

Writer: Michael Borkow
Director: Robby Benson
First US transmission: 30.01.97
First UK transmission (C4): 26.09.97

Guest Cast: Tom Selleck (Dr Richard Burke),
James Michael Tyler (Gunther), Markus Flanagan (Robert),
Gina Hecht (Richard's Date), Steven Harad (Clerk)

Summary: Returning a video to the store, Monica bumps into Richard (noticing that his 'lips went bald') and they begin chatting. It's obvious to both of them that they still get on like a house on fire and, although Monica suspects that it might be a bad idea, they decide to spend a little time together again – just as friends. One thing leads to another, though, and while they are both wrist deep in squished tomatoes, their hands meet and they realise that they're still attracted to each other. Only one course of action is left, so they stay friends. Friends that sleep together. When Richard announces that he's going on a blind date, though, Monica's jealousy becomes apparent and they have to decide once again whether to stay together or break up.

Phoebe has her own relationship problems when she meets Robert, a Californian sports fanatic who has a penchant for wearing shorts, even in the dead of winter. Not only that but, as Chandler is first to discover to his wide-eyed disgust, he doesn't like to wear anything under them. When Phoebe herself finally finds out about his love of the open air, she decides she has to find a way to tell him about it.

Rachel and Joey, throughout all this, have decided to swap their favourite novels with each other. Rachel has to read *The Shining*, while Joey tackles *Little Women*. And these are little women he finds particularly hard to get to grips with . . .

Freaky Monica: The poor honey has to cope with all her feelings over Richard coming back to the surface again. Her slightly weird obsessive streak is on display again, as she begins to plan a future for Richard and herself based around their being friends: 'Maybe someday,' she suggests, they could be 'friends who stood up in front of their other friends, and vowed to be friends for ever.' We love her put-down of the annoying video-store clerk: 'Y'know, in a weird way, you have too much power.'

Phoebisms: On being told that Monica and Richard just went for an innocent burger, Phoebe comments, 'There's no such thing as an innocent burger,' in reference to her refusal to eat anything with a face.

Slow Joey: He's read *The Shining* many, many times, but still gets frightened by it – so frightened, in fact, that he regularly has to hide the book in the freezer. (That's Joey logic for you.) When he is finally nearing the end of *Little Women*, and bad things are starting to happen to the characters, he turns up at Rachel's, close to tears. She offers to put the book in their freezer, and he accepts. The funniest moment in the episode comes when Joey and Rachel start to ruin the plot of each book to each other, after Joey accidentally let slip the ending of *The Shining*. (He was using a complicated code – 'when Jack almost kills them all with that "blank", but then at the last second they get away' – but *somehow* Rachel cracked it.) In a particularly bitchy swipe, Rachel tells him that Beth dies (sorry, reader!) and Joey's world nearly falls to pieces.

Chandleresque: On meeting Robert for the first time, he asks Phoebe's date why he's wearing shorts when it's so cold. He simply answers that he's from California, to which Chandler nods and says, 'Right, right. Sometimes you guys just burst into flames.' Later, when Phoebe gives Robert something new to wear instead of the revealing baggy shorts he always wears, Chandler's excitement at the idea of Robert's modesty being covered is palpable: 'Stretchy pants! Why, those are the greatest things in the world! If I were you, I would wear them every day, *every day*.' And of course, Chandler gives us all a new euphemism – 'showing *brain*'.

Yo Gunther!: He warns Robert about his revealing shorts, pointing out that Central Perk is a family place: 'Put the mouse back in the house.'

Generation X: Monica and Richard joke that one of the customers in the video store is likely to go rummaging in the porn section any minute, speculating that he'll probably rent *Citizen Kane* (Orson Welles, 1941), *Vertigo* (Alfred Hitchcock, 1958), and *Clockwork Orgy*, another of the writers' attempts to pun out for porn (see 'TOW The Free Porn'), inspired by *A Clockwork Orange* (Stanley Kubrick, 1971). Joey and Rachel read *The Shining*, the horror novel by Stephen King, and *Little Women* by Louisa May Alcott. For anyone who hasn't read these books, they *do* spoil the endings in this episode.

The Story So Far: Obviously there are some references to 'TOW Barry And Mindy's Wedding'. Ross reminds us that he's 29. According to Chandler, Monica and Richard split up six months ago.

The Last Word: One of the finer examples of this season's habit of the ongoing story overshadowing the comedy. Hey, viewers! Remember Richard? Remember how mad Monica was about him, and him for her? Remember why they broke up, and how distraught Monica was afterwards? Yeah? Yeah? Oh, hey! We forgot the jokes! Grrr. As affecting as this is, it leaves little room for anything actually funny. The plot about Robert's shorts is funny, but a one-joke thing (which is, erm, milked *four* times). So that just leaves us with the 'read-off' between Rachel and Joey. At least *that's* good. **Ahhh rating:** ***

French Title: 'Celui Où Monica Et Richard Sont Juste Amis' (as English)

German Title: 'Nichts als Freunde' (nothing but friends)

314
'The One With Phoebe's Ex-Partner'
#465266

Writer: Wil Calhoun
Director: Robby Benson
First US transmission: 06.02.97
First UK transmission (C4): 03.10.97

Guest Cast: Sherilyn Fenn (Ginger), E.G. Daily (Leslie),
James Michael Tyler (Gunther), Steven Eckholdt (Mark)

Summary: The gang are all impressed by Leslie, a new singer at Central Perk – all, that is, except for Phoebe. She reveals that Leslie used to be her singing partner, but she walked out on Phoebe to make money writing advertising jingles. Leslie has returned to patch things up with Phoebe and, although she feels reluctant at first, Phoebe soon remembers that her times with Leslie were the happiest in her life. The pair make a triumphant reunion appearance at Central Perk, but things go sour when Leslie tells Phoebe that she should sell 'Smelly Cat' to a kitty-litter advertiser. Chandler meets a beautiful girl called Ginger and they start to date. But Joey reveals to the others that he used to date Ginger, and he has a terrible secret shame about their date together. Ginger has an artificial leg, and one night Joey threw it on to the fire by accident. When Chandler himself finds out about the leg, he has to confront his own feelings over it. And Ginger has to face up to the fact of Chandler's own physical abnormality: his third nipple.

Rachel is deliriously happy to have finally found a job that she both cares about and is good at. But Ross is concerned that the job is pulling her away from him, so he begs Rachel to let him, instead of Mark, accompany her to a fashion lecture. She agrees, but Ross falls asleep there, later telling her that it was boring. When Ross says that he is worried that Rachel has a whole new part of her life that he doesn't belong to, Rachel tells him that she loves her new job, and he's just going to have to live with it.

Phoebisms: Before we learn of her history with Leslie, it's great to see Phoebe's disparaging comments about the obviously talented singer. When everyone says they like one of her songs, she snaps, 'A song with rhyming words. Ooh, I never thought of that before.' To everyone's surprise, Leslie announces the title of her next song: 'Phoebe Buffay, What Can I Say? I Really Loved When We Were Singing Partners, And I Shouldn't Have Left You That Way'. Phoebe, trying to cover, mutters that it's 'one of those "look for the hidden meaning" songs.' Explaining her out-of-hand dismissal of Leslie's attempts to get them back together, Phoebe says, 'Once you betray me, I become like the ice woman: very cold, hard, unyielding ... Nothing can penetrate this icy exterior.' For a minute she seems convincing, until she asks Monica for a tissue. A veritable album full of songs appear in this episode, including (of course) 'Smelly Cat', 'Sticky Shoe' and the apparently 'sad' song 'Magician Box Mix-up', which she must turn her guitar upside down to play. Although she claims to have no hard feelings over Leslie using 'Smelly Cat' in the cat-litter advert, when she debuts her new song it's obvious that she's lying. 'Jingle Bitch screwed me over,' she sings. 'Go to hell, Jingle Whore!'

Slow Joey: The highlight of the episode comes when Joey is explaining what happened between him and Ginger. He tells the story of the fateful leg-burning incident, and Monica and Phoebe are truly appalled at how terrible his actions were – they are even worse, it seems, than throwing Ginger's dog on to the fire (which, for a second, they think he did – Joey's only reaction to this is, 'I wish!').

Chandleresque: Just when he seems to have got over the fact that Ginger's leg freaks him out, their burgeoning relationship hits a major bump when she finds his third nipple. Driven then to have it removed (by a procedure he calls a 'nubbinectomy'), Chandler later finds a further problem when a very obvious joke is made, but not by him. Immediately, he suspects that the third nipple was the source of all his 'powers', and now he worries that his power might have gone. 'Oh dear God, what have I done?'

The Ballad of Ross & Rachel: Their argument after the fashion lecture is brilliantly entertaining. When Rachel complains that she was polite enough not to fall asleep when she went to a boring palaeontology lecture given by 'Professor Pitstains' ('Pittain,' corrects Ross), Ross counters with the factoid that 'a hundred million people went to see a movie about what I do', saying that there'd be no such interest in a film called *Jurassic Parka*.

The Story So Far: Joey hasn't seen Ginger since 'that night', four years ago. And, of course, from this episode on, Chandler no longer has his 'nubbin'. Phoebe has known Leslie ever since their mothers lived together on a barge.

The Last Word: Chandler on form, Phoebe having some great lines, and a funny argument-with-a-point between Ross and Rachel makes for not a bad episode. The lion's share of comedy belongs to Phoebe, though, whose bitterness over the break-up from Leslie is beautifully vicious. **Ahhh Rating:** *

French Title: 'Celui Que Les Prothèses Ne Génaient Pas' (the one who's not bothered by the prosthetic)

German Title: 'Geld Oder Freundschaft' (money or friendship)

315
'The One Where Ross And Rachel Take A Break'
#465263

Writer: Michael Borkow
Director: James Burrows
First US transmission: 13.02.97
First UK transmission (C4): 10.10.97

Guest Cast: Steven Eckholdt (Mark), Stephen Kearney (Mischa), Jim Pirri (Sergei), Angela Featherstone (Chloe), Maury Ginsberg (Isaac), **and introducing** Laura Dean (Sophie)

Summary: Phoebe's new enterprise of giving free massages outside the UN has paid off in an unexpected way: she's dating Sergei, a foreign diplomat who doesn't speak a word of English. On their dates, Mischa, his translator, keeps getting in the way and spoiling the moment, so Phoebe suggests to Monica that she come along to meet Mischa to give her and Sergei a little quality time alone. Unfortunately, Phoebe gets a little too much quality time: Monica hits it off with Mischa so much that Phoebe can't drag him away to chat on her behalf with Sergei.

Chandler and Joey, meanwhile, are obsessing about Chloe, the girl from the Xerox place. When she has figured out that they fancy her, she invites them both to a party at a nightclub. Ross, meanwhile, is still behaving jealously about Rachel's new job. On their first anniversary, Rachel can't get away from work to celebrate so Ross decides to take a picnic to her office instead. But this gesture is met with anger, and eventually Ross storms off upset. When Rachel arrives home, Ross forgives her for their earlier argument. Rachel, who was going to give *him* the chance to apologise, suggests that maybe they should take a break from the relationship. Ross leaves the apartment to join Joey and Chandler at the nightclub, where he meets Chloe again – he once had some work done at the Xerox place, and Chloe is obviously slightly smitten with him. When Ross phones Rachel to try to apologise, he hears Mark's voice in the background (he has come round simply to chat to Rachel) and overreacts. Slamming the phone down, he returns to the dance floor, where he kisses Chloe and decides to take her home . . .

Phoebisms: Her attempts to woo, and be wooed by, Sergei – with Mischa interrupting, necessarily, all the while – are terrific. Once Mischa is out of the picture, thanks to Monica, the awkwardness of her conversation with Sergei is brilliant: 'Plate,' he says, picking up a plate. 'See, we don't need them!' Phoebe asserts. Sergei then picks up a cup, saying 'Plate' again. Phoebe is wonderfully unimpressed.

Slow Joey: Contemplating a threesome with Chloe, Joey and Chandler have a marvellous conversation. Initially, they feel they should keep their eyes closed. But then, what if they fondled the wrong person? Then Joey wonders how they would work out where each of them would be during the act itself. Chandler suggests they toss a coin, but Joey wants clarification on what heads and tails would be. 'If you don't know that,' says Chandler, worried, 'then I don't want to do this with you.'

The Ballad of Ross & Rachel: It's all-out Ross-and-Rachel-Rama in this episode. Ross's unreasonable jealousy finally reaches a head, and Rachel is clearly painted as the innocent party. Quite why the producers decided to make Ross quite so unequivocally the bad guy is beyond us, but it does at least mean that, for ever after, the phrase 'We were on a break!' becomes one of the most successful catchphrases in the show.

Generation X: As Ross's infidelity begins, we hear Ross and Rachel's song, U2's 'With or Without You'. Sergei sings a version of Don McLean's 'American Pie' in his own language.

The Story So Far: Chloe is the Xerox girl mentioned by Chandler in 'TOW The Jam'. There's a reference to one of Phoebe's friends, a 'Spackle Back Harry', who Monica thinks is unattractive – Phoebe seems terribly protective of him, though.

The Last Word: Phoebe's fling with Sergei is not quite as funny as it should be, but the whole thing is redeemed by her and Monica's bitchiness as Sergei and Mischa separate. So, if that's not funny, it leaves us with the break-up of Ross and Rachel. The scene where Rachel suggests they take 'a break from us' is heart-rending; Aniston gives her all, investing Rachel once again with a great little-girl-lost fear, combined with the strength to make a decision (it has, after all, almost always been her who made the actual moves in their relationship). Oh, wait – that's not funny either. Well, there's always the fantastic scene where Joey and Chandler work out what they'd do if they had a threesome with Chloe. Now, *that* is funny. **Ahhh Rating:** ***

French Title: 'Celui Qui Vivait Mal La Rupture' (the one who took the break-up badly)

German Title: 'Kurzschluß' (short circuit)

316
'The One The Morning After'
#465264

Writers: Marta Kauffman & David Crane
Director: James Burrows
First US transmission: 20.02.97
First UK transmission (C4): 17.10.97

Guest Cast: Angela Featherstone (Chloe),
James Michael Tyler (Gunther),
Maury Ginsberg (Isaac), Cynthia Mann (Jasmine)

Summary: It's the next day (as if you hadn't guessed), and Ross has to come to terms with two things. First, he's slept with Chloe. Secondly, there's a message on his answering machine from Rachel, telling him how much she loves him and how she wants them to work things out. She tells him that she'll call at his apartment in the morning to talk about it. It's now morning, and Chloe's still there. Rachel arrives, and it's only by luck that she doesn't see the living proof of Ross's infidelity. Following the advice of Chandler and Joey, Ross resolves to make sure Rachel never finds out about what happened with Chloe. He chases around New York, begging everyone who knows not to tell Rachel – until he reaches Gunther and discovers that he has already told her.

Later at Rachel and Monica's, Ross and Rachel argue, discuss and pore over the situation. In Monica's room, the rest of the gang – gathered there by several unfortunate incidents involving waxing – listen in, trapped behind the door, unable and unwilling to interrupt the discussions outside. Finally, in the small hours of the morning, they can breathe again when Rachel makes her decision.

Freaky Monica: Monica is feeding fruit into a blender as she talks to Rachel when she suddenly leaps to the wrong conclusion: that her friend and Mark have slept together. The resultant shock makes her accidentally switch the blender on and spray her kitchen with banana. Momentarily anxious about the mess, she brings herself back to Rachel's problems, almost begrudgingly admitting that 'this is more important than fruit . . . on my ceiling.' When she is telling Phoebe about the new miracle pain-free hair-removal wax that she bought from an offer on the television, she explains that she has never fallen for such infomercial tactics before – except when she bought a mop (see 'TOW The Fake Monica').

Phoebisms: When told that Monica has banana on her ceiling, Phoebe instantly takes an interest: 'Wow,' she says. 'I have the spirit of an old Indian woman living in mine.' Monica tells her about her new wax, Phoebe gets all excited at its organic ingredients, particularly the pain-free formula developed using substances found in the rainforests – 'They have the best stuff in there!' Later, trapped in Monica's room, she has to phone the massage parlour to get someone to cover one of her appointments: 'It's, like, nine fifteen now, and I'm not there.' Of course, she should have expected all this turmoil. When told about the argument between Ross and Rachel, she says, 'I knew something had to be wrong, because my fingernails did not grow at all yesterday.'

Slow Joey: He knows all about covering tracks after cheating on people. You've got to find 'the Trail', the list of people who link the cheated-upon with the cheated-with. In the depths of everyone else's concern for Ross and Rachel, all Joey can wonder is whether he should develop a 'new walk', the kind that gets you noticed the minute you enter a room. Later, as he and Chandler sneak past an exhausted Rachel asleep on the couch, Chandler asks him if that is his new walk. 'No,' he whispers so as not to disturb Rachel, 'I really have to pee.'

Chandleresque: On the matter of when Ross should admit his fling to Rachel, Chandler comments that there is a right time for doing it: 'That's what death beds are for.' When Phoebe and Monica are screaming with anguish as they rip the strips of supposedly pain-free wax off their legs, Joey and Chandler rush in (ever the gentlemen), thinking that the girls are being attacked. While Joey is sensibly armed with a heavy brass pan, Chandler bizarrely wields a kettle. While they're all trapped in Monica's room, a screaming row progressing between their friends outside, Monica wonders whether they should do something. 'Yeah,' says Chandler. 'Never cheat on Rachel.'

The Ballad of Ross & Rachel: And that's just about the only thing that this episode is about. The scenes of their arguing are sometimes quite harrowing, but marvellously broken up by the comments of the listening friends in Monica's room. Rachel, quite rightly, has the script on her side, and Aniston seems to have a whale of a time delivering some of the episode's finest lines. When Ross says that it was just a mistake, she snaps, 'What were you trying to put it in? Her purse?' Later, when Ross tries to excuse himself by saying that he thought the relationship was dead, she says, 'Well, you sure had a hell of a time at the wake.' Crisply scripted and finely acted, the scenes of the end of their relationship are the highlight of this episode, if not the whole season. It's just a shame that the bitching and sniping, and this distinctly unfunny plotline, had to dominate the rest of the season.

Gunther's a BASTARD!: Our fine apron-clad friend is the one link in the Trail that Ross didn't get to in time. Yes, folks, we have him to thank for Rachel's discovering Ross's infidelity.

The Story So Far: (Take a big breath) Chloe works with a guy called Issac. Issac's sister is called Jasmine, and she works with Phoebe at the Healing Hands Massage Parlour. Obviously Phoebe is friends with Rachel – but Jasmine's roommate is Gunther, whose undying love for Rachel is what forced him to tell her. We saw Jasmine in 'TOW Frank Jr'.

The Last Word: This is the big event of the season, and it's not a happy one (echoing the tone of the season as a whole).

A fine script manages to deliver some terrible news, while also managing to be seriously funny in places. We defy the hardened viewer not to blub – even a little – at the final lines between Ross and Rachel. 'This can't be it,' says a confused and devastated Ross. Rachel stares back, finally realising that it's over. 'Then how come it is?' Sniff. **Aaah Rating** (note: that's a deeply harrowing 'Aaah', not a cuddly-fluffy 'Ahhh'): ****

French Title: 'Celui Qui A Survécu Au Lendemain' (the one who survives to live another day)

German Title: 'Der Seitenspringer' (the one with the bit on the side)

317
'The One Without The Ski Trip'
#465267

Writers: Scott Silveri & Shana Goldberg-Meehan
Director: Sam Simon
First US transmission: 06.03.97
First UK transmission (C4): 24.10.97

Guest Cast: Jane Sibbett (Carol Willick)

Summary: An icky situation for the friends, as Rachel invites them all (except Ross, of course) to her sister's ski cabin for the weekend, just before Ross suggests they have a laser-disc-cum-darts marathon that same weekend at his flat. Since Rachel asked first, they all awkwardly admit that they should go on the ski trip. The tension of his friends' break-up reminds Chandler of his parents' divorce, and his anxiety leads him back to smoking. As they journey up to the ski cabin in Phoebe's grandmother's cab, Chandler engineers a stop-off so that he can have another cigarette. They all get out into the cold night air, slamming the car doors behind them and locking the car keys inside. When Joey manages to break back into the car (ingeniously using the under-wire from Phoebe's bra), they prepare to set off. But the car splutters to a standstill as Phoebe tries to drive away. 'This has happened before,' she says, so Monica figures she must know how to fix it. 'Yep,' Phoebe replies, 'put more gas in.'

Cold, alone and lost in the middle of nowhere, their only salvation is Ross. If they call him, he can come and look for them and help them out. But Rachel is insistent that they don't ask for his help, so they have to resort to duplicitous means to save themselves.

Poor Ross: Or should that be 'Poor Carol'? He calls round unannounced at her flat, to find he is interrupting preparations for an anniversary dinner between her and Susan. He moans his excuse: 'Candles, champagne. Yeah, anniversaries are great. 'Cause you know love lasts for ever, y'know? Nothing like it in this lifetime, money in the bank, so Rachel and I broke up.' When Carol challenges him about sleeping with another woman, Ross retorts, 'You're the one to talk!'

Freaky Monica: Her idea of fun, when she offers to stay home and spend the weekend with Ross: 'We can make fudge!' which Ross understandably sees as pity for him on her part.

Spoilt Rachel: Rachel has a little rule explaining why she never uses public toilets: 'No tissue, no tushie.' When it is suggested that Ross come to pick them up, she says, 'I am not getting in a car with Ross. We'll just have to . . . live here.'

Phoebisms: Phoebe's attempts to understand both sides of the Ross-and-Rachel argument are brilliant. She likens the dilemma over taking sides to something she saw on *60 Minutes*: 'At first you're really mad at that pharmaceutical company for making the drug and then, y'know, you just feel bad for the people because they need it to make their hair grow.' In Central Perk a while later, she cunningly tries to defuse the situation by trying to trick Ross and Rachel into getting back together: in a quiet ventriloquist's mutter, she says, '[in a Ross-like voice] Um, Rachel I'm really sorry. [in a Rachel-like voice] That's OK, do you want to get back together? [back to Ross] Yeah, OK . . . Did anyone else hear that?' When she is sneakily phoning Ross for help, she has to talk with a really quiet voice so that Rachel can't hear her betrayal. Equally, she can't let Ross know that Rachel is being cranky and anti-Ross in case he refuses. So, she just croaks an apology: 'I ate a bug.'

Slow Joey: The opening exchange of the episode is pure, wonderful Joey. He sees Chandler reading a newspaper and asks, 'Can I see the comics?' Chandler, a little snobby and affronted, tells him that it's the *New York Times*, to which Joey replies, 'All right. *May* I see the comics?' Later, he marvels at the length of time it's taking Rachel and Ross to come to terms with things – it's been a week now: 'It's never taken me more than a week to get over a relationship.' 'It's never taken you more than a *shower* to get over a relationship,' says Monica. Two interesting facts about Joey's physiognomy come to light in this episode, the first one revealed when he tells a smoking Chandler to close the window because 'my nipples could cut glass'. Later, Chandler ensures that they stop so he can have a cigarette by pretending to be desperate for a pee. 'Come on,' he says, 'I *really* have to *go*.' There is a long pause, then Joey whines, 'Oh, now I have to go!' Some wonderfully twisted lateral thinking from Joey: trapped at the restrooms on an unknown road, Joey spells out a big 'HELP' using twigs. But he's spelt it 'PLEH': 'That's "help" spelt backwards, so that the helicopters can read it from the air.'

Chandleresque: 'You're smoking again?' gasps Joey early in the episode. 'Well, actually, yesterday I was smoking again,' Chandler replies. 'Today, I'm smoking still.' He started smoking after his parents' divorce and he's been driven back to nicotine by the constant bickering between Ross and Rachel. When Rachel chides him for taking up the habit again, Chandler just yells, 'Hey, shut up! You're not my real mom!' He also explains that it was the divorce that set off his habit of using humour as an emotional shield: 'So,' says Monica, 'if your parents hadn't got divorced, you'd be able to answer a question like a normal person?' One brilliant example of this is when he hears a knock at the door and worries that 'with my luck, that's going to be him'. 'Him?' says Phoebe. 'Him, Ross?' 'No,' replies Chandler acidly, 'Hymn 253: "His Eyes Are on the *Sparrow*".'

The Ballad of Ross & Rachel: It's that nasty period when the friends get dragged into the break-up, but Rachel and Ross do try their hardest not to involve people too much. Their resolution to be civil at the end of the episode is sweet, and a relief. It's surprising to see Rachel, particularly, thank Ross for letting them continue with their ski trip. It's not surprising, though, to see how Ross ensures Carol is on his side: he obviously paints himself as the innocent victim, making Carol believe that Rachel fell in love with Mark. But Phoebe sets the record straight for Carol, and she is rightly appalled.

Parents – Who Needs 'Em?: 'This is like when my parents got divorced,' Chandler explains. 'Man, I hope Ross doesn't try to kidnap me after Cub Scouts.'

Just Plain Weird: There's a sign in Phoebe's grandmother's cab that reads BEAM ME UP, JESUS.

Girl Power: After Joey asks for the wire from a bra to open the cab door with, the girls argue about who has the biggest breasts – all of them insisting theirs are smallest! Monica claims hers are 'non-breasts' compared with Rachel's. As the friends are trapped miles from anywhere, Monica discovers that the tampons in the restroom are only a penny each, suggesting they stock up.

Generation X: Although we can't see how it *could* be, Chandler's freaking out is supposed to represent Shelley Winters from *The Poseidon Adventure* (Ronald Neame, 1972), in which we see her swim underwater to save her friends, but die in the process. Yeah, *you* work it out!

The Story So Far: Chandler reveals that it was his parents' divorce that drove him to cigarettes in the first place – when he was nine years old. The cabin the gang go to belongs to Rachel's sister (see 'TOW The Dozen Lasagnes'). Ross remembers that Carol and Susan got married in January (see 'TOW The Lesbian Wedding').

The Last Word: A great episode, where everyone gets a fair crack at the whip. Perry and Kudrow are on good form, and have most of the best lines. Although this is an episode about the break-up, it's refreshingly low on bitchiness between Ross and Rachel, choosing to concentrate more on the plight of the people in the middle. Fine stuff. **Ahhh Rating:** **

French Title: 'Celui Qui Était Laissé Pour Compte' (the one who's left behind)

German Title: 'Einsam und Verlassen' (lonely and left alone)

318

'The One With The Hypnosis Tape'
#465269

Writer: Seth Kurland
Director: Robby Benson
First US transmission: 13.03.97
First UK transmission (C4): 31.10.97

Guest Cast: Giovanni Ribisi (Frank, Jr),
James Michael Tyler (Gunther), Jeffrey D. Brooks (Trent),
and introducing Jon Favreau (Pete Becker),
Debra Jo Rupp (Alice)

Summary: Frank Jr, Phoebe's weird half-brother, stops by Central Perk to give her some good news: he's going to get married. Although she is initially very excited about this, when she meets Frank's fiancée, she is secretly outraged and wants the wedding to be called off. Frank is going to marry Alice (or 'Mrs Knight', as he keeps calling her), his home economics teacher – a woman almost twice his age. Although they are obviously passionately in love, Phoebe sets about trying to persuade Frank that it's not a good idea. Or at least, she sets Ross and Joey the task, but things go awry and they end up agreeing to become ring bearer and best man respectively. Phoebe decides to confront Alice but, although it seems she has managed to convince them of their haste, the minute they see each other again they fall into an enthusiastic clinch and Phoebe has no choice but to give them her blessing.

Monica, while working at the Moondance Diner, tells Rachel that she is getting frustrated that she hasn't had a date in months. Pete, who sits nearby, once again offers to go out with her. Although she refuses, when she and Rachel later discover that he is a multimillionaire, Rachel manages to cajole her into going for dinner with him – in Rome. But even after that, she's still not attracted to him.

Chandler, meanwhile, tries self-hypnosis using a tape. It's surprisingly successful – but it does have one very strange side effect . . .

Freaky Monica: She's really hit the skids when it comes to dating. When trying to persuade her to go out with Pete (and this is before they even know he's rich), Rachel asks her what happened on last Saturday's *Walker: Texas Ranger*. Monica, laughing warmly at the memories, says, 'Well, Walker was looking for this big busload of kids . . . All right, I get your point.'

Spoilt Rachel: When Monica is bemoaning her lack of dates, she asks Rachel if she could set her up with someone at work. Rachel then points out something about her industry that has obviously escaped Monica's notice. 'Well, that shouldn't be a problem,' she replies. 'I mean, I work in fashion and all I meet are eligible *straight* men.' When Rachel finds out that Pete is rich beyond her wildest dreams, she realises that the $20,000 tip he left Monica is genuine: 'I can't believe this is a real twenty-thousand-dollar cheque. Oh, this is just so exciting.' 'Or incredibly offensive,' Monica points out. Grasping the cheque, Rachel just says, 'Oh yeah, sure, that too.'

Phoebisms: Phoebe's surprising summation of her brother's relationship: 'I don't want to be all judgemental, y'know, but this is sick. It's sick and wrong!' 'Is it the age thing?' Ross asks her. 'I'm fine with the age thing, until it starts sticking its tongue down my little brother's throat!' Phoebe's normal easygoing attitude to things goes out of the window when it comes to Frank's choice of wife, which shows a touching concern. At least, in the end, she comes around to the idea.

Slow Joey: When Frank asks him, 'Isn't sex better when it's with one person that you really, really care about?' Joey, incredulous, replies, 'Yeah, in a poem, maybe.' In the final scene we see how Joey, with the power of hypnotism at his fingertips, tries to get Chandler to make him a cheese sandwich every night (see 'TOW The Embryos').

Chandleresque: At Central Perk, he sits in front of Rachel and puts a cigarette in his mouth, preparing to light it. Rachel just pulls it out and throws it on the floor. He takes another one and puts it to his lips; again, Rachel grabs it and throws it away. 'OK,' he says, 'that's like the least fun game ever.' When Rachel gives him the hypnosis tape, he places it to his arm and watches it fall to the ground: 'Nope, that patch is no good,' he observes. When he consents to trying the tape, he plays it while sleeping: 'Cigarettes don't control you,' it proclaims. 'You are a strong, confident woman, who does not need to smoke. A strong, confident woman . . .' Chandler then starts to act very strangely, and Matthew Perry does a marvellous job with this new Chandler, totally at ease with his feminine side. When he shares Rachel's excitement at Monica's date with a rich guy, the look on everyone's face says it all.

The Ballad of Ross & Rachel: When Ross is confronted by Frank's love for Alice, his realisation that he's really messed up something special with Rachel is wonderfully done. Here, for once, they play the break-up for laughs, not bitterness. Earlier in the episode, Ross appears to deride hypnosis simply because Rachel supports it; he claims it 'is beyond crap'. Rachel reminds him of the time he appeared in a stage hypnotist's act, but he claims he wasn't actually hypnotised. 'Oh, right,' splutters Rachel, 'you *always* pull your pants down at the count of three and play "Wipeout" on your butt cheeks.'

Parents – Who Needs 'Em?: Phoebe gives her own suggestion for how to stop smoking: 'You have to dance naked in a field of heather, and then bathe in the sweat of six healthy young men.' 'Or what my father calls "Thursday night",' deadpans Chandler.

Just Plain Weird: Welcome back to Frank, whose grasp of the real world seems even more tenuous than his sister's. Joey, trying to persuade him to think again about the marriage, points out that 'you're eighteen, OK, she's forty-four. When you're thirty-six, she's gonna be eighty-eight.' Frank just says, 'You don't think I know that?' Frank gets some of the best lines in this episode, and it's great to see Giovanni Ribisi not going to waste. Alice is a scream, too – literally, as her trademark startling (but infectious) giggle makes its debut. Ladies and gentlemen: the wacky couple.

Joey's an Actor?: At the opening of the episode, he is practising his fake laugh. Soon, Monica is practising with him – and they both get the perfect opportunity when Chandler makes his first crack of the episode.

Gunther, Can You Spare a Match?: It seems Gunther is an ex-smoker. When he sees Chandler walking in, smoking, he walks over to him and tells him to put it out. Chandler agrees, but only if he can finish it first. Gunther's prepared to let him, if he'll give him a drag. The waiter takes a deep breath, and lets out the smoke with a sigh. 'Oh, dark mother,' he says. 'Once again I suckle at your smoky teat.' When he offers the cigarette back to the disturbed Chandler, he just waves it away. 'Why don't you hang on to that one?'

Generation X: Jon Favreau starred in the critically acclaimed film, *Swingers* (Doug Liman, 1997) and the blockbuster *Deep Impact* (Mimi Leder, 1998). 'Wipeout' was originally a hit for the Sufaris in 1963, though the Fat Boys and the Beach Boys teamed up to cover it in 1987. Monica has become hooked on the CBS action series *Walker: Texas Ranger*, which stars Chuck Norris. Pete Becker is a thinly veiled take on Bill Gates, the Microsoft king.

The Story So Far: Monica reminds Rachel that she's dated only two men this year, Richard (see 'TOW Barry And Mindy's Wedding') and Julio ('TOW All The Jealousy').

The Last Word: A good episode, featuring a fine turn from Kudrow as Phoebe tries to come to terms with something she thinks is wrong. Perry as the empowered Chandler is frighteningly brilliant, and it's a bit of a shame that more couldn't be made of this little plot. Still, there's a good balance between the heart-warming and the rib-tickling here. **Ahhh Rating:** ***

French Title: 'Celui Qui S'auto Hypnotisait' (the one who hypnotises himself)

German Title: 'Wie angle ich mir keinen Millionär?' (how not to pick up a millionaire)

319

'The One With The Tiny T-Shirt'
(a.k.a. 'The One With The Lousy T-Shirt')
#465268

Writer: Adam Chase
Director: Terry Hughes
First US transmission: 27.03.97
First UK transmission (C4): 07.11.97

Guest Cast: Steven Eckholdt (Mark), Jon Favreau (Pete Becker), James Michael Tyler (Gunther), Ethel Ayler (Hospital Administrator), **and introducing** Dina Meyer (Kate Miller), Reg Rogers (the Director)

Summary: Rachel asks Ross round to her apartment. He is convinced that this is the first step on the road to reconciliation, so he's upset when he discovers that all she wants to do is return a box full of his things. Unreasonably irate, he starts to demand everything back, including a FRANKIE SAY RELAX T-shirt he used to wear when he was fifteen. Although it's ridiculously small and Rachel uses it as nightwear, Ross storms off wearing the shirt.

Later, Mark admits to Rachel that he has had a crush on her for a while and – now that she's no longer with Ross – asks her out on a date. Ross gets wind of this, and spends that evening at Chandler's, ceaselessly staring through his peephole, waiting for Rachel's return. When she and Mark finally do get back, he watches them go inside together and Chandler has to physically restrain him from following them in. Telling him that he must finally let go, Chandler manages to convince Ross that Rachel is moving on. Meanwhile, Rachel tells Mark that, nice as he is, she just can't use him to get back at Ross. A little disappointed, Mark leaves.

Joey is having trouble with a fellow cast member in his new play. The beautiful, fiery Kate responds to all his efforts to get along with arrogant, snide comments. Joey can't stop talking about the woman, and Chandler points out that this might be because he has a crush on her.

Pete and Monica are still dating, but he is beginning to get a little impatient. He asks Monica whether their relationship is going anywhere, and she admits to him that she doesn't find him attractive. Filled with what seems to be misplaced confidence, Pete just says that he'll ride it through, and that her attitude may change.

Freaky Monica: It's revealed in this episode that Monica paints numbers on all her mugs, so that they can be easily tracked down. At one point, Monica is lamenting the fact that she can't get into a decent relationship – here's Pete, who's handsome, clever, funny, but she just feels nothing for him. 'Does it sound like there's something wrong with me?' she asks Phoebe. 'Yeah,' her friend replies. 'Kinda.'

Phoebisms: Apropos of nothing, Phoebe wonders at one point, 'Why isn't it Spiderm'n? You know, like Goldman, Silverman . . .?' This wonderfully twisted little conversation continues, with Chandler explaining that it's not his surname – 'it's not, like, Phil Spiderm'n' – and then Phoebe insisting there should be a superhero called Gold Man. Although it has nothing to do with anything, this little exchange is a nice little distraction.

Chandleresque: Chandler's own wonderment at the fact that he's in his late twenties, but still so childish, comes to the fore when he meets Pete for the first time. 'You're *our* age,' he keeps repeating, stunned by Pete's financial success. This little Peter Pan aspect of Chandler's character isn't touched on very often, but goes a long way towards explaining his behaviour. Like when he does a *High Chaparral* showdown, using the footrest on a leather armchair instead of a six-shooter. 'Draw!' he yells at the empty chair, and whips his own chair into its reclining position. Joey then walks in, and Chandler suddenly turns round and says cagily, 'I wasn't doing anything.' When Monica claims that Pete has everything, Chandler challenges her by asking if he has a life-sized Imperial Stormtrooper from *Star Wars* (Monica claims he has two!).

The Ballad of Ross & Rachel: So, what Ross suspected all along is true: Mark did want to go out with Rachel and, furthermore, she is at least partly open to the idea. But, as she explains to Phoebe later, she just couldn't do it. 'I mean,' she says, 'I'm standing there with this charming, cute guy, who's asking me to go out with him – which I'm allowed to do – and I felt guilty.' Phoebe thinks that she's obviously still not over Ross, and that she has issues with her father. When Rachel says she has no such issues, Phoebe – as if she had just performed some great feat of psychoanalysis – announces, 'It's probably just the Ross thing, then.' Ross, meanwhile, is quite clearly not over Rachel. His vigil at Chandler's peephole is wonderful: first he wants to see what happens, then he doesn't. Eventually, Chandler has to physically restrain him from going over to spoil Rachel's date. He throws one arm around Ross's neck, clambers on to his back, and takes hold of the foosball table with the other hand. Even with all this luggage, Ross still soldiers on towards the door. Finally, Chandler has a heart-to-heart with Ross, persuading him to let go of Rachel. (That this conversation is carried out while Chandler is resting on Ross's back, his legs braced halfway up his front door, brings a brilliant note of crazy comedy to the moment.)

Joey's an Actor?: Kate recognises Joey from the Milk Master 2000 infomercial (seen in 'TOW The Metaphorical Tunnel'), claiming, 'You're the guy who doesn't know how to pour milk!' Joey explains that this shows what a good actor he is, because of course he can pour milk. Then, Kate remembers that he 'choked on a cookie' during the commercial. Embarrassed, Joey admits, 'That was real.'

Gunther's There For You, Rachel: At the opening of the episode, Gunther is thinking to himself how he might approach Rachel for a date now that Ross is out of the picture. As he silently contemplates asking Rachel to come to dinner ('as my lover'), he watches Mark swoop in, admit his crush, and ask her for a date, and get a pleasantly stunned 'Wow' in reply. A hurt look on his face, he disappears into the bowels of Central Perk. We hear an almighty crash, as if ten Welsh dressers had just collapsed, and then he reappears. 'I dropped a cup.'

Generation X: Dina Meyer co-starred in the sci-fi movie *Starship Troopers* (Paul Verhoeven, 1998). The craze that was 'Frankie Says' was the product of Paul Morley's superb PR promotion of the band Frankie Goes To Hollywood. The T-shirts, like the group, were everywhere in the summer of 1984.

The Last Word: The Ross-and-Rachel stuff is getting boring by this point, which lets the episode down somewhat. Monica's problems with Pete are also too serious to be very funny, as are Joey's feelings over Kate. Altogether, this episode is a little too soapy: the only laughs are provided by Chandler and Phoebe, and their little random moments of comedy. **Ahhh Rating:** **

French Title: 'Celui Qui Avait Un T-shirt Trop Petit' (the one whose T-shirt was too small)

German Title: 'Männer Ohne Chance' (men with no chance)

320
'The One With The Dollhouse'
#465270

Writer: Wil Calhoun
Director: Terry Hughes
First US transmission: 10.04.97
First UK transmission (C4): 14.11.97

Guest Cast: Dina Meyer (Kate Miller), Reg Rogers (the Director), Jennifer Milmore (Lauren), Laura Dean (Sophie), **and introducing** Alison LaPlaca (Joanna)

Summary: Women trouble for Joey and Chandler: Joey wants one who doesn't want him, and Chandler doesn't want one who wants him. Of course, there are complications. Joey's fallen for Kate, one of his fellow actors in his current play, in a big way. But she's seeing the director, Marshall, and Joey's being torn apart – he can't understand why she doesn't want him. When their performances in rehearsal begin to suffer, Marshall storms out in overdramatic disgust and Kate and Joey wonder how they can spice up their acting. But they get a little too spicy, and end up in bed together. Joey is on top of the world, until he discovers that Kate is doing what he has done to a thousand women. It looks like she is now going to just cast him aside.

Chandler, meanwhile, meets Rachel's boss, Joanna. She falls for him instantly, and Rachel sets up a date for them. While Chandler is completely unimpressed by her, she is totally smitten – so much so that she fails to spot that Chandler is trying to give her the brush-off. He tells her he'll call, she thinks he means it. When Joanna clearly threatens Rachel's job, she has to persuade him to end it properly.

Ross and Monica's Aunt Sylvia has passed away ('Yes!' yelps Monica. 'She was a cruel, cranky, old bitch!') and left her dollhouse to Monica. She's delighted, because she was never allowed to play with it. She suggests to Phoebe that she should bring her dolls round so they can finally use the dollhouse for what it's for – playing. But Phoebe's choice of dolls (a dinosaur, a handkerchief ghost, and a three-storey dog) doesn't go down well with Monica, so Phoebe decides to build a dollhouse of her own.

Freaky Monica: When she throws Phoebe out of her dollhouse, it leads Pheebs to term Monica's house 'the House of No Imagination'. As everyone coos over Phoebe's house of wonder, Monica shouts, 'Hey, guys, guys, did you see my new china cabinet?'

Phoebisms: Her games with Monica's dollhouse involve its being built on both an Indian burial ground and a nuclear-waste dump. When Ross suggests that seems pretty unlikely, she comments that 'obviously you don't know much about the US government'. So, the giant dog has to protect the inhabitants from an attack by a tyrannosaurus, with a hand-kerchief haunting the attic all the while. When Monica freaks and says that Phoebe can't play with her house any more, Phoebe just builds her own (complete with slide, edible furniture, bubble-blowing chimney, fairy lights and an aroma room). When a spark from the aroma room causes her house to be burnt to the ground, she immediately tries to find out who survived the blaze. While nearly all her toys are OK, there's something lying under a handkerchief (probably the ghost) on the table. She lifts the hankie and screams as she sees the charred remains of the Foster puppets.

Slow Joey: Kate sneers at his choice of dates, by calling her understudy Kate 'the sweater'. Joey retorts, 'It's what's under the sweater that counts.' When Kate suggests there needs to be something more between their characters when they kiss, Joey suggests, 'Maybe he could slip her the tongue.' Subtle and charming as ever. At the end of the episode, when he knows how it feels to be tossed aside by someone you like, Joey sets about phoning all his ex-girlfriends to apologise.

Chandleresque: As Joey laments the fact that Kate is the first woman he wants who isn't interested in him, he turns to Chandler and asks, 'Is this what it's like to be you?' Monica is explaining that Aunt Sylvia would always say that the dollhouse was a thing to be looked at but not played with, to which Chandler says, 'My grandmother used to say that exact same thing to me.' When he is introduced to Joanna, she just repeats his surname like a timer going off: 'Bing!' Chandler explains that his name is 'Gaelic for "thy turkey's done"'. After he has had the date with Joanna, he tells Rachel that he *never* wants her to set him up with anyone, that from now on he makes his own dates. Then he adds, 'That's just a lot of big talk, you know?'

The Ballad of Ross & Rachel: When Rachel arrives home to tell Chandler that she wants to set him up on a date, she walks through the door and says, 'I need to talk to you.' Ross turns round and asks, 'What's up?' She tells him that she meant Chandler. There's an embarrassed exchange which ends with Ross saying, 'Well, if something comes up . . .' Chandler, breaking the tension, says, 'I'm glad you guys are past that little awkward phase.'

Parents – Who Needs 'Em?: When Chandler walks in to see Phoebe's dollhouse all lit up with fairy lights and blowing bubbles, he comments, 'Hey, my father's house does that!'

Just Plain Weird: Marshall, the manic director whom Joey likens to a cartoon character, starts rehearsals with the affirming 'All right, it's time to act, my talking *props*!'

Joey's an Actor?: Lauren, Kate's understudy, comes up to him and announces that she's a big fan of his, to which Joey gasps, 'What?'

Boys Will Be Boys: Chandler escorts Rachel to her desk so he can pick up a copy of her 'summer catalogue'.

Dinosaurs ROCK!: After the dinosaur attack on Monica's dollhouse is over, Ross politely points out to Phoebe that 'dinosaurs don't go "ruff!"'. Phoebe, with equal authority, states that 'the little ones do'.

Shut Up, Sophie!: With Joanna's debut, we see the start of the I-suck-up-to-you/I-see-through-you relationship between her and her other assistant, Sophie. When Sophie suggests that Chandler might be 'intimidated by really smart, strong, successful women', Joanna says, 'Sophie, will you please climb out of my butt?'

The Story So Far: Monica's Aunt Sylvia has previously been mentioned in 'TOW The Dozen Lasagnes' and 'TOW Old Yeller Dies'. Phoebe's jealousy for Monica's dollhouse is because when she was a child, all she had was a barrel – not to play with dolls in, just a barrel. Lauren refers to the time Joey played Dr Drake Ramoray on *Days Of Our Lives* and they dropped him down an elevator shaft (see 'TOW Dr Ramoray Dies').

The Last Word: A great episode for Phoebe, as Kudrow brings bucketfuls of relish to her games with the dollhouses. Phoebe's own dollhouse knocks spots off Monica's, and it's a great tragedy to see it go up in flames. (Ross's final solution of putting the fire out – by shoving it under the shower while Monica is in there – is brilliant. And yes, Monica, we believe you when you say you were 'just checking the shower massager'.) **Ahhh rating: ****

French Title: 'Celui Qui Courait Deux Lièvres' (literally the one who chases two rabbits – it means the one who has two goals but achieves neither)

German Title: 'Feuer gefangen' (catching fire)

321
'The One With A Chick. And A Duck'
#465271

Writer: Chris Brown
Director: Michael Lembeck
First US transmission: 17.04.97
First UK transmission (C4): 21.11.97

Guest Cast: Jon Favreau (Pete Becker),
James Michael Tyler (Gunther)

Summary: Working at the Moondance Diner has reached a new low for Monica. The management are now insisting that all the waiting staff wear roller skates. Monica, aided by Phoebe and Rachel, is practising her skating outside Central Perk when an interruption from Gunther causes her to crash into Rachel, sending them both tumbling to the floor. By the time she gets to work, she's still no better at skating and keeps falling over as she welcomes back Pete from his trip to Japan. It seems that her humiliation might come to an end, though, when Pete tells her that he's bought a restaurant and he wants her to be head chef. Once he's convinced her (by making up a story about meeting another woman) that he's not doing it just to win her over, Monica agrees and immediately leaves her job at the diner. Later, she finds out that Pete has been lying, and very nearly calls the whole thing off. Until a kiss changes her mind about everything.

Ross is excited because he's been asked to join a panel of palaeontologists on a television programme but, when he briefly calls in at Monica and Rachel's before the recording of the show, his plans are derailed when he sees the state that Rachel's in. It seems she took quite a beating when Monica skated into her; she needs to go to the hospital, but obviously needs someone to go with her.

There's happiness on the other side of the hallway, though, as Chandler and Joey greet a couple of new arrivals to their apartment. Joey decides to buy Chandler a fluffy little chick as an Easter present. They soon decide, however, that she is too much responsibility for them and Chandler tries to take her back to the store. They won't take her back, though, and when he tries the animal shelter, he discovers that they are likely to have her destroyed. So, back he comes with the chick, and another rescued animal – a fully grown duck.

Poor Ross: He turns up at Monica and Rachel's wearing an extremely cheesy white suit and red bow tie. When Rachel criticises his outfit, he points out that they're not going out any more, so he can wear whatever he likes. Rachel just says that he's right, he's free to look as stupid as he likes.

Freaky Monica: A little secret from her childhood is let slip when she reveals that she always used to dream of being a head chef: 'I mean, this has been my dream since I got my first Easy Bake Oven and opened Easy Monica's Bakery.' She doesn't, however, seem to notice the inappropriateness of her bakery's name.

Phoebisms: She manages to work out that Pete is lying to Monica when he says he has met another woman. When Pete implores her not to tell Monica, Phoebe says, 'Absolutely, I promise. Tell her what?' Thinking that she's pretending to have forgotten their whole conversation, Pete thanks her. 'No, I'm serious,' she replies. 'I mean, I'm intuitive, but my memory sucks.' At Central Perk, Phoebe announces to Monica, 'I have to tell you something' but 'I can't tell you'. She proceeds to have Monica try to guess what she can't tell her. As her methods of communication get increasingly strange, Monica gives up, saying, 'I feel like I'm talking to Lassie.' And of course, it was Phoebe's suggestion to the manager of the Moondance Diner that led to Monica being forced to wear skates!

Slow Joey: A smile of delight crosses Joey's face when he exits Central Perk just after the skating accident to find Monica writhing on top of Rachel. When he sees a news report about the plight of abandoned and ill-cared-for chicks on television, he takes it as an advertisement for a great gift idea.

Chandleresque: It's the first regular appearance of the short-lived goatee (after its brief appearance back in 'The One With The Flashback'). Maybe it's just that Matthew Perry was so thin at this point that it didn't work, but we definitely prefer him without it. (And this comes from two men, one of whom has had a goatee for two and a half years now, and the other – like Chandler – managed it for a month.) We agree with Joey when he says that 'with that goatee, you kinda look like Satan'.

The Ballad of Ross & Rachel: This is the one where they nearly get back together. With Rachel injured and in pain, Ross has to help her with her make-up (putting it on very badly), and then she asks him to help her get dressed. Rachel doesn't want him to see her naked, though, and Ross finds this ridiculous – after all, he has seen her this way many times before. He begins to gently freak Rachel out by closing his eyes and imagining her naked, until her pain finally drives him to take her seriously and suggest that she really should get to the hospital. He agrees to go with her, even though it means missing his television appearance. When Rachel finds out what he's given up for her, there's a second – just a second – where it looks like they are about to kiss.

The Chick and the Duck: When he and Joey get their first new pet, Phoebe asks if they know anything about chicks. 'Fowl? No,' says Chandler. 'Women [in a now-we're-talking tone] . . . no.' Later, he is alone with the chick as they both watch *Baywatch*. 'I know,' he says as the little bird chirps at the picture on the screen. 'That's Yasmine Bleeth. She's a completely different kind of chick. I love you both. But in very different ways.' This is the moment of inspiration where the chick is given its name: Yasmine. Chandler hauls the unnamed duck out of the apartment into the hallway as Ross and Rachel are passing by. 'You stay out here,' he yells at it, 'and you think about what you did . . . That chick is not a toy!'

Magna Doodle: Introduced this episode is the Magna Doodle message board, which is pinned to the wall by the door in Joey and Chandler's apartment. In later episodes it becomes the source of many hidden gags, but for its debut, someone's merely drawn a big happy face.

Yo Gunther!: He may be the one who unwittingly started to bring Rachel and Ross back together. If Gunther hadn't offered Rachel that coffee when she should have been catching the skating Monica, then she wouldn't have been distracted and Monica wouldn't have crashed into her, breaking her rib. The resultant care and attention she needed could only be given, of course, by Ross.

Cruelty To Animals: Chandler asks the gang if they know how to get a chick out of a VCR. Over the closing credits,

Joey arrives home to see Chandler giving the duck a bath, while Yasmine watches on from dry land. Joey wonders whether chicks can swim too, so they give it a try – only to discover that they can't. As Chandler cradles and comforts poor, drenched Yasmine, a look of horror crosses his face when he hears Joey turn on the hairdryer.

Dinosaurs ROCK!: When Ross announces that he's going to appear in a programme about 'these fossils they just found in Peru', Chandler seems excited. 'Oh my God!' he says, before adding, 'Who's going to watch that?'

Generation X: Joey watches *Quincy, ME*, the medical detective series. Monica compares Ross's white suit to something Colonel Sanders, founder of Kentucky Fried Chicken, might wear. When Joey cuddles the chick, Chandler warns, 'Easy, Lenny' – a reference to the character from John Steinbeck's *Of Mice and Men*. Chandler gives us an impromptu performance of 'Old MacDonald' ('Here a chick, there a chick . . .'). Something Joey and Chandler obviously don't know is that male chicks don't have external sex organs (see 'TOW The Embryos').

The Story So Far: A guy called Stu Vincent offered Monica a necklace when she was in seventh grade (she turned him down as he was her health teacher). According to Monica, Chandler keeps a sock by his bed – and we really don't want to know why.

The Last Word: Yay for the chick and the duck! This is a brilliantly scripted episode, especially the sequences where Joey and Chandler, like a married couple coping with a new child, begin to argue and worry that the chick is driving a wedge between them. Matthew Perry, though still not back on top form, gives one of his best performances of the season, as he gradually falls in love with Yasmine (chick, not Bleeth). The scenes between Rachel and Ross are genuinely sweet, and the script shows a marvellous warmth and understanding between them. One of the best episodes of this season, without a doubt. **Ahhh Rating:** ****

French Title: 'Celui Qui Avait Un Poussin' (the one who had a chick)

German Title: 'Ein Huhn und eine Ente' (a chick and a duck)

322
'The One With The Screamer'
#465272

Writers: Scott Silveri & Shana Goldberg-Meehan
Director: Peter Bonerz
First US transmission: 24.04.97
First UK transmission (C4): 28.11.97

Guest Cast: Jon Favreau (Pete Becker),
Dina Meyer (Kate Miller), Reg Rogers (the Director,
Marshall Talmant), June Gable (Estelle),
Jennifer Milmore (Lauren), James Michael Tyler (Gunther),
Ben Stiller (Tommy), Laura Cayouette (Cailin),
Jeffery D. Brooks (Stage Manager)

Summary: It's the premiere of Joey's new play and everyone is invited. When Ross announces that he's bringing along a date, Rachel lies and says she has a date too. Rachel finds and brings along Tommy and leaves him with Ross to find their seats. Ross alone witnesses him shouting hysterically at another audience member who has mistakenly sat in his seat. Ross continues to see Tommy scream at innocent victims, and tries to convince Rachel that her new man is psychotic. She believes that he's just acting out of jealousy, however, and it isn't until she sees Tommy shouting at the duck that she pays Ross's suspicions any attention.

Joey, meanwhile, is finally beginning to fall in love. His feelings for Kate are getting stronger, and they spend a night together, not sleeping but talking and learning everything about each other. But, the next day, Joey is devastated when Kate – whose understudy has suddenly taken her place in the play – tells him that she has a part on *General Hospital* and is leaving that night. Deeply upset, he directs his character's emotional departure speech to Kate, who stands in the wings, and watches his true love leave his life for ever.

Freaky Monica: Still high on finally getting together properly with Pete, when Joey asks how many tickets she wants for his play, she excitedly says, 'I need two. I'm bringing Pete. My boyfriend. I have a boyfriend now!' This little burst of glee is quite charming, and you can't help but smile along with her happiness.

Phoebisms: Throughout this episode, Phoebe suffers self-imposed confinement in Monica's apartment. She has broken her phone on the final day of her warranty, and is on hold with the manufacturer's support line to get help. She misses Joey's opening night, because the recorded voice has told her that she is the next caller in line. But she is the next caller throughout the entire night. This little diversion makes for some wonderful moments, especially when Phoebe puts the phone down and tries to put on a jumper in a panic: she ends up trying to squeeze her head through the sleeve, while shouting, 'I'm right here! Wait one second!' Caught in the jumper, she has to cry for Monica's help, claiming, 'I'm scared!' While she is on the phone, she takes a call for Monica from her father, telling her that 'he said call him as soon as you get a chance – he's at Flimby's.' When Monica says she doesn't know where Flimby's is, Phoebe explains that that's the word she uses when she can't remember the real thing.

Slow Joey: In preparation for meeting Kate again, Joey borrows some of Chandler's cologne. Chandler explains, though, that he has no cologne – Joey's actually used the duck's worm medicine.

The Ballad of Ross & Rachel: Rachel, not unreasonably, assumes that Ross's constant warning about Tommy's screaming habits are just jealousy. When he suggests that she stop seeing him, Rachel nods and says that, instead, 'Maybe I should stay away from *all* men.' Ross then says, deflating his argument somewhat, 'It's not just because I'm jealous.' For once, the viewer can sympathise with Ross, but the bitter memories of his behaviour over most of this season are still too fresh to be able to root for him totally.

The Chick and the Duck: Chandler brings Yasmine and the duck through to Monica's and asks if they can go to see Joey's play. When she says no, a vindicated Chandler looks at them and says, 'I just wanted them to hear it from somebody else.' Later, when Tommy is screaming at the innocent pair, we see that Chandler and Joey have left a little something in Yasmine's basket in case she gets bored – it's a Game Boy.

Just Plain Weird: Joey's agent, Estelle (one of our favourite guest stars), makes an appearance after the play, telling Monica and Rachel that she was really impressed with them. When they explain that, not only were they not in the play – they're not even actors – Estelle moans, 'What a shame! Because with her face [she points at Monica] and her chest [then at Rachel], I could really put something together.' When Marshall reads the review, he sees that his direction is criticised. True to form for a stage-director stereotype, he blames everybody else for ruining his life.

Joey's an Actor!: The after-show party for the first night of the play drags on until the early hours when the reviews are printed. Marshall, the director, runs in with the first one and reads, 'Mr Tribbiani is not the worst thing in this production.' Delighted, Joey shouts, 'Yes!' and punches the air. Later, he keeps the newspaper for himself – obviously as a memento of his best review yet.

Gunther Plays Cupid: In a totally unconnected scene, Gunther brings a cup of coffee to Chandler, explaining that it's been bought by a woman at the bar. He looks over at her, and the woman whispers something to Gunther: 'Sorry,' he says, taking the coffee away, 'she thought you were someone else.'

Generation X: Ben Stiller appeared in and directed the Jim Carrey vehicle *Cable Guy* (1996).

The Last Word: Quite good fun, particularly Phoebe's telephone traumas and Tommy's insanity – the point where he's screaming at Ross outside Central Perk, with him tapping on the window to try to catch Rachel's attention is priceless. The best part, though, is Joey's fond farewell to Kate – for this alone, the episode deserves an **Ahhh Rating:** ****

French Title: 'Celui Qui S'énervait' (the one who got annoyed)

German Title: 'Der Choleriker' (the bad-tempered one)

323
'The One With Ross's Thing'
#465274

Writers: Andrew Reich & Ted Cohen
Director: Shelley Jensen
First US transmission: 01.05.97
First UK transmission (C4): 05.12.97

Guest Cast: Jon Favreau (Pete Becker), Kevin McDonald (Guru Saj), Matt Battaglia (Vince), Robert Gant (Jason), Richard Gant (Dr Rhodes), Carole Goldman (Pete's Mom, billed as 'Woman'), Doug Looper (Fireman)

Summary: Having discovered what can only be described as a 'thing' on his butt, Ross seeks advice from Joey and Chandler. When they fail to identify it, he decides to bite the bullet and see a doctor. But the doctor is as clueless as his friends, so he calls in a colleague. Then he calls another. And another. Before long, the whole hospital is staring at Ross's backside, but to no avail – they just can't work out what it is. Eventually, he agrees to see Phoebe's herbalist, Guru Saj, whose first attempts to cure it seem only to 'anger' it. Then Saj decides to treat it with love, waving his hands above the thing: the method works, but only because Saj catches the thing on his watch and rips it right off.

Pete is away, and Monica heads round to his house to talk to him over the videophone – it turns out he has something important to tell her. The gang go with her, just to check out his pad. Joey happens across a cheque made out to 'Hugo Lindgren Ring Design', and Rachel is immediately convinced that Pete is going to propose to Monica. Mulling over it for a while, Monica decides that her answer would be 'yes', but when Pete returns he tells her that he is planning to become the world's Ultimate Fighting Champion, and that he's even had his own ring designed.

Phoebe, meanwhile, is high on the fact that she's dating two men at once. She can't decide between the two: Vince, a fireman, has an incredible body, while Jason, a teacher, is sensitive, kind and intelligent. Eventually, she plumps for the brains, and tells Vince that she has to call it off. The news brings him close to tears, and he leaves to write his feelings down in his journal – he too is sensitive. Phoebe falls into even deeper confusion when she walks in on Jason to find that he has Adonis's body. Eventually, the decision is taken out of her hands when they discover that she's seeing them both at once.

Spoilt Rachel: Her excitement at the idea that Monica might be marrying Pete is classic rich-girl material. 'Monica's going to marry a millionaire!' she yells, with open glee. She suggests that they should have a themed wedding, her idea for the theme being 'Look How Much Money We've Got!' At one point in the middle of an unconnected conversation, she flings her arms into the air and screams with joy. 'Sorry,' she says, 'I was just imagining what it'd be like to catch the money bouquet.' Rachel even goes to the lengths of picking out a dress that Monica could wear: Phoebe is so taken with the frock that she suggests to Monica that she buy it whatever, 'for clubbing'.

Phoebisms: Phoebe's not quite being herself here, as she plays the man's game of going out with two people at once. She describes herself, with not a small amount of pride, as an 'oat-sowing, field-playing juggler'. Later, she is performing a song at Central Perk which is probably best titled as 'Crazy Underwear (Creeping Up My Butt)'.

Slow Joey: When Pete announces to Monica that he has something serious to talk about, she immediately thinks that her relationship is over. Joey, showing just how amoral he can be, says that maybe it's not that bad – 'Maybe he just cheated on you.' When Chandler offers to go over to Pete's apartment to 'water' the plants in retaliation for this supposed dumping, Joey – characteristically – misses the point and says, 'Or, we could go over there and pee on them!'

The Chick and the Duck: The duck, here named Dick, is taken to see Guru Saj as he has a 'bad cough'. When Saj asks if the duck would be prepared to eat a whole bat, a marvellous synchronity occurs: the duck starts to flap its wings in a mad panic, with Le Blanc having to hold it tightly. The look on Perry's face here is brilliant – just like it was when Joey was about to blow-dry the chick in 'The One With A Chick. And A Duck'.

Just Plain Weird: Guru Saj is simply not funny. On seeing *Friends* for the first time, it's quite easy to see Phoebe as a kook and nothing more. Repeated exposure to our favourite weirdo, though, brings her closer to your heart – Kudrow is funny and warm, and has exceptional ability to deliver her lines just so. Kevin McDonald, who plays Saj, though, has none of these charms. Get him off our screens! Oh, and Joey's pondering about what to call the offspring of a chick and a duck is quite weird too.

Gunther's Got Style, He's Got Grace!: He does nothing but appear in the background – but he's wearing the best tie in the world, ever!

The Story So Far: When Ross tries to warn Monica against rushing into marriage, Rachel spitefully reminds him that he married a lesbian.

The Last Word: Ross's Thing itself makes for little more than tedious viewing: it's a dully scripted plot that Schwimmer seems only half concerned about getting his teeth into. Phoebe's flings with Jason and Vince are entertaining, but still the most laughs come from Monica's thoughts about marrying Pete and, more specifically, Rachel's reaction to the whole thing. All told, it's a fairly run-of-the-mill half-hour.

Ahhh Rating: **

French Title: 'Celui Qui Avait Un Truc Dans Le Dos' (the one who had something on his back)

German Title: 'Zuviel des Guten' (too much of a good thing)

324

'The One With The Ultimate Fighting Champion'
#465273

Writers: Mark J. Kunerth & Pang-Ni Landrum (story),
Scott Silveri & Shanan Goldberg-Meehan (teleplay)
Director: Robby Benson
First US transmission: 08.05.97
First UK transmission (C4): 12.12.97

Guest Cast: Robin Williams (Thomas), Billy Crystal (Tim),
Jon Favreau (Pete Becker), James Hong (Hoshi),
Sam McMurray (Doug), Steve Dark (Phil), Joe O'Connor
(Stevens), John McCarthy (Referee), Bruce Buffer
(Announcer), **and introducing** Christine Taylor (Bonnie)

Summary: Monica begins to think Pete is going insane: he's still determined to become the Ultimate Fighting Champion. She goes with him to his first fight and watches him get soundly trashed. Despite the fact that he has been beaten to a bloody pulp, Pete obstinately carries on in his dream. Monica finally realises she can't watch someone she cares about so much go through it all, so they agree to go their separate ways.

Chandler has a new boss at work, who keeps insisting on patting him on the behind after every meeting. Though Joey insists that it's just a male bonding gesture, Chandler is deeply uncomfortable with it. Chandler eventually decides to tell his boss that the other men in the office are getting jealous of all the attention lavished on Chandler, but this plan seems to backfire.

Phoebe asks Rachel if she can set Ross up with Bonnie, a friend of hers. Rachel checks that Bonnie is the girl with the shaved head, which Phoebe confirms; knowing that, Rachel's more than happy for the two of them to go out on a date. When Bonnie turns up, though, her hair has grown back – into long, beautiful blonde locks. She and Ross hit it off, and Rachel can do nothing but watch helplessly from the sidelines.

Freaky Monica: On the balcony of her apartment, Ross prepares the barbecue for everyone to eat as they watch Pete's second fight on television. In a reference to her past obsessive eating habits, Monica asks for four hot dogs. 'I'm really nervous,' she explains.

Phoebisms: When she hears that Pete is to become a wrestler, she seems quite excited. But once it is explained that, in this kind of professional fighting, they don't have costumes like those on WWF, she is immediately disappointed. Is this some hitherto unknown kink of Phoebe's, or does she simply like the bright colours and patterns? We think it's the latter. When she is trying to distract Rachel from staring at Ross and Bonnie hitting it off, she points to the pavement and shouts, 'It's a line of ants!' It's a weak distraction, and it doesn't work. When Rachel is finally dragged away, they sit on the kerb and Phoebe realises with brilliant sorrow that, when they sat down, they killed all the ants.

Slow Joey: He suggests to Chandler that, to avoid the butt-slapping of his boss, he could cover his behind with something that smells bad, so that the boss would end up with bad-smelling hands. 'Now,' wonders Joey, 'what could you rub on your butt that would smell bad?'

Chandleresque: After Chandler tells the gang about the way his boss keeps slapping him, Rachel supports him, saying that if Monica made a great stew she wouldn't congratulate her by, say, grabbing her boob. Chandler agrees: 'For a really

great stew you just, y'know, stick your head in between 'em.'
Good one, Chandler.

The Ballad of Ross & Rachel: This time, it's Rachel who's
the all-out loser. Her feelings about Ross and Bonnie getting
together quietly pave the way for the wonderful events of the
episode that follows. Even so, as with Ross's whining when it
goes on too long, there are elements to her jealousy that are
neither entertaining nor interesting. It's at times like these you
wonder what the producers were thinking when they broke
these two up in the first place.

Just Plain Weird: The episode opens, as they invariably do,
with the gang chatting in Central Perk. Monica is trying to tell
the others about Pete's plan to become the Ultimate Fighting Champion, but she is interrupted when a couple of
noisy guys muscle in on their sofa. One of them thinks that
his wife is having an affair with her gynaecologist. The
other then reveals that it is in fact he who is sleeping with
his wife. Despite the fact that these men are played by
Billy Crystal and Robin Williams (who puts on a ridiculous
European – probably – accent), this just isn't funny and
smacks of opportunistic guest-star wrangling. Hoshi, Pete's
fighting trainer, apparently used to be an assassin for hire.
When Pete tells Monica this, Hoshi loudly complains that his
secret is out and Pete corrects it to 'house painter'.

Generation X: The comedians Robin Williams and Billy
Crystal both started out their careers on *Saturday Night Live*,
but shot to fame on sitcoms: Williams in a bit part in *Happy
Days* as Mork, an alien from Ork (which was the inspiration
for Willams's series *Mork and Mindy*); Crystal in the classic
spoof series, *Soap*. It was, of course, for this reason that they
appeared in this episode, and not because they wanted to plug
their latest movie, *Father's Day* (Ivan Reitman, 1997). Rachel
claims to have been served a pretzel from one of the kids
from *Fame*.

The Story So Far: Phoebe reminds Rachel that she met
Bonnie at Pheebs's birthday party two years ago (presumably
the one shown in 'TOW Two Parts', Part 2).

The Last Word: Focusing mainly on Monica's having to choose between staying with Pete and saving herself the pain of watching him being regularly beaten to a pulp, this episode is really quite touching in places. Her final speech to him ('I've got to do this,' he says. 'Then I've got to go,' Monica replies), considering how long it took for her to realise how much she liked him, is very moving. Perry is beginning to get back on form as Chandler, and his facial expressions that accompany each butt-smack are a wonder to behold. The appearance of Billy Crystal and Robin Williams, though, might have looked like a great idea on paper, but it is painfully unfunny in the realisation, as the guest stars seem to be enjoying themselves a little too much and the regulars just look plain embarrassed. **Ahhh Rating:** ***

French Title: 'Celui Qui Voulait Être L'ultime Champion' (the one who wants to be the ultimate champion)

German Title: 'Kampfspiele' (fighting games)

325
'The One At The Beach'
#465275

Writers: Pang-ni Landrum & Mark J. Kunerth (story),
Adam Chase (teleplay)
Director: Pamela Fryman
First US transmission: 15.05.97
First UK transmission (C4): 19.12.97

Guest Cast: Christine Taylor (Bonnie),
James Michael Tyler (Gunther), Teri Garr (Phoebe Abbott)

Summary: One of Phoebe's clients invites her and her friends to use his beach house for a weekend. The gang, with Bonnie, all pile down for a few days of sun and sand. All they get is sand, though, as there's been a flood which has pushed a pile of sand inside the beach house. While she is there,

Phoebe intends to look up Phoebe Abbott, a woman who appears in a photograph of her dead mother. After their first meeting, they agree to go for dinner the next day, so Phoebe can learn more about her mother and father. But Phoebe Abbott pulls out. Pheebs is very disappointed and decides to break into the other Phoebe's house and snoop about for more information on her parents. When Phoebe Sr catches her creeping about she eventually admits that she is in fact her biological mother.

Rachel manages to convince Bonnie that the shaved-head look really suited her, and that she should do it again. When she does, proudly showing the results to a disgusted Ross, Ross accuses Rachel of engineering the whole thing. Rachel claims she did it because she thinks she still has feelings for him. They kiss, but are interrupted by Chandler and Joey. Rachel goes to her room and, later, Ross is faced with a choice of doors – Rachel's on one side of the hall, Bonnie's on the other . . .

Freaky Monica: Post-Pete, Monica is worried that she'll end up alone and 'die an old maid', but Chandler tries to reassure her that won't happen – although she might die 'an old spinster cook'. He suggests that maybe he might be suitable 'boyfriend material', getting only a laugh from Monica as response. He finds the laugh somewhat annoying, and spends the rest of the episode trying to convince her that he could be her boyfriend.

Phoebisms: Phoebe throws a brilliantly ineffectual tantrum when Phoebe Sr tells her that she's not going out to dinner with her: she simply pushes a stool gently, and watches it thud quietly on the sand-covered floor.

Slow Joey: His suggestion to lift the boredom at the beach house is a characteristic one: why don't they play strip poker? When they find out that they have no cards, they change it to a game of strip Happy Days. Of course, it backfires on him terribly and he ends up completely naked while everyone else is fully dressed. When he falls asleep after the game, drunk on Margaritas, the gang cover him in sand and mould it so that it looks like he's got the body of a mermaid. When he wakes, he looks down at his new breasts and smiles in appreciation. Later, he tries to suggest to Chandler that they practise one-on-one strip poker, but Chandler point-blank refuses.

Chandleresque: He tries to give Ross advice on how to handle the developing situation with Rachel, but he seems to realise the futility of his involvement. As he talks on, he says feebly of his own experience in such things, 'Take it from a guy who's never had a long-term relationship.'

The Ballad of Ross & Rachel: Well, this is it. After nearly a year of bitchiness, Ross and Rachel finally realise what everyone else has known from the minute they broke up – they're still crazy about each other. The scene where Rachel chases Ross around the room, intending to paint his toenails, closes with a wonderfully surprising moment. Ross collapses on the sofa, and Rachel tumbles on top of him. They hold a look for a second before Phoebe arrives to interrupt them. In that second, although we've known all along it could happen, Aniston and Schwimmer manage to remind us why we ever thought the idea of Ross and Rachel was a good one, and it's enough of a reminder to make us forget the months of tiring nastiness we've gone through to get here.

Just Plain Weird: Teri Garr as Phoebe Abbott is an example of intelligent, perfect casting – she's obviously carefully studied Kudrow's role, and successfully emulates her unique take on wackiness. Particularly impressive is when she leaps to her feet and suggests making sangria as a tactic to avoid talking about Phoebe Jr's heritage. This line alone brilliantly shows how she's got a handle on Phoebe's habit of trying – and often failing – to avoid a topic by desperately going off on a tangent (just check out last episode's line of ants).

Dinosaurs ROCK!: Playing the Happy Days game, Ross shakes the dice in his cupped hand and mutters, 'Daddy needs a new pair of electromagnetic microscopes for the Prehistoric Forensics Department.' When everyone looks at him like the sad man he is, he shuts up and plays the game.

Generation X: Teri Garr starred in, among other movies, *Tootsie* (Sydney Pollack, 1982), which is sadly not the story of Chandler's father.

The Last Word: With this episode, it's as if the memories of all the bad things about this year are erased. Phoebe finding her real mother, and Ross and Rachel so nearly getting back together, are the dramatic highlights of the entire season. And, like all the best *Friends* has ever been, all this serious stuff is handled with style, wit, panache and a bellyful of laughs. The cliff-hanger itself (we see Ross go into one of the girls' rooms, and say, 'Hi' – but we don't know who to) is a brilliant moment, guaranteed to make you hold your breath until the conclusion. **Ahhh Rating:** ****

French Title: 'Celui Qui Allait À La Plage' (the one who went to the beach)

German Title: 'Entscheidung am Strand' (decision at the beach)

Fourth Season

1997–1998

24 Episodes

401

'The One With The Jellyfish'
#466601

Writer: Wil Calhoun
Director: Shelly Jensen
First US transmission: 25.09.97
First UK transmission (Sky One): 08.01.98

Guest Cast: Christine Taylor (Bonnie),
Teri Garr (Phoebe Abbott), Lisa Kudrow (Ursula)

Summary: Ross chooses Rachel's door, but is surprised to find Bonnie there too – Rachel's massaging lotion into Bonnie's burnt scalp. Bonnie returns to her and Ross's room, leaving Ross to tell Rachel that he wants her back and that he's decided to finish with Bonnie. Ross returns to Rachel after telling Bonnie they're over. Rachel has written a huge letter detailing her feelings over their relationship and says she won't consider getting back with Ross unless he agrees with her. But Ross falls asleep and doesn't get to read the letter by the time Rachel gets up. Rather than admit he fell asleep, Ross claims to agree with everything Rachel has written – even the 'does it' part. Unfortunately, by the time he has had chance to read the letter, he realises that he absolutely 'does not'! Unable to reconcile their differences, Ross and Rachel split up again.

An understandably upset Phoebe confronts her newly discovered 'birth mother'. Apparently, Phoebe Sr, Lily and
Frank Sr were 'a couple', and, when she discovered she was
pregnant, Phoebe Sr panicked and handed her twins over to
Frank and Lily. Phoebe Sr is keen to try to make it up with her
daughter, but Phoebe Jr is unforgiving and leaves, having told
her mom that she never wants to see her again. When Phoebe
Sr follows Phoebe to New York, though, she manages to
convince her daughter that maybe they have a lot of things in
common after all and that maybe they could begin again from
scratch.

Back at the girls' apartment, the gang begin to get suspi-
cious about the behaviour of Chandler, Monica and Joey.
Something happened at the beach, but none of them will say
what . . .

Poor Ross: After Ross reminds everyone that he and Rachel
were 'on a break', Chandler warns: 'If you say that one more
time, *I'm* gonna break up with you!'

Freaky Monica: After Monica was stung by a jellyfish, her
wrath gets the better of her: 'Damn the jellyfish – damn *all*
the jellyfish!' Trying to rebut Chandler's advances one final
time, Monica reassures him by saying that she thinks he's
sweet and smart, and that she does love him, 'but you will
always be the guy who peed on me'.

Phoebisms: Pheebs sings a song about the 66 colours of her
bedroom – two of which are fuchsia and mauve.

Slow Joey: Joey tries to explain to us what happened at the
end of the last series, only to give up and go looking for
Chandler to help out. Later, we see how his excitement over
the hole he's dug prevents him from being any help to the
distressed Monica. When the trio try to explain what happened to the other three, Joey justifies himself: 'She's my
friend and she needed help! And if I had to, I'd pee on any
one of you!'

Chandleresque: Still asking Monica if she'd consider going
out with him, he poses the question in the context of his being

the last man left after a nuclear holocaust: 'I've got canned goods,' he adds persuasively.

The Ballad of Ross & Rachel: In Rachel's eighteen-page odyssey, she asks Ross to accept full responsibility for their break-up: 'Does that seem like something you can do? Does it?' Chandler convinces Ross that it's something he *must* do, if he wants to avoid losing the best thing that's ever happened to him. But when Rachel labours the point about how much it means to her, Ross screams, '*We were on a break!*', and the relationship ends once again. Rachel, of course, gets the last word when she tells Ross (and anyone else who's listening) that 'it's not that common, it doesn't happen to every guy and it *is* a big deal!'

Just Plain Weird: Joey has seen a documentary on jellyfish on the Discovery Channel. Weirder – he remembers the facts from it!

The Story So Far: Phoebe gives her birth mom a potted history of what it was like when she was eighteen: 'My mom had killed herself, and my dad had run off, and I was living in a Gremlin with a guy called Sidney who talked to his hand.' Phoebe is now 29. We see Phoebe's older twin, Ursula, again (see 'TOW Two Parts', 'TOW The Jam'). Ursula already knew about Phoebe Sr, but she lies to Phoebe when she claims to have Lily's suicide note. Both Phoebes claim to like the Beatles and pizza, and they both think puppies are '*so* cute!' (see 'TOW Phoebe's Uterus'). Rachel reminds Ross that he cheated on her with the girl from the photocopy place (see 'TOW Ross And Rachel Take A Break'). In drawing Rachel's attention to the difference between 'your' and 'you're', Ross reminds us that Rachel's spelling is pretty poor (see 'TOW Mrs Bing').

The Last Word: So it's off, and on, and off again in rapid succession, though it's doubtful that we really care any more. As later episodes will show, they're far funnier at each other's throat with anger than with love. The playful sexual tension between Monica and Chandler resurfaces once more at

the end, but it's probably best left alone for the moment. Strangely, no one notices that Chandler's hair has become sunbleached and that he's gained about a stone in weight (thank God!) overnight. But picky continuity problems aside, it's just reassuring that with one episode many of the third series' detractors are silenced. Best scene has to be the moment where Monica *et al* reveal just what happened at the beach; the way they pace the floor and build upon the melodrama, punctuated by the others' cries of 'Euuuwww!'
Ahhh Rating: *

402
'The One With The Cat
#466602
(*Dedicated to the memory of Dorothy Kauffman*)

Writers: Jill Condon & Amy Toomin
Director: Shelley Jensen
First US transmission: 02.10.97
First UK transmission (Sky One): 15.01.98

Guest Cast: Dan Gauthier (Chip Matthews),
James Michael Tyler (Gunther), Mathew Kaminsky (Tony),
Ken Weiler (Peter), Marc Unger (the Thief)

Summary: Having torn his jacket on Joey's entertainment centre one time too many, Chandler decides it's time to get rid. Joey is adamant that they mustn't throw it out, but he agrees to sell it. While making a sale he shows a prospective buyer that the unit is big enough for a grown man to fit into, and is promptly locked in by the buyer, who proceeds to steal everything of value from the place – even the reclining chairs!

Monica bumps into Chip Matthews, Rachel's prom date in high school, and agrees to go out on a date with him. Rachel is annoyed by this, considering how badly that prom went for her and Chip, but reluctantly consents to letting Monica go anyway. However, Chip hasn't changed much since high school: he still thinks wedgies are funny and still works at the local multiplex because he gets free posters for his room. Monica returns home to tell Rachel the joyous news: she got to go out with Chip from high school – and got to dump him!

Phoebe, meanwhile, becomes drawn to a cat that she swears has a smile just like her dead mother, Lily. Strangely enough, it also looks a lot like Julio, the lost cat of a little girl from SoHo, but no one can bear to tell Phoebe . . .

Freaky Monica: Monica tells Rachel that she feels she owes the fat girl inside her, as she never lets her eat.

Spoilt Rachel: Not thinking of Monica's feelings for a second, she asks her if she could help her get some kind of revenge on Chip Matthews by leaving him somewhere to have sex with someone else, just like he did to Rachel at the prom.

Phoebisms: She sings a song ending in the words '. . . dumb drunken bitch!' Lovely! She later feels certain that the cat is the reincarnated spirit of her dead stepmother, based on some pretty dodgy thinking involving an orange felt-lined guitar case and the fact that cats like fish (!). To spare the feelings of the cat, Phoebe tells her friends she's going to call her mom at the B-E-A-C-H, before realising that she should have spelt out the word 'M-O-M'. Reasserting her belief that the cat is her dead mother, Pheebs also forces Ross to accept that he's not always right about everything and spells out some simple rules about being a friend. 'Even if I'm wrong, who cares? Just be a friend, okay? Be supportive.'

Slow Joey: Joey can't help but point out that the cat that Phoebe believes is her 'mom' has got a 'huge peni–' 'Let it go,' warns a tactful Chandler. Joey's selection process for the new owner of the entertainment centre is a little strict. Chandler notes, 'Apparently, not everyone is qualified to own wood and nails.' Joey not only falls for the same 'trapped inside the unit' trick, he actually tells the thief how to do it! Joey is understandably upset when all their stuff is stolen: 'If I ever run into that guy again, do you know what I'm gonna do?' 'Bend over?' cries Chandler, having lost his patience with his friend's stupidity.

Chandleresque: After the robbery, Monica asks Chandler what happened: 'Um, Joey was born, and twenty-eight years later, I was robbed!' Ross asked him what his insurance company said about it all: 'They said, uh, "You don't have insurance here, so stop calling us."' When Phoebe tells her 'mom' that she's welcome back any time, Chandler tells her they'd really appreciate it if her mom could come back as a couch next time.

Chandler's Job: Joey believes Chandler has undervalued the entertainment centre: 'And you call yourself an accountant,' he mocks. 'Noooo!' replies Chandler, but apparently no one else knows what he does either – although Rachel knows it's 'something to do with numbers'.

The Ballad of Ross & Rachel: Rachel sarcastically complains to Ross that she has an eight-page report to read and doesn't want to fall asleep (a reference to her eighteen-page letter in the previous episode). Ross rebuts with, 'Why? Did *you* write it?' Rachel gets her own back later, as she tries to prove Ross's obsession with always having to be right by tempting him with a sadistic '*Jurassic Park* could happen.'

The Chick and the Duck: They're housed inside the entertainment centre, with their own disco ball and fairy lights.

Magna Doodle: The thief leaves the boys a rather cruel message: 'Thanks for all your stuff!'

Generation X: Chandler refers to Gepetto, 'father' of Pinocchio (see 'Pilot').

The Story So Far: We saw a young Chip briefly in 'TOW The Prom Video', where he was Rachel's prom date (played by a different, uncredited actor). Chip apparently went missing on Prom Night, leaving Rachel alone. She eventually discovered he'd been having sex with a girl called Amy Welch. Monica's band uniform in school had to be specially made because she was so fat, and Rachel was in the home economics class that had to make it. Chip reminds Monica of his old schoolmates: Simmons, Zana, Spindler, Devane, Kelly, Goldie, Steve Brown, Zuchoff, McGuire, J.T., Breadsley and Richard Dorfman (who is now an architect). Rachel and Ross allude to the letter, again (see 'TOW The Jellyfish'). Phoebe's mother died seventeen years ago. Joey tells the thief about the time Chandler trapped Joey inside the entertainment centre (see 'TOW Frank Jr'). According to Chandler, Joey is now 28. As a result of the robbery, the guys acquire a canoe to replace their chairs.

The Last Word: Oh, will Ross ever learn? Surely he realises by now that Phoebe can never be dissuaded from believing anything she wants to (see, for example, 'TOW Heckles Dies'). He is actually a little cruel in the force he uses to shatter Phoebe's illusions. One good thing about the break-up of Ross and Rachel is the way their bickering can result in some of the funniest scenes in an episode, in this instance, the glee with which Rachel informs Ross that *Jurassic Park* could happen – that's really underhand, but he was really asking for it! The main thread of this plotline, the cat, is a little far-fetched, even for Phoebe, but the joy it gives her far outweighs any need for logic. **Ahhh Rating:** **

403
'The One With The 'Cuffs'
#466603

Writer: Seth Kurland
Director: Peter Bonerz
First US transmission: 09.10.97
First UK transmission (Sky One): 22.01.98

Guest Cast: Alison LaPlaca (Joanna), Penn Jillette (the Salesman), Laura Dean (Sophie), Christina Pickles (Judy Geller)

Summary: Desperate for money, Monica agrees to cater a

party for her ever-critical mother. To avoid getting hassle about biting her nails, she wears false ones, but then one of them goes missing and it can only be in one of the quiches that she's just made for the party. Monica's mother then makes the situation worse by revealing that she had frozen lasagnes on standby, just in case her daughter 'pulled a Monica'.

Chandler starts dating Rachel's boss, Joanna, again, despite having previously called her a 'big, dull dud'. Rachel is really annoyed about this, because last time she nearly lost her job over the way Chandler led Joanna on. But Chandler is drawn to Joanna's bossy ways and ends up fooling around with her in her office, and when she's called away to a meeting she handcuffs Chandler to a chair and leaves the keys out of arms' reach.

An encyclopedia salesman calls at No. 19 – but only Joey's at home. The salesman asks him if he ever feels left out of conversations because he doesn't know what his friends are talking about. If only he knew . . .

Spoilt Rachel: Monica cries, 'How desperate am I?' to which Rachel says that it's a good thing Chandler's not there as 'he always wins at this game'. Worried that she might get fired, she demands that Chandler dump Joanna, oblivious to the fact that, presumably, this would put her job in greater danger than if he kept on seeing her. Having phoned Phoebe and Monica to tell them about Chandler's predicament, Rachel manages to get him back in the handcuffs through blackmail: 'When they ask me what I saw, I can be very generous . . . or very *stingy*'.

Slow Joey: As a replacement for all of their stolen furniture, Joey procures some rusty patio furniture and some bubble rap: '. . . and some of it is not even popped!' he cheers. When the salesman asks him if he ever feels people are talking above his head, Joey has a flashback to a few incidents that illustrate the problem. After the flashback we realise that Joey's been reminiscing in real time, leaving the salesman waiting for two and a half minutes. Joey thought Van Gogh cut off his ear because his paintings must have sucked. In response to the question, 'Where does the Pope live?' Joey answers, 'In the woods . . . No, wait, that's the joke answer.' And of course 'Vulcanised rubber' is 'Spock's birth control'. When the salesman tells Joey that the full set of encyclopedias will cost $1,200, Joey is not impressed: 'I'm home in the middle of the day and I got patio furniture in my living room. I guess there's a few things you don't get from book learning!' But even after Joey has swotted up on volcanoes, vivisection and the Vietnam War, he still finds he's left out of the conversation when Monica asks if anyone saw the documentary on the *Korean* War – maybe you should have bought the volume dealing with K, Joey.

Chandleresque: An unsympathetic Rachel tells Chandler he'll have to get himself out of the handcuffs: 'You must have me confused with "The Amazing Chandler"!' Despite being in such discomfort, he still takes time out to look up the skirt of a small statue near Joanna's desk.

Parents – Who Needs 'Em?: Monica agrees to cater for her mother because she needs the money and 'thought it'd be a great way to get rid of that last little smidgen of self-respect'. Judy Geller's tactlessness strikes again: she tells Monica that she'd just assumed that Richard raved over her catering because he was sleeping with her, but that she paid attention when she heard about the catering at the lesbian wedding (from Sandra Green, Rachel's mother) as she assumes she wasn't sleeping with anyone there: 'Though at least that would be something,' she adds.

The Chick and the Duck: Dick the Duck comes to see what Joey's up to. Joey, without looking, waves him back into the bathroom and he waddles back in despondently.

Magna Doodle: Someone has drawn a big smiley face again (see 'TOW A Chick. And A Duck').

Shut Up, Sophie!: Joanna's other assistant, Sophie, tries to be nice to her intolerable boss. When she brings Joanna a macaroon, she's told, 'Great! I'll keep it in my butt with your nose!'

Generation X: Chandler's quip about the 'Algonquin kids' table' in Joey's flashback is a reference to the literary intelligentsia of the 1920s, which included the notorious wits Dorothy Parker and Robert Benchley (father of the *Jaws* author, Peter). They used to meet at the Algonquin Hotel and became known as 'the Vicious Circle'. The salesman is played by Penn Jillette, one half of the blackly comical magicians Penn & Teller. Mr Spock is the Vulcan from *Star Trek*. Milton Berle is otherwise known as 'Mr Television', having been one of TV's first great stars. He's also renowned for his 'romantic' links to a number of Hollywood's biggest names (including Marilyn Monroe and Lucille Ball).

The Story So Far: Judy Geller tells her daughter that her blue nails look just like her grandmother's when they found her (see 'TOW Nana Dies Twice'), and recalls Richard's party and Carol and Susan's wedding (see 'TOW Ross And Rachel ... You Know' and 'TOW The Lesbian Wedding'). Chandler and Joanna dated a couple of times in 'TOW The Dollhouse'. Monica has, at one time, been in therapy with a Dr Weinberg. When Mark left (see 'TOW Phoebe's Ex-Partner'), he gave Rachel the keys to Joanna's office – but Joanna doesn't know Rachel has got them. Chandler still doesn't know Joanna's last name by this point. We see how Monica's room back at her parents' house has been transformed into a gym (see 'TOW The Prom Video').

The Last Word: Joey's simulation of the creaking noises from Chandler's room are superb – especially when he adds a new one to simulate the sounds Chandler makes on his own. Matthew Perry reminds us how great he is with the physical comedy – how many other actors could be so animated while handcuffed to a chair? Apparently a lot of women have worn out their tapes of this episode trying to freeze-frame all the scenes with Perry trouserless. Luckily for him, it's not possible to tell whether Rachel would have been lying or not.
Ahhh Rating (Poor Joey): **

404

'The One With The Ballroom Dancing'
#466604

Writers: Andrew Reich & Ted Cohen
Director: Gail Mancuso
First US transmission: 16.10.97
First UK transmission (Sky One): 29.01.98

Guest Cast: Jason Brooks (Rick), Michael G. Hagerty
(Mr Treager – billed as 'Treeger'), Rhoda Gemignani
(Mrs Potter), E.J. Callahan (Mr Simon), Brien Perry (Gym
Employee), Christopher Carroll (Bank Officer),
Amber Smith (Maria), Hope Allen (Karen Lambert),
Cheryl Francis Harrington (Interviewer)

Summary: Mr Treager, the superintendent of the apartment
block, roars at Rachel after she blocks a garbage shoot he's
spent half an hour unblocking. When Rachel returns to her
apartment crying, Joey becomes her knight in shining armour
– only to worsen the situation and risk getting the girls
evicted. Joey offers to do anything for Mr Treager to keep the
girls in their home – but isn't expecting 'anything' to mean
becoming Treager's dance-practice partner.

Chandler is a member of a gym that he never goes to but
still pays $50 a month for. With Ross in tow for moral
support, Chandler tries to quit the gym, only for Ross to be
conscripted too. Their attempts to cut the gym off at source
by closing their bank accounts are similarly unsuccessful –
they end up opening a joint account together.

Pheebs is distracted by one of her clients at the massage
parlour as she finds him very attractive and provokes her to
want to do things to him she's 'not allowed to charge for'. But
then she finds herself biting his backside mid-massage and
she has to tell him how she feels . . .

Spoilt Rachel: She has never, in the three years she's been
living there, taken out the trash, as she presumed Monica

liked doing it. Treager mocks how pampered she is: 'Daddy buy me a pizza, Daddy buy me a candy factory. Daddy, make the cast of *Cats* sing "Happy Birthday" to me!' Rachel is driven to tears, and later complains to her friends that his comments were only 'partly true'. Joey defends Rachel because Treager made her cry, but Monica is wonderfully unsympathetic, pointing out that Rachel *always* cries!

Phoebisms: Phoebe has made herself swear a 'Masseuse Oath': No fooling around with clients and always be prepared' (she stole the last one from the Boy Scouts). Trying to excuse the fact that she's paid extra-special attention to her feet (because that's the only part of her the client sees), Phoebe claims that it's Arabian Princess Day at work. After spending half an afternoon, Pheebs tells her client that it had been only an hour: '. . . in Really Long Hour World'. Finally, she tells a prospective employer that she left her previous job because her boss thought she was a whore. Good going, Pheebs!

Slow Joey: Trying to explain away letting slip about the chick and the duck to Treager, he tells him that they're nicknames – he's the chick and Chandler's the duck. Treager is surprised – he thought it would have been the other way round! When Treager asks Joey to be his dancing partner, Joey asks if that's 'prison lingo'. When Joey's trying to avoid getting too overexcited during sex, he thinks of sandwiches, baseball and Chandler to calm himself down.

Chandleresque: He describes Maria at the gym as being a 'lycra spandex gym treat'. Standing up to Ross's temptation of the thought of having a 'washboard stomach and rock-hard pecs', Chandler cries weakly that he just wants 'a flabby gut and saggy man-breasts'.

Generation X: The sexy client of Phoebe's is a supporter of the environmental campaign group Greenpeace. The superintendent's annual dance is called the 'Super Ball' (hahaha). Treager and Joey practise their dancing to Cole Porter's 'Night and Day'.

The Story So Far: Treager knows that Monica is subletting her grandmother's apartment (her father's mother) (see 'TOW The Flashback'). Joey, Chandler and Ross all use the same bank (according to Joey, they're 'bank buddies'). Prior to this episode, Phoebe has never been sacked from a job before.

The Last Word: Joey clearly enjoys learning how to dance, despite not knowing how to lead (hence the one asterisk in the **Ahhh Rating** below). We love the bit where Treager swings Joey around and he gives out a little 'Wheheyy!' We also love Chandler's mantra of 'I wanna quit the gym!' which should be put on to T-shirts and bumper stickers now! As for Rachel, well maybe it's about time she was mocked for crying at the drop of a hat. Good call, Monica. **Ahhh Rating:** *

405
'The One With Joey's New Girlfriend'
#466605

Writers: Michael Curtis & Gregory S. Malins
Director: Gail Mancuso
First US transmission: 30.10.98
First UK transmission (Sky One): 05.02.98

Guest Cast: Laura Stepp (Amanda), James Michael Tyler (Gunther), Brian 'Fish' Smith (Josh), Charles Thomas Allen & John Christopher Allen (Ben)
And Introducing: Paget Brewster (Kathy)

Summary: Chandler tries to chat up a beautiful woman at Central Perk only to discover she's Joey's new girlfriend, whom he met in acting class. Chandler really likes her – though the rest of the gang suspect he actually loves her. He tries avoiding her, but Joey thinks that he mustn't like her and tries to get them to spend time together. When Chandler finally confesses just how he feels for her, Joey thinks that he's just making too much of an effort to be nice, much to the frustration of his lovelorn friend.

Rachel starts dating a guy who is still in college and might be stealing from her, while Ross meets a really sexy woman . . . who uses him as a babysitter. Phoebe catches a cold, which, she discovers, makes her voice all husky and sexy. So when her cold clears she tries anything to catch another one!

Poor Ross: Thinking tonight might be the night, Ross is left literally holding the baby when he realises that Amanda wants him only as her babysitter.

Phoebisms: She starts to make shoes by getting old ones and tarting them up with really tacky decorations. She sings 'Smelly Cat' (the sexy, bronchitic remix) and has new songs too – 'Sticky Shoes', 'Plaiting Goats' and 'Pepper People', in which she sneezes as part of the last verse. At the end she sings a song about a 'papier-mâché man' à la Brigitte Bardot. She feels that with her new sexy voice she should write about something sad but claims that nothing sad has ever happened to her – forgetting, of course, her mother's suicide and the time she spent living rough.

Chandleresque: When Rachel reveals that Chandler told her that Ross and Amanda didn't even kiss on their 'date', Chandler explains that he tells people secrets: 'It makes them like me.' He tells Kathy that whenever he sees women in fishnet stockings it reminds him of his father.

The Ballad of Ross & Rachel: Ross tries to make Rachel jealous by showing off a piece of paper with the phone number of a 'really hot girl' on it. Ross waves it annoyingly in her face, so when Phoebe starts to sneeze, Rachel snatches the paper out of Ross's hand for Phoebe to wipe her nose on.

The Chick and the Duck: Chandler lifts the chick into the canoe. When Kathy asks 'What about the duck?', he explains that the duck can swim. Later on he plays an unsuccessful game of hide and seek with the pets.

Gunther Sneezes!: Only for Phoebe to snog him senseless in the vain hope of catching his cold. Torn up with guilt, Gunther tells Rachel about it to just check that she's 'cool' about it. Rachel, of course, has no idea what he's going on about.

Cruelty to Animals: Kathy goes off to buy hamsters – she works for a medical researcher part-time, which Phoebe thinks is nice: 'It's great that the medical community is finally trying to help sick hamsters,' she says, missing the point somewhat.

Generation X: As Chandler runs towards Kathy we hear the theme tune from *The Mod Squad*, a crime drama series that ran in the States from 1968 to 1973 in which young offenders were given a second chance by joining an underground counter-culture that fought crime. Chandler sits watching the classic B movie, *Attack of the 50-Foot Woman* (Nathan Hertz, 1958).

The Story So Far: Rachel's birthday is 5 May, and Ross's is some time in December (but see 'TOW George Stephanopoulos'). Ross introduces the gesture he used to do as a kid to Rachel – where he'd bang the sides of his fists together so that he could give 'the finger' to his parents without their knowing. Monica claims she cried the night he made that up, as she finally realised she was cooler than he was. This sign is used regularly throughout the rest of the season. Joey tells Kathy about the time Chandler got drunk and fell asleep with his head down the toilet (but we've all done that . . . haven't we?). Monica recalls that Phoebe was living rough when she was fourteen. When Ross was in high school he organised the football team's schedules on his Commodore 64 computer.

The Last Word: It's a little unfair to keep harping on about Chandler's show-stealing abilities, but if one episode justifies it, it's this one, just for the scene where he runs after Kathy, colliding with a car, a hot-dog vendor, the leads of a pack of dogs and a big pile of garbage, *just* to say 'Hi!' to her. But by the end of it, the laughter has stopped for Chandler as he finds it harder and harder to hide his feelings for her. **Ahhh Rating** (Chandler's revelation to Joey, which passes him by completely): ********

406
'The One With The Dirty Girl'
#466606

Writers: Scott Silveri & Shana Goldberg-Meehan
Director: Shelley Jensen
First US transmission: 06.11.97
First UK transmission (Sky One): 12.02.98

Guest Cast: Paget Brewster (Kathy), Rebecca Romijn (Cheryl), Gretchen Wyler (Mrs Burkart), James Michael Tyler (Gunther)

Summary: Ross starts dating a beautiful woman, but when he gets back to her place he's sickened to discover that she's the most untidy, unhygienic person in the world. Meanwhile, when Monica is forced to turn down a catering job because she can't afford the stuff she needs, Phoebe offers to lend her some money. Accompanying her to a wake, Phoebe helps out when Monica has difficulty getting paid by a merry widow. Realising how great a team they make together, they decide to form a partnership.

Chandler buys Kathy a first-edition copy of her favourite childhood book for her birthday, but when Joey only buys her a tacky watch/pen, Chandler realises that his present might make his feelings towards her too obvious, so he allows Joey to give her the book. But Kathy guesses who got her what and thanks Chandler. It's slowly becoming obvious to both of them that they are very much attracted to each other, but Joey's in their way.

Rachel spends her time completing a crossword puzzle without help from any of the others – even if they do actually end up giving her most of the answers.

Poor Ross: His description of Cheryl's apartment is enough to make you itchy, so she really has a cheek saying his apartment has a weird smell [it still smells of Marcel?]. When Cheryl creeps up behind him and says, 'Guess who,' his only response is a hopeful 'Department of Sanitation?' After Chandler tells Rachel not to touch the book, because she's got 'destructive oils' on her fingers, Rachel tells him not to get it near Ross's hair.

Freaky Monica: After Ross and Cheryl split up, Monica calls round and practically begs to clean up for her – she's been having sleepless nights just at the thought of it!

Phoebisms: When Rachel tells her she wants to complete the crossword without help, Phoebe huffily tells her that she won't let her help create her new universal language (and you just *know* she means a language that can be spoken anywhere in the universe). When Monica suggests that she cooks in their partnership while Phoebe looks after the money, Pheebs says how it'll be like she has a wife in the 1950s.

Slow Joey: He offers girlfriends coupons for an hour of 'Joey love' in lieu of a real present. When Chandler tells him that the first-edition book he got Kathy cost 'an even twenty [dollars]', Joey can't believe it: 'That's almost as much as a *new* book!' When he finally gives Kathy the book, he says it's because he knows she likes both rabbits *and* cheese, completely missing the point that it was her favourite book as a little girl.

The Ballad of Ross & Rachel: Rachel guesses that maybe Cheryl had a bet with her friends as to which of them could bring home the biggest geek, which is fine by Ross as he hopes she wins.

Gunther's There For You, Rachel: When Rachel finally finishes her crossword, she audibly bemoans the fact that there's no one there for her to hug – cue Gunther, who pushes customers out of the way to get to her, slips and disappears down the back of the couch. As the rest of the gang walk in and congratulate her, we just see Gunther slope back to work.

Cruelty to Animals: Ross pulverises a rat hiding underneath the rubbish in Cheryl's flat.

Dinosaurs ROCK!: Ross's date, Cheryl, is a palaeontologist, specialising in the Cenozoic era (which Chandler jokes is the easiest era to study). They do a variation on the 'Is the pope Catholic/Do bears . . . etc' joke with 'Did *Homo erectus* hunt with wooden tools?'

Generation X: Chandler buys Kathy an early edition of *The Velveteen Rabbit (or How Toys Become Real)* by Margery Williams. The 1996 Tony Award winner was, of course, *Rent*, which won four awards that year, including Best Musical. The Tonys are the Oscar equivalent for stage productions. The grieving widow is heard singing the patriotic standard 'You're a Grand Ole Flag' and the sprightly 'Jeepers, Creepers' (Murrell-Sheller-Canfield-Peu-Archer)

The Story So Far: Chandler still owes Phoebe a present for her last birthday. Joey claims his ex-girlfriend, Angela Delvecchio, never had a birthday while they were dating – for three years! (See 'TOW The East German Laundry Detergent', 'TOW The Dozen Lasagnes'.)

The Last Word: Chandler's (lack of) love life still dominates the plot (and it's great to see ongoing storylines that don't just focus on Ross and Rachel). But there is one part of this episode it would have been nice to follow up on at some point – we'd really like to see Monica and Phoebe fighting crime as 'Hard Ass and Wuss'. **Ahhh Rating** (Poor Chandler, Part II, in the way he tells Kathy that Joey is his 'best friend'): ***

407
'The One Where Chandler Crosses The Line'
#466607

Writer: Adam Chase
Director: Kevin S. Bright
First US transmission: 13.11.97
First UK transmission (Sky One): 19.02.98

Guest Cast: Paget Brewster (Kathy),
James Michael Tyler (Gunther)

Summary: Ross reveals to the gang how he created his 'sound' – basically a cacophony of crappy sound effects which mean far more to Ross than anyone else with hearing. But Phoebe thinks his noise is the mark of a genius, causing her to lose confidence and refuse to play at Central Perk. Realising how unhappy she is, Ross 'deliberately' plays badly and asks Pheebs if she'll continue his set. Meanwhile, Joey has arranged a date with another woman, explaining to Chandler that he and Kathy are not exclusive. When Joey is delayed, leaving Kathy alone with Chandler, the two begin to reveal their feelings for each other and end up kissing. Feeling guilty, Chandler buys a new entertainment centre, stereo and TV to replace the one that was stolen. But when Kathy dumps Joey for 'another guy', Chandler feels that he must confess what happened.

Poor Ross: He warns his friends that his 'sound' is about 'communicating very private emotions' and that they should be thought of as 'wordless sound poems'.

Freaky Monica: Listening to Ross talk about his 'sound' makes Monica laugh while drinking: 'Orange juice just came out of my nose, but it was totally worth it!' she gurgles.

Phoebisms: After Chandler sits on the worktop in Monica's kitchen, moaning about accidentally seeing Kathy in the shower, Phoebe waits until he leaves before asking everybody else if they could see up his bathrobe. Pheebs sings a song about a tiny Tarzan swinging on a nose hair. Euch! Being the only person who thinks Ross's music is any good, Phoebe complains that she can't follow his act, comparing it to the bicycle-riding chimps that followed the Beatles. She later bemoans the fact that Ross is evidently unappreciated in his own time: 'I would give anything not to be appreciated in my own time!' The girls tell her honestly that she sucks too, but the ever-certain Phoebe sees this as an attempt by them to make her feel better.

Slow Joey: Chandler tells Joey he must 'make a choice, pick a lane', to which Joey asks, 'Who's Elaine?' When Kathy finished with Joey he thought she was acting a scene so he let her break up with him in front of everyone else.

Chandleresque: When Phoebe says that Ross's stuff is so different from what you usually hear, Chandler quips 'like *music*?' He tells Kathy that he watches *Baywatch* only for the articles. She offers to cut his hair for him, but jokes that she trained at her aunt's dog-grooming salon: 'OK,' says Chandler, 'but don't make my tail too poofy.' She tells him he has great hair: 'Thanks, I grow it myself' (he just can't stop himself!). After the kiss, Kathy starts to tell Chandler how she feels, but he stops her mid-sentence, saying that she's confusing him: 'I'm starting to yearn!' he protests.

The Ballad of Ross & Rachel: Hearing Ross's 'sound' for the first time she suggests he should play in public – what a bitch! Later, she says that she can't believe she ever let him touch her with his fingers and claims that rats in the basement are hanging themselves because of his music.

The Chick and the Duck: The duck starts quacking during *Baywatch*, prompting Chandler to reassure him that his breasts are just as firm and juicy as Yasmine Bleeth's.

Magna Doodle: There's a message from 'Treager' telling the guys to 'clean up duck feathers in hallway!' (Up 'till now his name has been spelt 'Treeger' on the credits, but we suspect he knows better than a credit writer.) Chandler later replaces this with a cartoon of his own face with the words 'I love you, man!' next to it.

Boys Will Be Boys: Chandler tries to convince Joey that 'having sex with an endless line of beautiful women must be very unfulfilling', only to realise how utterly lame that sounds. Joey later spells out to his best friend that kissing his girlfriend is worse than sleeping with her: 'How is that worse?' asks a desperate Chandler. 'I don't know,' says Joey, 'but it's the same!' The tragedy is that every other friend of Joey seems to have known that Chandler could have told Joey how he felt for Kathy and he would have stepped aside.

Generation X: 'Play That Funky Music, White Boy', mentioned by Phoebe, was a 1976 American No. 1 for Wild Cherry, which was covered by Vanilla Ice in 1990. Ross's 'sound' is inspired in part by the German synth masters Kraftwerk and by the late seventies/early eighties King of the Vocoder, Peter Frampton. Joey watches Lynda Carter in the eighties superhero series *Wonder Woman*.

The Story So Far: Ross began 'playing' keyboards in high school. His father soundproofed the basement for him to practise in (and now Monica is really grateful to her dad for that!). Chandler is now 29 years old.

The Last Word: The eternal-triangle storyline continues with Chandler and Kathy finally kissing. We can entirely understand Joey's reaction – despite the fact he was with another woman when it happened, Joey *does* have a basic code of honour which Chandler broke. But our sympathies are, of course, with Chandler, who, let's face it, would be far better with Kathy than Joey. But it ain't over yet! **Ahhh Rating:** ****

Oh, and Ross, you are *not* talented – your music stinks! (That feels *so* much better, now.)

408

'The One With Chandler In A Box'

#466608

Writer: Michael Borkow
Director: Peter Bonerz
First US transmission: 20.11.97
First UK transmission (Sky One): 26.02.98

Guest Cast: Michael Vartan (Dr Tim Burke),
Paget Brewster (Kathy), James Michael Tyler (Gunther),
Marcy Goldman (Nurse)

Summary: As Phoebe and Monica have very little money this Christmas, Pheebs suggests they play 'Secret Santa', meaning they each buy one present, but they won't know who they're getting a gift from. Phoebe is desperate to swap with anyone for Rachel, claiming that she always exchanges anything she's bought for something else. When Ross discovers that she exchanged a gold necklace he bought her he's in a bad mood throughout dinner – until Rachel shows him all the mementos she *did* keep from their relationship.

Monica gets a chip of ice in her eye, forcing her to go to the eye doctor. Having checked that Richard is away, she's surprised to discover that the on-call doctor is actually Richard's son, Tim. Against the advice of her friends, she invites Tim to their Thanksgiving dinner, but after kissing him she is reminded of his father and suddenly gets all grossed out.

Joey has been refusing to talk to Chandler, even by phone. Chandler tries every way he can think of to get Joey to forgive him, and as a last attempt suggests he pay his penance by sitting inside a wooden box for the duration of Thanksgiving, *in silence*, to help him concentrate on his great betrayal of his best friend. But while he's in there, Kathy comes to tell him that she doesn't want to come between such good friends and tells him she can no longer see him . . .

Freaky Monica: In one of the series' all-time best lines, Monica compares her decision to date the son of her ex-lover with the mistakes of her friends: 'Judge all you want to but, [to Ross] married a lesbian, [to Rachel] left a man at the altar, [to Phoebe] fell in love with a gay ice dancer, [to Joey] threw a girl's wooden leg in a fire, [to Chandler] living in a box!' Priceless!

Spoilt Rachel: She claims that just watching Monica work hard makes her sleepy. We discover that she exchanges every gift she ever received. She asks Ross, 'Isn't it better that I exchanged it for something that I enjoy, and that I can get a lot of use out of?' When Ross asks what, she replies, 'Credit'.

Phoebisms: Due to the accident, Monica hands over the Thanksgiving duties to Phoebe. Pheebs claims she has to call her mom to ask her a 'left-handed cooking question'.

Slow Joey: Our Italian friend exclaims '*Va fa Napoli*, which we presume is the Italian equivalent of 'Go to Hell' (though why he should equate Naples with Hell we're not sure). He later teaches the same phrase to Rachel. Ross discovers that Joey has sentenced Chandler to five years: 'Don't do the crime if you can't do the time!' Joey preaches.

Chandleresque: Phoebe goes to answer a knock at the door only to find it's Chandler knocking the inside of his box. Later on, Chandler tries to break the tension by claiming to be mooning everyone from inside the box.

The Ballad of Ross & Rachel: Rachel offers to get Chandler a hands-free headset for his phone, prompting Ross to ask if they can all expect Christmas gifts that she can steal from her office: '*You* shouldn't,' Rachel replies, bitchily. Later on, she shows Ross her keepsake box with little treasures from their relationship. 'Maybe I exchange gifts sometimes, but I keep the things that matter!' Ross apologises, but can't help adding that the piece she kept from their first time together was from the museum and strictly speaking she shouldn't have taken it.

The Chick and the Duck: The feathered fowl, clearly distressed, walk in on Chandler and Joey's row. Chandler begs Joey to stay for their sake: 'They have had a very difficult year, what with the robbery and all.' It's probably a good job they didn't wander next door – the sight of the Thanksgiving dinner might emotionally scar them for life!

Magna Doodle: Chandler has written 'I'M SORRY I'M SORRY I'M SORRY' over and over again on the Magna Doodle board.

Gunther's Confused: He always thought Joey was Chandler.

The Story So Far: Chandler still has a downer on Thanksgiving (see 'TOW Underdog Gets Away'). Rachel claimed that a backpack that Chandler got her was stolen by a dog, and she exchanged a gold necklace that Ross got her for store credit. However, she also kept the movie stub from her first date with Ross, an artefact from the museum from the first time they slept together (see 'TOW Ross And Rachel . . . You Know') and the eggshell from their first breakfast in bed. Richard's son was mentioned in 'TOW Joey Moves Out'. Monica reminds her friends about their past mistakes (see 'Pilot', 'TOW Phoebe's Husband', 'TOW Phoebe's Ex-Partner', and every episode with Carol and Susan). Chandler claims that Joey knows only the bad words in Italian.

The Last Word: Proving that Matthew Perry can make any situation funny, the writers must have been wetting themselves when they came up with the idea of putting him inside a box for half an episode. As we'd probably expect, even this doesn't stop him, though some have commented on his 'wooden performance' (sorry, couldn't resist that). Star of the show, though, is Courteney Cox, who captures effortlessly the way some of us regress to childhood when confronted by an all-knowing, all-powerful doctor. The way she carries herself in the scene in Dr Tim's surgery reminds us of how vulnerable we feel when putting our health in someone else's hands. Yet, back home, she is the bossy, frenetic woman we all know and love. As we've illustrated above, that outburst of hers is one of the all-time best speeches the show has offered us. **Ahhh Rating** (lucky Chandler!): *****

409
'The One Where They're Gonna PARTY!'
#466609

Writers: Andrew Reich & Ted Cohen
Director: Peter Bonerz
First US transmission: 11.12.97
First UK transmission (Sky One): 05.03.98

Guest Cast: Alison LaPlaca (Joanna), Taylor Negron (Allesandro), Richard Fancy (Mr Posner – man on hiring committee), Jennifer Rhodes (Mrs Lynch – woman on hiring committee), Laura Dean (Sophie), James Michael Tyler (Gunther)

Summary: Gandalf, 'the Party Wizard', is coming to town

and Chandler and Ross are very excited. It seems Gandalf is wild and always takes them on adventures where they can wind up literally anywhere. The guys decide to book the day off work and prepare for the ultimate night of recklessness and debauchery. But then Gandalf phones to cancel. Joey tries to arrange a wild night out instead, but after hitting only a few bars, the guys come to realise that maybe they're not as young as they once were.

Rachel is up for a job as purchaser for Junior Miss at Bloomingdales, but her boss, Joanna, totally rubbishes her abilities in the interview. Upset, Rachel confronts Joanna, only to find that she's a lot more valued than she'd thought. As an apology, Joanna offers to create a post for Rachel that would still allow her to work for her, but before she can set the wheels in motion, Joanna is knocked down by a cab and killed. Rachel is desolate – though more for the loss of her dream job than her boss's death.

Monica offers to fill in for a restaurant critic friend and do a few reviews. When she slates an Italian restaurant, the owner comes to demand a retraction. But when Monica shows him how to cook proper Italian food, he ends up offering her the job of head chef. Now all she has to do is find a way of dissolving her partnership with Phoebe . . .

Freaky Monica: In her scathing restaurant review, she says that if she ever returns to Allesandro's, she'd need to order two meals, one for her and one for the guy pointing a gun at her head.

Phoebisms: Monica claims that Phoebe doesn't need her for the business, but Pheebs rightly points out that she's the cook – 'Without you,' she explains, 'it's just me driving up to people's houses with empty trays and asking for money.' But eventually, Phoebe realises that Monica really wants the head chef's job: 'I don't wanna be the reason you're unhappy. That would make *me* unhappy and I *really* don't wanna be the reason I'm unhappy!' Pheebs reconciles herself with the thought of forming the new A-Team.

Slow Joey: Joe claims to know the woman who posed for the illustration on Phoebe's van. When Ross asks him if he read *Lord of the Rings* in high school, he brags, 'No, I had sex in high school.' Chandler once paid Joey $50 to eat a book.

Chandleresque: In anticipation of Gandalf's arrival, Chandler tells Joey, 'I am *so* excited – I may vomit!' Trying to fill out his day after Gandalf has stood him up, he claims he spent his time giving first names to all the foosball players.

Just Plain Weird: Allesandro, owner of an Italian restaurant, is actually Lebanese.

Dinosaurs ROCK!: Ross tells Chandler that he wants to watch a documentary on bumblebees on the Discovery Channel.

Shut Up, Sophie!: During the interview, Rachel says she loves working with designers. Joanna corrects her: 'With them, under them, what's the difference, eh, Rach?' After she's left the room, Joanna claims that Rachel enjoys 'the occasional drink . . . –ing binge'. As Rachel complains about her boss's behaviour in the interview, Joanna calls Sophie into her office and then claims Rachel is making Sophie uncomfortable. When Sophie denies this, Joanna snaps, 'Congratulations – you've just crossed the line into "completely useless"!' After Joanna dies, though, Sophie gets the last laugh – and laugh she does.

Generation X: Gandalf is the wizard in J.R.R. Tolkein's epic *Lord of the Rings* trilogy. Kenny G. is a rather bland saxophonist. *The A Team* was an action-adventure series from the mid-1980s starring George Peppard, Mr T, Dirk Benedict and Dwight Schultz as mercenaries on the run in a customised van, wanted 'for a crime they didn't commit'. It was a major smash in the UK for a while, until complaints about the levels of violence got it taken off. It's unlikely Phoebe would have fitted in anyway. Taylor Negron (Allesandro) is well known on the comedy circuit and appeared in the movie *Punchline* (David Seltser, 1988).

The Last Word: 'I'm getting too old for this . . .' was the catchphrase of Murtaugh in the *Lethal Weapon* films. It could easily become the catchphrase for the boys here, as they realise that they had much more energy when they were younger. If the show tells us one thing, it's that in our twenties there are so many opportunities open to us, but that they slowly disappear as we get older. It's a sobering thought, but one that the guys take quite easily. We feel so sorry for Rachel as her dreams pass her by thanks to the intervention of fate, but once again, Monica gets some excellent scenes, notably at the end of the episode, when she begins to suspect that her dream job might not be as dreamy as she first thought. 'Are you going to kill me?' she asks nervously.

Ahhh Rating (poor Rachel – hah, poor Joanna!): ***

410
'The One With The Girl From Poughkeepsie'
#466612

Writer: Scott Silveri
Director: Gary Halvorson
First US transmission: 18.12.97
First UK transmission (Sky One): 12.03.98

Guest Cast: Fred Stoller (the Waiter), James Michael Tyler (Gunther), Jamie Kaler (Mike), Micheal DiMaggio (Drew), Shannon Maureen Brown (the Woman on the Train), Amy Smallman (the Kitchen Worker), Yasemin Baytok (the Poughkeepsie Woman), Vic Helford (the Conductor)

Summary: Ross has started dating a girl from Poughkeepsie, and another from upstate, but due to the amount of time he spends travelling to see them both, he keeps falling asleep. Having decided to finish with both of them, he misses his stop and ends up in Nova Scotia – where he meets another girl!

Monica is still suffering harassment at work, so Joey suggests she hire him just so she can fire him and assert her authority over the staff. They come up with a plot, but when

Joey gets his first tips he shrinks away from Monica and backs out of the deal. Eventually, after the staff have played one too many tricks on her, Joey lets Monica fire him in full view of the rest of the staff and it seems to have the desired effect.

Chandler sets Rachel up on a date with a guy from work, but makes the mistake of letting him know that she just wants a fling. When Rachel hears this she is furious – but not half as furious as she becomes when Chandler tells the date that she wants a serious relationship and he dumps Rachel out of panic.

Freaky Monica: Upset about the victimisation she's suffering at work, she sobs that she hasn't been picked on this much since kindergarten, when they had to bring someone from junior high to do the seesaw with her.

Spoilt Rachel: When Chandler says that he'd always thought girls didn't just want a fling, Rachel complains, 'Believe me, it's a long time since I've been flung.' When he tells her that her blind date Patrick's father invented the magnetic strip they use on credit cards, she yelps, 'I like credit cards!' Rachel later tells Chandler that with him telling everyone that she wants a fling – and with her 'putting out' on the first date – Patrick is '*so* gonna get the wrong idea'.

Phoebisms: She is writing a seasonal song featuring all her friends, but she moans to Rachel that 'nothing rhymes with your stupid name!' She asks her if maybe she ever had a nickname, like for instance 'Budolph'. Monica shows her what her staff wrote on her chef's hat. Phoebe tries to make her feel better by guessing they were trying to write 'Qui*et*, Bitch!'

Slow Joey: He beats his previous 'personal best' by stuffing fifteen Oreos into his mouth at once. When he starts work at the restaurant, he tells the staff that his name is 'Dragon' because he fancies the idea of having a cool nickname. He asks Chandler if Orson Welles ever directed Burger King commercials, to which Chandler replies, 'Yes.'

Chandleresque: Asking one of his work colleagues if he's dating anyone, Chandler reassures him that he's not gay. 'I didn't think you *were* gay,' he replies. 'I do now.' He describes ice hockey to Rachel as 'angry Canadians with no teeth'. Later, he asks Rachel if she's ever been with a woman. She's shocked: 'So there is no good time to ask that question?'

Chandler's Job: His company has a Fine Foods division. Thanks to a mix-up, Phoebe is convinced they have robots there who work for them.

Gunther's There For You, Rachel: When Rachel declares that she wants 'somebody', Gunther hovers behind her. But when she says, emphatically that she wants a '*man*!' we see Gunther slope away, depressed.

Dinosaurs ROCK!: When Chandler offers to fix Rachel up with a date, she says she doesn't want anyone from legal, or anyone with a boring job. Chandler reminds her, 'Ross was, like, what? A *lion-tamer*?'

Generation X: Oreos, for those who haven't had the pleasure, are two layers of circular chocolate biscuit with a layer of cream in between. Orson Welles was the acclaimed director of such masterpieces as *Citizen Kane* (1941) and *The Magnificent Ambersons* (1942). He later provided the distinctive and much-imitated voice-overs for a series of adverts for Carlsberg lager.

The Story So Far: Phoebe casually mentions that she once lived in Prague and, on noting Chandler's reaction to this, says playfully, 'There's so much you don't know.' Apparently, Chandler took Rachel to the last Christmas party. Chandler points out to Phoebe that he's not Jewish (which kind of ruins one of her rhymes).

The Last Word: Our hearts go out to Monica, who suffers the cruelty of bullies in the workplace with ever decreasing grace. Strangely, Rachel's subplot is not nearly as involving because of the way she rounds on Chandler, who, after all, is just doing exactly what she asked him to (he's a guy – of *course* he'd think the fact she wants a fling would be a selling point). In spite of this (and the fact that Chandler has taken to answering Phoebe's and Joey's dumb questions with a terse 'yes'), Chandler's touchy-feeliness with her just makes him all the more perfect a friend. In fact the selflessness from both Chandler and Joey makes this episode what it is. Ross, on the other hand, actually surpasses Rachel in being just so self-obsessed that it borders on annoying. Is that why they were so perfect for each other? we ask ourselves. We just find it unlikely that it'd be Rachel who can't get a date and Ross having three on the go. As if! **Ahhh Rating** (Monica's burning hat): **

411
'The One With Phoebe's Uterus'
#466610

Writer: Seth Kurland
Director: David Steinberg
First US transmission: 08.01.98
First UK transmission (Sky One): 19.03.98

Guest Cast: Teri Garr (Phoebe Sr), Giovanni Ribisi (Frank Jr), Debra Jo Rupp (Alice), Paget Brewster (Kathy), Sherri Shepherd (Rhonda, the Tour Guide), Miles Marisco (the Smart Kid), Jack Ong (the Older Scientist, with the pear), Jim Bentley (Another Tour Guide), Chip Chinery (Another Scientist)

Summary: Phoebe's half-brother Frank tells her that he and his girlfriend, Alice, have just got married. He also asks her if she'll consider being a surrogate mother for them, as they've already been trying for a year and a half and they are unable to conceive. Phoebe tells her friends about it, but they're a little worried for her and suggest she get some advice from her birth mother. Phoebe Sr tries to show how difficult it was for her to give Phoebe up by lending Phoebe a puppy, thinking that if she can't return the puppy then no way will she be able to give up her child.

Ross gets Joey a part-time job as a tour guide at the museum. Looking forward to having lunch with Ross at work, Joey's shocked to find that there's a colour code, and that people in white coats don't sit with people in blue blazers. He's certain that this won't apply to him and Ross, but when Ross chooses to sit with the other 'white coats', Joey is offended. Explaining the situation to his friend, he encourages Ross to try to break down the barriers between the workers at the museum, with mixed results.

Chandler still hasn't had sex with Kathy yet, as he's intimidated by the fact she dated Joey. Monica teaches Chandler the real facts of life, and ends up all sixes and sevens. Well, mainly sevens . . .

Freaky Monica: Seizing the moment, when Chandler uncharacteristically fluffs his joke, Monica crows, 'You're stoopid!' Ross tries to explain his point to Joey by asking Monica if the waiters ever sit with the chefs in her restaurant: 'I eat by myself in the alley,' she confesses, 'because everybody hates me.'

Phoebisms: When her friends are less than enthusiastic about her becoming pregnant, Pheebs is disappointed: 'You guys were a lot more supportive when I wanted to make denim furniture.'

Slow Joey: When Joey hears his friend referred to as 'Dr Geller' he presumes it's a nickname. Rachel claims that when they're in the audience, Joey doesn't talk to them, but he does sometimes wave.

Chandleresque: When Phoebe tells the gang that she wants to give her brother and sister-in-law the greatest gift she can, Chandler asks if she's getting them a baby *and* a PlayStation. Chandler speculates that either Joey's great in bed, 'or Kathy just likes to agree with him a lot', whereas when he's with her he claims she's more like 'I see your point, I'm all right with it.' Ahhhh.

Just Plain Weird: One of the scientists, in Ross's 'Oprah' moment, confesses his compulsion to flip the light switch on and off seventeen times to prevent his whole family from dying.

Dinosaurs ROCK!: Practising for his new job, he claims that *Tyrannosaurus Rex* came from the Jurassic period. When Ross corrects him (it was from the Cretaceous period), Joey explains that he can pronounce 'Jurassic'. Taking a party round the museum, Joey confuses the (fictional) semi-late Jurassic period with the Pleistocene epoch (and the bratty kid almost pronounces this correctly). Finally, in the cafeteria, Joey is encouraged by Ross to proclaim that he knows 'squat' about dinosaurs.

Generation X: Rachel compares Phoebe's dilemma to *Sophie's Choice* (Alan J. Pakula, 1982), a movie in which Meryl Streep plays a refugee forced by the Nazis to choose one of her children to leave behind. Chandler compares the squidgy-faced puppy to Karl Malden, the actor who appeared in *The Streets of San Francisco*. Can't think why . . .

The Story So Far: Phoebe's mom makes erotic pottery. Frank Jr used to have a dog called Tumour (see 'TOW The Bullies').

The Last Word: Just a couple of things to note here – that puppy is just adorable and he and Phoebe playing together make the thought of her giving him up even more painful. But Frank and Alice seem to love him just as much, so that's OK. Monica's explanation of the seven erogenous zones is, erm, educational, though there must be *so* many guys who never get a woman to pant 'seven' like she does. **Ahhh Rating:** **

412
'The One With The Embryos'
#466611

Writers: Jill Condon & Amy Toomin
Director: Kevin Bright
First US transmission: 15.01.98
First UK transmission (Sky One): 26.03.98

Guest Cast: Giovanni Ribisi (Frank Jr),
Debra Jo Rupp (Alice), Cindy Katz (Dr Zane)

Summary: Having been woken up in the early hours of the morning by Yasmine the Chick's crowing, everyone's just a little crabby with each other. Joey is certain that it's Monica's wash day and that she's wearing her grubbiest underwear, which annoys Monica because she can't believe his arrogance, thinking he knows more about the girls than they do about the boys. After a brief proof of their perspicacity (see box below), the guys win a $10 bet, but Monica wants a rematch – and wants the stakes upped to $100! Ross designs a gameshow-style quiz in which each team has to pick a question from a set of categories. The game goes extremely well, with the guys and the girls locked at nine points each, so when Ross reveals his tie-breaker lightning round, Monica and Chandler begin to play one-upmanship with the stake – if the girls win, the boys' birds have to go; if the boys win, they get Monica's apartment!

Phoebe is inseminated with the embryos and has to wait to see if she will become pregnant. As her friends descend into a ferocious row, Phoebe prepares herself for bad news . . .

Freaky Monica: According to Chandler, Monica will eat Tic-Tacs only in even numbers. When Alice and Frank buy Phoebe a lollipop and a home pregnancy test kit, Monica warns them not to get the two mixed up or they'll really ruin the lollipop.

The Showdown: Boys v Girls!

Before the competition even begins, Chandler correctly guesses that Rachel carries a half-eaten box of cookies in her handbag. He and Joey then go on to name every remaining item (a bag of apples, tortilla chips, yoghurt, diet soda and Scotch tape). Ross sets up the competition with categories 'Fears and Pet Peeves', 'Ancient History', 'Literature' and 'It's All Relative'. The info run-down goes as follows: Monica's pet peeve is animals dressed as humans, whereas Chandler's is Michael Flatley, Lord of the Dance ('His legs flail about as if independent to his body'). Monica and Ross's nana, who died, was called Althea (see 'TOW Nana Dies Twice'). The literature question refers to the *TV Guide*, which gets delivered to the boys' apartment each week, addressed to 'Miss Chanandelor Bong'. Chandler's father owns an all-male burlesque in Las Vegas called Viva Las Gaygas.

Monica's nickname on the hockey team was 'big fat goalie'. Rachel claims her favourite movie is *Dangerous Liaisons*. Her actual favourite movie is *Weekend at Bernie's*. Monica once got a pencil stuck in her ear. Monica has eleven categories of towel (including 'everyday', 'fancy', 'guest' and 'fancy guest').

Joey's favourite food is sandwiches (see 'TOW The Ballroom Dancing'), Chandler was nineteen when he first touched a girl's breast, Joey had an imaginary childhood friend called Maurice who was a Space Cowboy and Chandler's job is ... well it's not a 'Transpondster' as Rachel claims, thereby losing the tournament for the girls.

Spoilt Rachel: Woken up by the sound of crowing, Rachel goes on the warpath. When Monica comments that Rachel is not a 'morning person' she roars, *'Back off!'*, kind of proving Monica's point. When Pheebs warns the guys that their feathered pets shouldn't be living in an apartment, Rachel snaps, 'Especially not with all of these knives and cookbooks around!' After losing the bet, Rachel delivers her most damming assessment of her former friends: 'You are mean boys who are just being mean!'

Phoebisms: Pheebs gives a pep talk to the embryos, and warns them that if 'next time you see me I'm screaming, don't worry – that's supposed to happen.' She later explains the risks to the gang, saying that Frank and Alice 'are literally putting all their eggs in my basket!' She also claims that her body is a little faster than Western medicine.

The Chick and the Duck: Yasmine the Chick is going through some changes. 'She' turns out to be a rooster. Considering he's called Yasmine, that chick's going to have a rough time when he starts school!

Boys Will Be Boys: The guys stayed up late the night before making scary faces with the aid of Scotch tape (don't try this at home, kids – it can get very scary!). Frank Jr suggests that Phoebe should get drunk to help her get pregnant: 'That worked for a lot of girls in my high school.' When the girls unwillingly move into the boys' old apartment they find 'something' locked away. Rachel doesn't know what it is, 'but maybe if we keep that drawer shut it'll die,' she says, less than hopefully.

Generation X: *Dangerous Liaisons* (Stephen Frears, 1988) starred Glenn Close, John Malkovich and Uma Thurman, was based on the French classic *Les Liaisons Dangereuses* by Pierre Choderlos de Laclos and was a high-brow tale of scandal in the upper classes. *Weekend at Bernie's* (Ted Kotcheff, 1989) wasn't.

The Story So Far: The guys move into the girls' apartment and we see Joey's porcelain greyhound again (see 'TOW Eddie Won't Go'). Everyone now knows Ross's fist-smash gesture (see 'TOW Joey's New Girlfriend'). Monica lets slip that they steal Chandler's *TV Guide* each week. See also the box opposite.

The Last Word: Phoebe's storyline would be a major feature in most other episodes, but, of course, this is no normal episode as the Battle of the Sexes dominates the story. This is a sure-fire contender for best episode of all time with each question revealing a shocking or just plain bizarre fact about the people we claim to know so well. Not one to be missed under any circumstances, this is like a seven-horse accumulator coming in on the day you win the lottery on a rollover week. But without the money. **Ahhh Rating:** ***

413
'The One With Rachel's Crush'
#466613

Writers: Shana Goldberg-Meehan
Director: Dana deVally
First US transmission: 29.01.98
First UK transmission (Sky One): 02.04.98

Guest Cast: Paget Brewster (Kathy),
Paxton Whitehead (Mr Waltham), **and introducing**
Tate Donovan (Joshua Bergen)

Summary: Rachel's department is closed down (after the death of Joanna), and she's forced to accept a position as a 'personal shopper' for all the snooty rich people who need advice on what to buy. But then she gets allocated to her dream man, a recent divorcee called Joshua who needs to buy a whole new wardrobe. Rachel is really excited – but he's showing no signs of asking her for a date and she feels nervous about asking him out. On Joey's suggestion, she gets two tickets for the next Knicks game and offers them to him, but he misunderstands the offer and takes the second ticket for his nephew.

Chandler is distressed when he sees Kathy in a sex scene in a play and begins to feel insecure about their relationship. Asking Joey for advice (!), he learns that everything will be OK as long as there's chemistry onstage – if actors are doing it offstage, they lose the sexual tension onstage. But in the next performance, Chandler is sure Kathy and her co-star are acting really cool towards each other, which can mean only one thing . . .

Freaky Monica: She uses a fan to blow the freshly baked-cookie aroma across the hall. She also buys the latest *Playboy* magazine to tempt the guys back over to her apartment. She works for almost two days straight to completely redecorate the guys' old apartment and polish their floor.

Spoilt Rachel: Rach threatens to quit because she had to help an 81-year-old woman into a thong that she didn't even end up buying. When she sees Monica hauling a floor-polishing machine towards their apartment, Rachel makes toward the boys' place, then adds as an afterthought, 'Ohh, I just feel bad, I never vacuum.'

Phoebisms: Phoebe tactlessly asks if she can have some of Monica's old clothes from high school because maternity dresses are so expensive.

Slow Joey: In defence of his 'heat on stage' theory, Joey claims that there are plenty of theories that don't work: 'The Lone Gunman, communism, geometry . . .'

Chandleresque: Having just seen Kathy simulate sex in a play: 'It's like someone literally wrote down my worst nightmare and then charged me thirty-two dollars to see it!' An offended Kathy tells Chandler to call her when he grows up: 'Well don't expect *that* to happen any time soon!' shouts Chandler, missing her point somewhat.

Generation X: Ross and Joey come up with a list of actors and actresses who met on a film and got together after-wards: Susan Sarandon and Tim Robbins met on the set of *Bull Durham* (Ron Shelton, 1988). Alec Baldwin and Kim Basinger's relationship became public knowledge after alleged sex romps on the set of *Too Hot To Handle* – a.k.a. *The Marrying Man* – (Jerry Rees, 1991). Tom Cruise and Nicole Kidman were already married by the time they made *Far and Away* (Ron Howard, 1992). At the time this aired, Jennifer Aniston was dating Tate Donovan (Joshua), which might account for Chandler's storyline. Chandler calls Kathy a 'devil woman', possibly in reference to the 1976 song by Cliff Richard. Tate Donovan was the star voice in Disney's *Hercules* (Ron Clements, John Musker, 1997).

The Story So Far: The guys have been to every play Joey's ever appeared in. Rachel claims she's never asked a guy out before, but Phoebe has, 'thousands of times'.

The Last Word: Typical Chandler, he gets the best relationship of his life so far and he ruins it by being unnecessarily jealous, and then giving her cause to go off with someone else (and if Ross says the words 'on a break' once more we'll break *him*!). Rachel's new position will have quite an effect on her love life and, by association, that of one of her friends too (clue: her new boss, Mr Waltham is a significant factor). **Ahhh Rating:** *

414
'The One With Joey's Dirty Day'
#466614

Writer: Wil Calhoun
Director: Peter Bonerz
First US transmission: 05.02.98
First UK transmission (Sky One): 09.04.98

Guest Cast: Charlton Heston (himself), Tate Donovan (Joshua Bergen), Paxton Whitehead (Mr Waltham), Carlos LaCamera (Assistant Director), Rocky McMurray (Cigarette Guy), **and introducing** Helen Baxendale (Emily Waltham)

Summary: Chandler is depressed after breaking up with Kathy and is stuck in what Joey calls Phase One, where he won't change out of his sweatpants for days on end. Joey decides to go fishing, promising to be back in time for Phase Two – going to strip clubs and getting drunk. But Joey comes back from the trip late, stinking of fish and worms, and then he oversleeps and has to go to a film shoot still smelling from his trip. Discovering that the star of the picture (Charlton Heston) has his own shower, Joey sneaks in to use it. Heston returns to his dressing room and catches Joey half naked. Joey explains that he had to have a shower – he stinks! But Heston thinks he's just having a crisis of confidence and gives him a pep talk.

None of this helps Chandler, who is now ready for Phase Two. Distraught that his best buddy isn't available, Chandler is left to go to the strip clubs with the girls – who have a better time there than he does! As the girls discuss how much fun they had, Chandler suddenly finds himself jumping from Phase Two to an unprecedented Phase Four!

Rachel seems to be making headway with Joshua – he invites her to the opening of a nightclub, promising to leave her name at the door. But she's also promised her boss that she'll escort his niece, Emily, visiting from England, to the opera. In desperation she asks Ross if he'll step in and go with Emily. Reluctantly, Ross agrees, unaware that his life is likely to change for ever . . .

Spoilt Rachel: Hearing that Ross and Emily have flitted off to Vermont the day after they first met, Rachel is shocked. But when Monica reminds her that she 'flitted off' to Vail with Barry when they first met, a tired Rachel snaps back, 'Would you just for *once* not remember every . . . little . . . *thing*?'

Phoebisms: She gets her morning sickness in the evening (figures!). She thinks that at one point she feels her baby kicking for the first time, only to realise that the elastic on her underwear had just snapped. She discovers that Pheebs is short for Phoebe: 'I thought that was just what we called each other!'

Slow Joey: We're not fishermen, so we don't know if Joey is being serious or if he just made up names for fishing equipment, but we agree with Phoebe, 'guggly worm' and 'glow-pop giggly jammer' are hilarious.

Chandleresque: Joey is disappointed at missing the chance to go to a strip club with Chandler, but his friend reassures him, 'You're gonna have plenty of chances – there are literally thousands of women out there just waiting to screw me over.'

The Chick and the Duck: They follow Chandler into the bathroom: 'Will you give me one minute?' says an irritable Chandler.

Cool Britannia: Rachel's boss, Mr Waltham, tells Rachel that Emily is from London. 'Well, Shropshire, really,' he corrects himself. Surely, being English, he'd know that geographically speaking there's quite a difference between the two places (and we're not just talking pottery versus smog here). Emily turns up at Rachel's looking like a drowned rat having been strip-searched at JFK Airport: 'Apparently, to you people, I look like someone who's got a balloon of cocaine stuffed up their bum!' she rants.

Boys Will Be . . . erm, Girls?: Monica and Phoebe offer to be one of the guys to cheer Chandler up: 'You don't wanna be guys: you'd be all hairy and wouldn't live as long.'

Generation X: Of the three tenors, Luciano Pavarotti, José Carreras and Placido Domingo, the two who performed Strauss's *Die Fledermaus* (meaning 'The Bat') are most likely to have been Domingo and Pavarotti. In an epic career, Charlton Heston has played Moses, in *The Greatest Story Ever Told* (George Stevens, 1965), the eponymous hero in *Ben Hur* (William Wyler, 1959 – winner of more Oscars than any other film to date except *Titanic*, which equalled it with eleven awards), and, in the first two *Planet of the Apes* movies, he played the first astronaut ever to get a snog off a chimpanzee. Joey claims to be the veteran actor Kirk Douglas, in a flawed attempt to excuse his presence in Charlton Heston's shower. Helen Baxendale shot to fame in the UK as the acerbic Dr Maitland in the medical drama *Cardiac Arrest*, and later starred in *The Investigator* and *An Unsuitable Job For A Woman*.

The Story So Far: Rachel and Barry went to Vail when they first met, just like Ross and Emily went to Vermont. Rachel doesn't like people calling Joshua just 'Josh' (see 'TOW Joey's New Girlfriend').

The Last Word: There'll be some people out there who find the whole idea of spending a whole episode talking about strippers a little tacky. If so you're watching the wrong show! The dream sequence at the end is choice, with Chandler directing his fantasy, having his female friends while cavorting with strippers who shout 'Chandler is the King!' (though typically, he can't help torturing himself by receiving unwarranted advances from the smoking man as part of the fantasy). We're sorry for all the *Friends* fans out there who don't share our enthusiasm for this episode, but this is what a lot of blokes are really like! **Ahhh Rating** (funny, but a little distasteful): *

415
'The One With All The Rugby'
#466617

Writers: Andrew Reich & Ted Cohen (story),
Wil Calhoun (teleplay)
Director: James Burrows
First US transmission: 26.02.98
First UK transmission (Sky One): 16.04.98

Guest Cast: Maggie Wheeler (Janice), Helen Baxendale (Emily Waltham), Mark Thomas (Liam), Adamo Palladino (Devon), Robin McDonald (Ticket Counter Attendant)

Summary: Rachel persuades Chandler to accompany her to a beauty parlour, where he bumps into Janice. But to avoid getting back with her he tells her his company is sending him to Yemen. This seems like a pretty good excuse to Chandler – until Janice decides she's going to see him off at the airport.

Ross finds himself volunteering to play rugby just to impress Emily. As everyone expected, he gets beaten to a pulp, but when Emily encourages him to play dirty and gives him a few sly tips, Ross manages to survive the experience – just!

And Monica discovers a mysterious switch in the boys' old apartment and is driven to tearing down the walls just to find out what it's for . . .

Poor Ross: Having reassured Emily that New York is safe, he panics when two large guys run towards them – only to discover they're friends of Emily. When Ross boasts that he's man enough to play rugby, Joey says, 'Dude, you're not even man enough to order the channel that carries the sport!'

Freaky Monica: She plugs things in around the house to see what gets switched on or off by the switch, then she goes down to City Hall, waits for three hours and pays for a copy of the electrical plans to their apartment. When Rachel comes home, she finds pictures hanging on the walls to cover the massive holes Monica made trying to find where the cables lead! After hiring a $200-an-hour electrician, asking Treager's advice and suffering several electric shocks, Monica gives up.

Spoilt Rachel: At the manicure parlour, Rachel finds that she's sitting on a huge fingernail: 'I hate to think what this woman was scratching when this broke off!' Rach asks Joey what the silver knob on the toilet is for. When he tells her it flushes the toilet, she asks him, 'When you come over, would you mind actually using it?'

Phoebisms: As Monica absently flicks the switch on and off, we see the TV in the boys' apartment switching on and off (the switch controls the plug in that apartment!). Phoebe is watching the TV and repeatedly blinking in the belief that her eyes now control the TV.

Slow Joey: When Ross claims that the other rugby players don't look bigger than himself, Joey explains, 'Maybe that's because you're closer to you, so you look bigger to you from where you are.'

Cool Britannia: Ross jokes that although they don't have rugby in the USA, they didn't have freedom until 1776 (the War of Independence).

Generation X: Janice sang 'Old Man River', a song tradition- ally identified with a deep bass singer such as Paul Robeson. Ross recalls the gang all going to see *Dances with Wolves* (Kevin Costner, 1990).

The Story So Far: Janice is now divorced (see 'TOW The Race Car Bed'). Rachel reminds Ross that he once hurt himself playing badminton with her dad (though Ross claims it was because her mother's dog was psyching him out). Joey and Chandler's . . . er, Monica and Rachel's apartment is above that of a Mrs Chatracus, who presumably lived opposite Mr Heckles all those years. Ross claims he washed his father's Porsche with rocks when he was four (his father managed to get a replacement Porsche years later – see 'TOW Ross And Rachel . . . You Know').

The Last Word: Ross is a fool, but you've gotta admire his eagerness to please Emily. Chandler's desperation to rid himself of Janice reaches ludicrous proportions and Monica's obsessions reach fever pitch. It comes to something when Joey is the most normal member of the gang. It must be a warning for the end of civilisation as we know it . . . or just a fairly average episode of *Friends*. **Ahhh Rating:** *

416
'The One With The Fake Party'
#466615

Writers: Alicia Sky Varinaitis (story),
Shana Goldberg-Meehan & Scott Silveri (teleplay)
Director: Michael Lembeck
First US transmission: 19.03.98
First UK transmission (Sky One): 23.04.98

Guest Cast: Helen Baxendale (Emily Waltham),
Tate Donovan (Joshua Bergen),
James Michael Tyler (Gunther)

Summary: Phoebe discovers her baby doesn't like vegetarian food and is forced to eat meat. Joey helps her out with a few sandwich recipes, but she's still upset about the ethics of eating. Joey volunteers to become a vegetarian for as long as Phoebe is pregnant to even out the numbers.

It's Emily's last few days in the country and Ross wants to spend as much time with her as possible. Unfortunately, in a last-ditch attempt to seduce Joshua, Rachel arranges a surprise leaving party for Emily to give her the excuse she's needed to invite Joshua to meet her away from work. Emily is bowled over by what she believes to be Ross's generosity and really enjoys herself, to the extent where the evening draws on and there's no time left for any of the things Ross had planned. Rachel tries every trick she can think of (and at least three different dresses) to seduce Joshua, but all of them go horribly wrong. Eventually she comes clean and confesses her less-than-honourable intentions towards him. Joshua is relieved – he's been coming back to her department and buying suits just so he could see her. But he also explains that his marriage has just ended and that he doesn't feel ready for a relationship yet.

Phoebisms: Joey tries to cheer her up by telling her she has 'that cool, pregnant-lady glow', to which Phoebe says, 'That's sweat. You throw up all morning, you'll have that glow too.'

Slow Joey: Joey eats a bologna and pickle sandwich in the shower. When Ross explains that he and Emily knew they had only two weeks together, Joey boasts, 'That's what all my relationships are like.' Chandler has to remind him that in Ross's case, they *both* know it's just for two weeks. Having agreed to become a vegetarian for Phoebe's sake, he checks one last detail: 'There's no meat in beer, right?' He later asks Phoebe, 'If a cow should die of natural causes, I can have one of those, right?' 'Not if I get there first,' challenges the ex-vegetarian.

Chandleresque: She changes into her lucky dress. When Monica asks if 'lucky' means more cleavage, Chandler quips, 'Does for me!'

Cool Britannia: Emily's ever-so-English uncle drags her and Ross to a museum of Victorian doorknobs.

Gunther's There For You, Rachel: At the party, Rachel begins to illustrate the rules of Spin the Bottle by going to kiss Gunther, but when she sees the look of expectation on his face she decides against it. Ahhhh. When Rachel performs a less-than-successful cartwheel, Gunther's the only one who claps. He can't help himself. He also tells Emily that Rachel is his girlfriend.

Generation X: Joey gets *Footloose* (Herbert Ross, 1984), starring Kevin Bacon, confused with *Flashdance* (Adrian Lyne, 1983), which starred Jennifer Beals. At her party we hear Comershop's 'Brimful of Asha'.

The Story So Far: Encouraged by Emily, Ross signed himself up for helicopter classes. Monica tells Emily that Ross used to dress up like an old lady and throw tea parties when he was a boy (see 'TOW The Metaphorical Tunnel'). Rachel still uses her high school cheerleader's outfit to seduce men. She is 28 by this episode.

The Last Word: Despite the fact that this episode shows just how far Rachel will go to get her own way, it's good to see her having to work for a relationship instead of just having one appear in front of her. The best scene is probably where we see Ross and Rachel as friends for the first time since they took a break. Many fans have commented that it was about time. **Ahhh Rating:** **

417
'The One With The Free Porn'
#466616

Writers: Mark J. Kunerth (story), Richard Goodman (teleplay)
Director: Michael Lembeck
First US transmission: 26.03.98
First UK transmission (Sky One): 30.04.98

Guest Cast: Helen Baxendale (Emily Waltham),
Giovanni Ribisi (Frank Jr), Debra Jo Rupp (Alice),
Michael G. Hagerty (Mr Treager – billed as 'Treeger'),
Shirley Jordan (the Doctor)

Summary: Joey and Chandler suddenly find their lives freeze when they acquire a pornography channel for free. Terrified that they'll lose it if the TV set is switched off, they mount an all-night vigil. Meanwhile, Phoebe discovers that the baby she's carrying for her brother and his wife is actually triplets. Frank and Alice are thrilled, until they realise that three babies means three times the expense.

Monica persuades Ross to catch Emily before she leaves for England. At the gate, Ross tells her he loves her, but she seems really underwhelmed. Later he speaks to her on the phone and only then does she tell him there's 'someone else'. He is bullied by his sister into going to London, only to find that Emily has dumped her English boyfriend, having realised that she loves Ross, and rushed back to New York! Which doesn't help Ross much, as he sits outside her London flat.

Phoebe and Rachel come up with an enterprising way to use Pheebs's van and make money – mobile massages!

Poor Ross: After discovering Emily has a boyfriend back in London, Ross tells Monica he won't listen to her advice any more, blaming her for his putting his fist through the wall. Chandler asks, 'You put your fist through the wall?' 'No,' confesses Ross, 'I missed and hit the door, but it opened really hard!'

Freaky Monica: Monica wants Ross to live out her fantasy for her and tells him he must get to the airport before Emily leaves. Describing what she imagines might happen when the two lovers are reunited, Monica suddenly balks at the style of her narration, confessing, 'I've been watching way too much porn.'

Spoilt Rachel: She kindly takes the massage table out of Phoebe's tired arms, only to hand it straight to Monica.

Phoebisms: When her obstetrician discusses with her the possibility of multiple births, Phoebe at first misses his point: 'Why don't we take care of this one, and should I get pregnant again I'll hold on to your card, OK?'

Magna Doodle: 'Knock knock. Who's there? FREE PORN.'

Just Plain Weird: Frank Jr's response on hearing they're expecting triplets: 'I finally got my band!' He tells Phoebe he's enrolled in college – refrigerator college.

Boys Will Be Boys: Treager explains that he once got a free porn channel too and describes it as being like finding money: 'Like finding money with naked people on it!' suggests Chandler. When Treager tells them he lost the channel after he turned the TV off, a baffled Joey asks, 'Why would he turn off the TV?' Eventually the effect of the porn starts to addle what minds the boys still have. Chandler is dismayed to discover that the really sexy teller at the bank doesn't invite him to 'do it with her in the vault' and Joey is shocked when the 'woman pizza delivery guy' delivers the pizza and leaves without asking to inspect his bedroom.

Generation X: The writing team had been keen to use a fake porn film title for the one Joey appeared in (see 'TOW Phoebe's Husband'), but we get a much better selection here. *Good Will Humping* is inspired by *Good Will Hunting* (Gus Van Sant, 1997), while *In & Out & In Again* is an obvious nod to *In & Out* (Frank Oz, 1997), which starred Kevin Kline. As Monica explains her fantasy to Ross it echoes the movie *Only You* (Norman Jewison, 1994), which starred Robert Downey Jr and Marisa Tomei (if you squint really hard, Robert Downey Jr *could* be Ross!).

The Story So Far: Emily had a British boyfriend called Colin.

The Last Word: OK, so this goes one step further than the strippers in 'TOW Joey's Dirty Day', but it is funny, especially the bogus film names that pop up (oo-er) here and there. But our favourite scene is where Phoebe tries to tell the gang her new money-making idea, while trying to stop

Rachel from blowing the surprise. When Rachel claims it was her idea to call it 'Relaxi-Taxi' Phoebe nearly rips her head off when she shrieks: 'You did *not*! Oh No! You came up with "Relaxi Cab"!' When Rachel explains that she meant 'Relaxicab, like "taxicab"' Phoebe visibly backs down. One of the websites on the Internet comments on the way we can hear Emily's phone 'with amazing clarity' from outside her apartment, speculating that the walls in British apartments must be very thin. If this is the only thing of note they have to say, it doesn't exactly reflect well on how interested we are in Ross and Emily's love story, does it? However, Baxendale tries her best, and though the writers think they've written her terribly, terribly English, it does come across as slightly twee when they give her expletives like 'bugger off'. Well we like her, anyway. **Ahhh Rating:** **

418
'The One With Rachel's New Dress'
#466620

Writers: Andrew Reich & Ted Cohen (Story), Jill Condon &
Amy Toomin (teleplay)
Director: Gail Mancuso
First US transmission: 02.04.98
First UK transmission (Sky One): 07.05.98

Guest Cast: Tate Donovan (Joshua Bergen),
Jane Sibbett (Carol), Helen Baxendale (Emily Waltham),
Jessica Hecht (Susan), Debra Jo Rupp (Alice),
John Bennett Perry (Mr Bergen), Pat Crowley (Mrs Bergen),
Charlie Allen & Jack Allen (Ben)

Summary: Alice and Frank have chosen names for two of their triplets, but they want Phoebe to name the third. Asking Joey and Chandler for advice, she unwittingly provokes the boys to fight over whom she should name the child after. When Joey ridicules Chandler's name he suddenly becomes defensive and vows to change his name by deed poll. To stop him making such a rash decision, Phoebe tells him that she likes his name so much she's decided to name the third child after him. The second she leaves, Chandler breaks into a big smile – it has all been a ruse to get his own way.

Ross is concerned when Emily meets Susan for the first time and she offers to show his ex-wife's partner around London. Ross convinces himself that Emily, like Carol before her, has fallen for Susan. Expressing his fears to the gang, they all think he's paranoid. The only person who believes it's possible, ironically, is Carol.

Rachel plans a major seduction of Joshua for their first night together, but when he tells her about his morbid fear of fowl (brought to the fore by the chick and the duck), he suggests they both go over to his parents' house, as they're out of town. But just as Rachel undresses down to her undergarments, Joshua's parents come home and she's forced to pretend she's wearing a fashionable dress – to dinner!

Poor Ross: Emily worries about Ben getting the wrong idea if he sees her bra on Ross's shower rail. A pragmatic Ross says, 'If Mommy can have a wife, Daddy can have a bra.' Susan tells Emily that Ross doesn't like her: 'Oh come on!' says Ross. 'That's – that's . . . true.'

Freaky Monica: When Rachel asks her advice on which nightgown she should wear for her 'first time' with Joshua, Monica says that she feels creeped out by the thought of choosing other people's 'sex clothes'.

Spoilt Rachel: In preparation for her first night with Joshua, Rachel boasts that she's had her hair coloured, bought new sheets and that she's cooking him a fancy meal – only to turn to Monica to ask her what 'she' is cooking. It turns out that she's persuaded Monica to prepare an entire menu on her behalf, and Monica warns her that if she bitches about it, then she'll find herself making her 'famous baked potato and Diet Coke' instead. 'Wow, I really get crabby when I cook,' notes Rachel.

Phoebisms: Phoebe takes to playing a drum as she's too pregnant to play the guitar any more. This brings a whole new interpretation to 'Smelly Cat'. Phoebe's suggestions for the baby's name include 'Cougar', 'Exxon' and 'Chanoey', a combination of Joey and Chandler. When Joey suggests 'The Hulk', Pheebs says that she likes the idea of a name starting with 'The'.

Slow Joey: Joey asks Chandler to name one famous person with his name. When he names Raymond Chandler, Joey demands it should be someone he 'didn't make up'.

Parents – Who Needs 'Em?: The Bergens seem massively dissatisfied with Europe. Asked how he enjoyed France and Italy, Mr Bergen responds with, 'It sucks!'

The Chick and the Duck: Yasmine and Dick still 'migrate' over to their old apartment every now and again, which really freaks Joshua out – he's afraid of farm birds!

Just Plain Weird: Alice tells Phoebe that they've chosen the name Leslie for one of the babies, and that Frank wants to name one of the boy babies 'Frank Jr Jr'. When Chandler asks her if that would make him 'Frank III', Alice sighs 'Don't get me started.'

Girl Power: Rachel tells the girls that when she went to dinner with the Bergens, the waiter spilt cold water down her back and one of her boobs popped out. Her friends try to console her, but she's OK: 'I got nice boobs,' she tells them confidently – and the girls have to agree with her.

Generation X: In reference to Emily and Susan, Ross mentions *Personal Best* (Robert Towne, 1982) in which Mariel Hemingway hops in between the beds of her male coach and her female competitor. When Phoebe claims that Ross and the Hulk have very little in common, Ross refers to 'Issue 72' (before everyone looks at him as if he's a geek). There never was an Issue 72 of *The Incredible Hulk*. *The Incredible Hulk* Vol. 1 lasted a mere six issues, though the character returned as a strip-only character in *Tales To Astonish*. As he was by far the most popular character in it, *Tales To Astonish* was renamed *The Incredible Hulk* as of Issue 102 (so, Ross isn't always right!). Raymond Chandler was a celebrated crime author, whereas Joey Buttafucco, who sounds made up, most definitely isn't. He was an auto mechanic who alleged that after a young girl called Amy Fisher developed a crush on him, she murdered his wife in a jealous rage. She alleged that he'd seduced her, driven her to prostitution and bullied her into the murder. He became the butt of many jokes in the States, and she found her life story transformed into three lurid TV movies. And Joshua's father is played by John Bennett Perry, famous as the 'Old Spice guy' in a series of adverts. He also appeared in the film *Fools Rush In* (Andy Tennant, 1997) opposite his son, one Matthew Perry.

The Story So Far: Ross reminds Chandler and Phoebe that for six months before they split up, all he heard about from Carol was how great Susan was (see 'TOW The Flashback'). Rachel reminds Ross of how he got jealous of Mark even though nothing happened between them (see 'TOW All The Jealousy') and Monica reminds him that back in high school all of his girlfriends were cheating on him and he never got jealous once.

The Last Word: Rachel's quick thinking in this episode is very impressive, as she tells Joshua's parents that her undergarment is a new dress from Milan, and that she's just product-testing it: 'Obviously in this case, I am going to report back, "USA not ready".' The effort she goes to (OK, the effort she and *Monica* go to) is nice to see, considering that she's never really had to work this hard for a relationship. Ross, meanwhile, seems not to have grown at all. Hearing that Susan and Emily have gone to a poetry reading together, he cries, 'Poetry? Susan's gay! They're being gay together!' His irrational jealousy is getting tired by now, and Rachel's spiteful response to his behaviour is, for once, spot on – 'I hope Emily *is* a lesbian!' she cries. **Ahhh Rating: ***

419
'The One With All The Haste'
#466618

Writers: Wil Calhoun & Scott Silveri
Director: Kevin Bright
First US transmission: 09.04.98
First UK transmission (Sky One): 14.05.98

Guest Cast: Helen Baxendale (Emily Waltham),
James Michael Tyler (Gunther), Michael Connor (Singing Man)

Summary: The girls are really getting tired of living in the boys' old apartment and try anything to get their old home back. Having tried bribing them with Knicks tickets, they eventually find themselves caught in another 'Winner Takes All' bet. The boys win again and get both the apartment *and* the tickets! But while they're at the game, the girls plan a little house-swapping and get both apartments as they used to be in record time!

Ross, meanwhile, is beginning to find seeing Emily for only a couple of days at a time emotionally draining. He considers asking her to move to America, but after discussing it with her they agree to go the distance and get married! What will Rachel's reaction be when she finds out?

Poor Ross: When Joey sees Ross's earring for the first time he asks him, 'We don't make enough fun of you already?' And Chandler asks him if he was aware that Wham! broke up.

Freaky Monica: They sure know how easy it is to get men to do what they want. As a last-ditch attempt to keep their apartment, Monica and Rachel agree to kiss in front of the guys for one minute! Phoebe speculates that if they'd just done that right after the last contest, they could have kept their apartment. Monica looks at her murderously and asks her to pretend that 'that's not true'.

Spoilt Rachel: Boy does she go overboard this episode! She roars at a man who's singing joyfully early in the morning, then rants at Joey, 'I hate this apartment! I hate the colour of these walls! I hate the fact that this place still smells like bird! I hate that singing guy!' Then threatens to kill Joey. She is *so* not a morning person.

Phoebisms: She buys a pile of maternity clothes from a used-clothes store, only to find that the maternity pants she bought (complete with a list of names, both naughty and nice) are the bottom half of a Santa costume. Her idea of a suitable question to decide who gets the nice apartment is to ask each pair in turn what their favourite things about trees are. When Joey offers 'they're tall', Pheebs marks him down because she was going for 'leafy'.

Chandleresque: Monica asks him what she should wear to a Knicks game: 'A T-shirt that says "I don't belong here",' he suggests. After Ross tells the guys about his intention to ask Emily to live with him, Chandler claims that he has a carton of milk he's had a longer relationship with. When Joey begs Chandler to risk the bet with the girls, on account of his being his best friend, Chandler relents: 'All right, but you can't use that [excuse] again for a whole year.'

Generation X: Wham! was the name of George Michael's early 1980s double act with his childhood friend, Andrew Ridgeley. One of their biggest hits was 'Wake Me Up Before You Go-Go'. *Flowers for Algernon* was a novel by Daniel Keyes about a mentally disabled man who is used in an experiment to increase his intelligence. The fact that Joey has not read this book *is* relevant.

The Story So Far: Ross has an earring from this episode on (having evidently overcome his fear of needles – see 'TOW The Baby On The Bus'). Rachel claims that her mother got her father's Knicks season ticket in the divorce (though she's possibly lying). Joey bemoans the fact that when he was a kid, his father's work used to award the best salesman with a season ticket, and that his father never won. Of course, his father didn't actually work in the sales division anyway. By this point, Ross and Emily have known each other for six weeks.

The Last Word: Phoebe's reaction to Ross and Emily's news is what we're sure most of us would say to a friend who's decided to get married after only six weeks: 'Are you pregnant too?' But of course, it's Rachel's response that everyone is waiting for, and the relief of the whole gang when Rachel wishes them both well is almost tangible. Obviously, that's not what everyone remembers this episode for, is it? *Monica and Rachel snog*! Admittedly, we don't get to see it, but the thought of it is possibly enough for many viewers. **Ahhh Rating** (Ross's marriage proposal, where he tries to substitute his earring for an engagement ring, is just as cute as anything!): ****

420
'The One With All The Wedding Dresses'
#466621

Writers: Adam Chase (story), Michael Curtis &
Gregory S. Malins (teleplay)
Director: Gail Mancuso
First US transmission: 16.04.98
First UK transmission (Sky One): 21.05.98

Guest Cast: Tate Donovan (Joshua Bergen),
James Michael Tyler (Gunther), Christina Moore (Marjorie),
Anne Betancourt (the Saleslady), Thea Mann
(Sleep-Clinic Worker)

Summary: Joey's snoring is getting so bad that Chandler is having trouble sleeping, so he forces Joey to go to a sleep clinic. In preparation for the clinic, Joey mustn't sleep – something he's having trouble with. Chandler takes his friend to the clinic, and there, he meets an attractive woman, and because Joey can't help falling asleep, he manages to arrange a date with her. Chandler's happy with himself, not least because the woman talks in her sleep, which keeps Joey awake!

Ross asks Monica to pick up Emily's wedding dress – being the groom, he's not supposed to see it until his wedding day. Monica is only too happy to help him out, especially when the shop assistant thinks it's for her and allows her to try it on. Soon both Monica and Phoebe are wearing wedding dresses.

Trying to prove how 'OK' she is about Ross's impending marriage, Rachel speaks to Joshua about their future, pressurising him just a little into thinking about getting married. As he's only recently got divorced this almost frightens him away, but Rachel luckily manages to convince him that she wasn't that serious after all. But after she joins in with the girls and puts on a wedding dress, Joshua calls round, sees what she's wearing and runs off in a panic.

Freaky Monica: Monica tries to get Rachel to do the dishes, just once: 'I don't care if those dishes sit in the sink until they're all covered with [realises what she's saying] ... I'll do them when I get home!' We see Monica wearing Emily's wedding dress and admiring herself in the mirror – until eventually the shop assistant tells her that the store is closing. 'I wish there was a job where I could wear this all the time,' she tells her friends. 'Maybe one day, there will be.'

Slow Joey: When Ross tells the gang the date of his wedding, Joey tells him that's the day after he stops menstruating – before realising that he's reading someone else's diary.

Chandleresque: (After Marjorie tells him she talks in her sleep): 'What a coincidence, I *listen* in my sleep.'

The Ballad of Ross & Rachel: Rachel surprises her friends by stating that she doesn't believe that Ross and Emily will even *get* married. 'You're gonna be dancing at my wedding before you're dancing at theirs,' she boasts. Later, she tells Monica that she'd kind of expected her and Ross to get back together again. Monica reassures her friend, 'I think we all did.'

Magna Doodle: In a magic moment, the Magna Doodle is blank when Ross enters the guys' apartment, but the shot immediately after he's told his friends he and Emily have set a date, the board reads 'GET OUT!!' in surprise.

Just Plain Weird: Phoebe rents a wedding dress just for the fun of it from a shop called It's Not Too Late. Joey and Chandler have a disagreement about the noise a whip makes (!). Chandler goes for 'Whapahhh!', whereas Joey favours a more traditional 'Whitushhh!' – madness! Anyway, Joey's right.

Gunther's There For You, Rachel: Overhearing Joshua reject Rachel's marriage proposal, Gunther shrieks: 'You *idiot*!'

Generation X: Joey hums 'Here Comes the Bride'.

The Story So Far: Monica reveals that she sometimes snores. Joey sleeps naked (see 'TOW The Boobies'). Rachel unpacks her own wedding dress (see 'Pilot').

The Last Word: The self-destructive side of Rachel strikes again as she frightens away a perfectly good boyfriend just to compete with Ross. The seed is sown for a dramatic finish to the season at Ross's wedding! An episode that is supported by loads of superb visual gags, notably where Monica and Phoebe throw bouquets to each other in a mock end-of-wedding celebration. **Ahhh Rating:** **

421
'The One With The Invitation'
#466619

Writer: Seth Kurland
Director: Peter Bonerz
First US transmission: 23.04.98
First UK Transmission (Sky One): 28.05.98

Guest Cast: Helen Baxendale (Emily Waltham)

Summary: Ross and Emily are sending out their wedding invitations and discuss whether inviting Rachel is such a good idea. Trying to decide, Ross remembers some of the most prominent moments from his relationship with Rachel. He posts her invitation anyway. Rachel meanwhile is deciding whether she's actually going to go. As she realises how much she still feels for Ross, she tells the rest of her friends that she's decided to stay with Phoebe and look after her.

Phoebisms: Pheebs dampens the boys' spirits by pointing out that climbing Everest costs over $60,000 and that it's possible they might die: 'And you *would* die!' she says, not at all reassuringly.

Slow Joey: Phoebe tells them that expectant mothers are not allowed to fly once their pregnancy reaches the third trimester, and Chandler confesses he didn't know that. Joey claims that he did, much to everyone's surprise, only to blurt, 'I *so* didn't know that, but you should see your faces!' Good one, Joe.

Chandleresque: Realising that so many of his friends are doing things, he feels dissatisfied that the only thing he's achieved in his life is leaving his 'ass print' on a chair. After Joey suggests they might climb Everest, Chandler feels enthused enough to say, 'It would be nice to leave an ass print on Everest!'

The Ballad of Ross & Rachel: Rachel tells the gang that she won't be going to the wedding: 'I mean, it's Ross. How can I watch him get married . . .?'

Cool Britannia: The lame Brit-jokes start here. Emily offers Ross some tea: 'Earl Grey?' 'Yeah, fine. Invite whoever you want.'

Generation X: Joey and Chandler suggest renting the video of *Die Hard* (John McTiernan, 1988).

The Story So Far: The Gellers have an Uncle Nathan, whom nobody likes. Ross remembers events from 'Pilot', 'TOW The Blackout', 'TOW The East German Laundry Detergent',

'TOW Ross Finds Out', 'TOW Ross And Rachel Take A Break', 'TO The Morning After', 'TOW The Jellyfish' and finally 'TOW The Fake Party'. Rachel's memories begin with 'TOW Rachel Finds Out', then go through 'TOW Ross's New Girlfriend', 'TOW Ross Finds Out', 'TOW The List', 'TOW Ross And Rachel . . . You Know', 'TO The Morning After', 'TO At The Beach', 'TOW The Jellyfish' and finally 'TOW The Prom Video'.

The Last Word: This episode was largely a series of clips, which some fans felt cheated by, but it serves as a nice reminder of Ross and Rachel's past. If nothing else, it must have helped them afford the English episodes. **Ahhh Rating:** ****

('The One With The Invitation' and 'The One With The Worst Best Man Ever' were shown by Sky One in the UK as a double bill.)

422

'The One With The Worst Best Man Ever'
#466622

Writers: Seth Kurland (story), Michael Curtis &
Gregory S. Malins (teleplay)
Director: Peter Bonerz
First US transmission: 30.04.98
First UK Transmission (Sky One): 28.05.98

Guest Cast: James Michael Tyler (Gunther),
Lisa Rotondi (the Stripper), Robert Koch (the Doctor),
Helen Baxendale (Emily Waltham – credited but
does not appear)

Summary: Ross asks the guys to organise a bachelor party and Joey reminds him that he should pick a best man before he starts thinking about a party. But Ross has already picked Chandler. After Joey makes a lot of fuss, Ross agrees to let him be the best man and mind the wedding ring. Joey quickly starts arranging the party, and when the girls discover they're not invited they decide to throw a baby shower for Phoebe and get her gifts that she can use after the births. Unfortunately, Phoebe is suffering from mood swings and just gets upset at the thought of not being able to use any of her presents for two months.

The bachelor party goes much better, but after Joey sleeps with the stripper he discovers that the wedding ring is missing and that the stripper must have stolen it. However, when they finally trace her, she claims to know nothing about it. In all of this, one suspect remains unchallenged – no matter how loudly he quacks his confession . . .

Phoebisms: Her mood swings (which she actually denies having) are hilarious. At one point, Monica and Rachel shrink away from her, suspecting that she'll actually attack them. After the disastrous baby shower, the girls cheer Phoebe up by pointing out that as she's only a surrogate mother, she's free of all the worries about saving for their education or disciplining them, while she'll always be the one they turn to to talk about sex. She'll be their 'cool Aunt Phoebe'. 'I am pretty cool,' notes Pheebs.

Slow Joey: Joey, discussing the party, tells Chandler that Ross 'didn't say anything about no strippers'. When Chandler points out that 'no strippers' was exactly what Ross *did* say, Joey says that he 'chose not to hear that'. He gets T-shirts printed that say 'Ross Geller, Bachelor Bash 1998', which have a huge picture of Joey's face on the back under the heading 'Best Man'. The morning after the party, Chandler asks Joey the most naïve question ever: 'You slept with the stripper?' to which Joey replies, 'Of course!' Discovering that the ring is missing, Joey phones the emergency services, only to be laughed at: 'They said they're gonna look for it right after they've solved all the murders,' he explains to Ross.

Chandleresque: After the stripper tells the guys that she makes $1,600 a week Chandler begs her to marry him.

The Ballad of Ross & Rachel: Rachel tells Pheebs that she's not going to Ross's wedding, and Phoebe initially says that it's just like when she was living rough and a man offered to buy her food. When Rachel asks her how that's the same as her problem, Pheebs has to agree that it isn't, '. . . because, you see, *that* was an actual problem and yours is just, like, y'know, a bunch of high school *crap*'.

The Chick and the Duck: They hide in Joey's room while the party is on. Joey tells the stripper that he has them totally trained, and proves it by getting Dick the Duck to stare at the wall, hardly move and 'be white'.

Magna Doodle: At Ross's bachelor party, the words 'Another one bites the dust' can just be made out.

Gunther's There For You, Chandler: Trying to choose a best man for a wedding he's not having, Chandler picks his 'best friend', Gunther. When Gunther asks him if he knows what his second name is, Chandler replies 'Central Perk?' He later thanks Ross for not marrying Rachel.

Generation X: As the guys reminisce about the duck, we hear Barry Manilow's 'Weekend in New England', and the end credits are played over a shot of Dick enjoying a paddle in his water pail to the 'Trumpet Hornpipe' (known to Brits as the theme from *Captain Pugwash*).

The Story So Far: Chandler was Ross's best man at his first wedding. As the guys worry about Dick's health we see flashbacks to some of their memories of him, in which we see clips from 'TOW A Chick. And A Duck', 'TOW The Cat' and 'TOW Joey's New Girlfriend'. The wedding ring that Ross is going to give to Emily was originally his grandmother's.

The Last Word: A nice introduction to the madness that will become Ross's wedding, with Dick the Duck giving his best performance so far. When we wait with baited breath to see if he'll survive the ring removal, the flashback sequence is both emotional and somewhat distressing. Also distressing is witnessing what pregnancy is doing to our Pheebs. It's comical here, but neither of us would want to be in the same building as someone whose moods could switch so suddenly. **Ahhh Rating** (poor Dick): ****

('The One With The Invitation' and 'The One With The Worst Best Man Ever' were shown by Sky One in the UK as a double bill.)

423
'The One With Ross's Wedding', Part 1
#466623

Writers: Michael Borkow
Director: Kevin S. Bright
First US transmission: 07.05.98
First UK transmission (Sky One): 31.05.98

Guest Cast: Sarah Ferguson (the Duchess of York),
Richard Branson (the Vendor)

Summary: The gang prepare for their London trip while Phoebe and Rachel stay behind. Ross tries to talk Rachel into coming with them all, but she fobs him off with an excuse about having to work. Joey is visibly excited by the prospect of going to London, but his enthusiasm is already grating on Chandler's nerves before they even leave their apartment.

Joey and Chandler explore London. Joey insists on recording everything with his new video camera, much to Chandler's annoyance, and when Joey spies a hideous Union Jack hat, Chandler has had enough, warning him that he doesn't want to be seen with Joey if he buys it. Joey petulantly tells his best friend that, if it's a choice between him and the hat, the hat wins and the two end up spending the rest of the day apart. When Joey finally returns to the hotel room, Chandler is apologetic, saying that he'd had a terrible day. But if he expected Joey to say the same he's sorely mistaken – Joey's too excited about meeting Fergie, as his video recording of the moment shows.

Emily is distraught to discover that the church they've booked is being demolished and suggests putting the wedding off. Ross tells her that this isn't an option, which upsets her even more. It takes Monica to explain to her brother that, for women, it's essential that their wedding day be perfect, as most of them have been practising it since they were five years old. Ever-resourceful Ross finds a solution. Persuading the demolition company to put off their work till the day after, Ross arranges for fairy lights to be placed strategically around the shell of the church, a romantic gesture which persuades Emily to go ahead with the wedding.

Back in New York, Phoebe tries to help Rachel overcome her feelings of love for Ross. Rachel denies having any such feelings and when she discovers that, actually, she does, she's shocked. Rather than quell Rachel's remaining feelings, Phoebe's aversion therapy only provokes Rachel to rush to the airport intent on stopping the wedding . . .

Freaky Monica: Monica tries to get the guys to rush their packing: 'The flight leaves in four hours! It could take time to get a taxi! There could be traffic! The plane could leave early! When we get to London, there could be a line at customs!' Chandler notes that a six-hour flight is 'a lot of Monica' to put up with. When Phoebe tries to explain to Rachel how obvious her love for Ross was to everyone, she tells her that it would be like telling Monica, 'Hey, you like things clean.'

Spoilt Rachel: Monica leaves Phoebe by telling her where she keeps the vacuum cleaner and bin bags. When Pheebs asks why she can't just ask Rachel where they are, Monica laughs, 'Yeah, OK, give *that* a try.' She tries some shopping to clear her head of Ross, and when Pheebs asks her if it worked, she moans that 'Manhattan does not have enough stores.'

Phoebisms: Monica remarks on the way her mother always got her to pack her bags, realising that it's quite weird. Phoebe claims that her mother used to stick her head in the oven. 'Well, actually,' she corrects herself, 'she only did it the one time. But it was pretty weird.' She gives up trying to stop Rachel spoiling the wedding and sighs, 'Like I can really chase you. I'm carrying a *litter*.'

Slow Joey: When Chandler asks Joey if he's got his passport,

Joey tells him that it's in the third drawer of his dresser. Chandler glares at him and it takes him a painfully long time to realise that he should have his passport *with him* for the journey. Phoebe tells Joey that she phoned out for pizza and ordered 'the Joey Special'. 'Two pizzas?' cries Joey.

Chandleresque: Joey tries to record Chandler with his video camera and tells him to 'do something': 'I am,' says Chandler. 'I'm ignoring you.' By the time they reach Westminster Abbey, Chandler's patience is wearing thin – he tells Joey that they're thinking of renaming the Abbey. Joey falls for his bait and asks, 'To what?' and Chandler roars, 'To "Put the Camera *Away*"!' As Joey contemplates the horrible hat, Chandler murmurs, 'Well, I don't have to buy that "I'm with stupid" T-shirt any more.'

The Ballad of Ross & Rachel: You'd have thought that Ross's impending marriage would have put an end to this category – but no! Phoebe's attempts to distract Rachel from her feelings for Ross are superb, trying to get her to remember what it was like running her fingers through his hair. 'Eew-oh, gross, it's some kind of grease!' Phoebe spits helpfully, but Rachel defends him, claiming that Ross's hair was 'always more crunchy than it was greasy'. Phoebe notes that this will be harder than she first thought.

Cool Britannia: When Ross gives Emily the 'time out' signal, she misunderstands and cries, 'Well, up yours, too!'

Generation X: Sarah Ferguson is also known in the States as a TV presenter (she was asked to stand in for Jerry Springer on his infamous talk show). Richard Branson (playing the hat vendor) is the Virgin tycoon who has, at one time or other, had a finger in pretty much every pie possible. Joey watches an episode of *Cheers*, famous for being the place 'where everybody knows your name'. As the gang reach London we hear the Clash's anthem-like 'London Calling'.

The Story So Far: We can infer that Phoebe's mother gassed herself (this has never actually been stated before this episode).

The Last Word: Although this was shown on first broadcasts
as an hour-long special, it was actually made as two separate
productions, hence the separate entries here. All the signs
were pointing towards a traditional 'they drive on the wrong
side of the road'-style show, but thankfully they (largely)
veered away from that. We still have to endure the obligatory
tourist scenes which kind of work – Sarah Ferguson's great,
playing it down naturally. Matthew Perry's Chandler is evidently not having a good time stuck with the overenthusiastic
Joey, but his declaration that he refuses to be embarrassed any
more (promptly falling backwards into a flower stall) more
than makes up for his glum face in this episode. But there are
too many 'best moments' to list in detail: Monica's explanation to Ross about how important the perfect wedding is to
girls stands out, as does Phoebe's attempt at aversion therapy,
where she holds up a picture of Ross and then smacks Rachel
around the head. 'How do you feel now?' Pheebs asks
optimistically. 'Well, I like *you* less!' snaps Rachel. Thankfully, the best it yet to come. **Ahhh Rating:** ***

424

'The One With Ross's Wedding', Part 2
#466624

Writers: Jill Condon & Amy Toomin (story),
Shana Goldberg-Meehan & Scott Silveri (teleplay)
Director: Kevin S. Bright
First US transmission: 07.05.98
First UK Transmission (Sky One): 31.05.98

Guest Cast: Helen Baxendale (Emily Waltham),
Elliott Gould (Jack Geller), Christine Pickles (Judy Geller),
Tom Conti (Steven Waltham), Jennifer Saunders
(Andrea Waltham), June Whitfield (the Walthams'
Housekeeper), Hugh Laurie (Gentleman on the Plane),
Olivia Williams (Felicity), Jane Carr (Ticket Agent),
Daniel Caltagirone (the Waiter), Heathcote Williams
(Older Guest), Peter Eyre (Registrar)

Summary: As Phoebe tries to phone London to warn them of the impending arrival of Rachel, Joey begins to get homesick until he meets a 'hot bridesmaid' at the pre-wedding dinner. Ross and Emily's parents have decided to split the costs of the wedding, but when the Gellers find charges for new carpets, lawn ornaments and a wine cellar, Jack Geller is outraged. Ross manages to peace-broker an agreement between the two families, though his father is (justifiably) adamant about the wine cellar.

After a minor false start, Rachel books herself on to a plane to London, intent on telling Ross just how she feels. But when she arrives, she sees Ross and Emily together and can only wish her ex-boyfriend an emotional 'congratulations'. To everyone's relief, the wedding takes place and the happy couple read their vows to each other. Surely nothing can go wrong now . . .

Meanwhile Chandler and Monica get friendly . . .

Spoilt Rachel: Realising she's left her passport at home, she tries in vain to bribe the ticket agent with $20. Having sat through Rachel's self-pitying story during a seven-hour flight to London, the passenger next to Rachel (guest-star Hugh Laurie in a show-stealing performance) feels compelled to tell her, 'You are a horrible, *horrible* person!'

Phoebisms: After trying to warn the Walthams' housekeeper about Rachel, Phoebe is given a lesson in telephone etiquette. Losing patience, Phoebe roars that she's going to come over there and kick her 'snooty ass all the way to New Glocken . . . shire.' When the housekeeper hangs up, Pheebs realises that 'she knew I could kick her ass'.

Slow Joey: The man-child Joey takes homesickness to extremes: 'I miss my family,' he tells Chandler. 'I miss the coffee house. I can't even remember what Phoebe looks like.' Chandler points out to him that it's been only three days.

Chandleresque: His best-man speech is a joy, especially as it falls flat on the humourless crowd. Telling them he remembers Ross's first girlfriend, he jokes that he thought things were going to work out, 'until the day he overinflated her'.

Parents – Who Needs 'Em?: The Gellers arrive late, with Judy apologising. 'I insisted on riding the tube,' she explains, only for Jack Geller to misunderstand. 'Judy, the *kids*!' he warns, before she explains that she was referring to what New Yorkers would call 'the subway'. Judy can't help but undermine Monica's confidence at every opportunity, telling the Walthams that Ross's wedding 'may be the only wedding we get to throw'.

Cool Britannia: After becoming exasperated by the Walthams' bill for half the wedding costs, Jack Geller fortunately manages to avoid any xenophobic slurs against the British couple: 'You thieving would-be-speaking-German-if-it-weren't-for-us, cheap little man!' No diplomatic problems there then.

Just Plain Weird: Understandably, Andrea Waltham is a little confused when Phoebe tells her that she's carrying her brother's babies. 'Am I on the radio?' she asks cautiously.

Generation X: Tom Conti played Costas in the film *Shirley Valentine* (Lewis Gilbert, 1989). Jennifer Saunders is known in the States solely for playing Edina Monsoon in the comedy series *Absolutely Fabulous* alongside June Whitfield, who played her mother. Hugh Laurie, one half of the comedy partnership Fry and Laurie, appeared in the remake of *101 Dalmations* (Stephen Herek, 1996) and was also a familiar face as a regular member of the *Blackadder* cast. Jane Carr (the ticket agent) played Louise, the sexually obsessed organiser of the lonely hearts club in the American version of the sitcom *Dear John*, one of Londo's wives in *Babylon 5* and, as a teenager, she played Mary MacGregor in the film *The Prime of Miss Jean Brodie* (Ronald Neame, 1969). Monty Hall is another name for the 'three doors' problem, where a con man places a good prize and two bad ones behind three doors, and invites the punter to guess which door is hiding the good prize (we didn't get Chandler's joke either). One of the guests mistakes Chandler for Leonardo Di Caprio, congratulating him on his performance in *Titanic* (James Cameron, 1997). When Felicity asks Joey to talk in a New

York accent for her, he quotes Al Pacino's 'Forget about it' line from *Donnie Brasco* (Mike Newell, 1997).

The Story So Far: Rachel bores the passengers on the plane with her story about her and Ross, referring to when she proposed to Joshua ('TOW All The Wedding Dresses'). In a scene that the studio audience obviously adored, the passenger next to Rachel tells her that in his opinion it was quite obvious that they were 'on a break' (see 'TOW Ross And Rachel Take A Break').

The Last Word: So the last episode of the season ends on another cliffhanger, and in an action-packed special episode, more than just Ross and Rachel have an emotional tangle to sort out. Most viewers we've spoken to said that they didn't know what was more shocking – Ross's faux pas at the altar or the discovery that two of the other friends ended up in bed together.

Many people have already complained that the show is called *Friends*, not *Lovers*, and that maybe the gang shouldn't enter into relationships with each other, but we disagree. It's inevitable that a small group of people like the Central Perk gang will, at one time or another, pair off. While everyone has focused on Ross and Rachel since day one, there has always been a possibility of another couple, notably in one scene in 'TOW The Birth' in which we see Chandler and Monica discuss getting married when they're forty. The fact that the new couple are so perfectly suited to each other should add to some interesting events in the fifth season, especially as they seem intent on keeping it quiet from their other friends. Personally, we think they'll make a much better match than Ross and Rachel. Time will tell. **Ahhh Rating:** What else but *****!

References

Although we used many different sources in our research, we must acknowledge the books by David Wild (*Friends*, which looks at Season 1) and Penny Stallings (*Previously on Friends*, which provides an overview of Seasons 2 and 3). Both volumes give a tremendous amount of insight into behind the scenes on *Friends*.

Friends on the Internet

As one might expect, there is a huge amount of interest in *Friends* on the Internet: shrines dedicated to individual cast members, discussion groups and e-mailing lists all showing their love for the show.

All *Friends* fans should visit the informative official website at the **Warner Bros Virtual Lot** (www.virtuallot.com/cmp/comedy/friends/fr.htm), which is where we were able to get the American transmission dates. It also carries links to other Warner shows, such as *E.R.*, *Seinfeld* and the superbly original *Animaniacs*.

Many websites carry transcripts of the episodes – pretty much all of these are taken from **The Friends Script Index**, which was started by Guineapig and later taken over by Eric Aasen. Eric's **The One With All The Scripts – The Complete Friends Script Index** was an absolute godsend in the creation of this book (you can find this superb site at http://thecfsi.com). Eric's site also contains some excellent fan fiction and is one of the best on the web.

In addition, there's the **Friends Episode Guide** page (www.friends-tv.org/epguide.html) created by Andy J. Williams and maintained by Darcy Partridge, which you might want to check out. There's a similar site for all you Francophiles at www.fanfr.com.

A beautifully designed site, **The Friends Café** (www.

friends-cafe.com), was a great help in our survival of this book, specifically the notes for the *Friends* Drinking Game.

British fans might want to dip into Rob 'JustcallmeRob' Wilson's **UK Friends** site, which can be found at www.cynic.demon.co.uk. In addition to a list of Channel 4 transmission dates, Rob also carries a link to the **Friends Mailing List**, which is a friendly informal e-mail group who discuss (but don't limit themselves to) all the latest rumours, merchandising and general points of interest for the average fan.

Finally, there's another UK site run by Tina Nellis (fly.to/angelsfriends/). Tina stores loads of really interesting press articles and a great links page (and she's a jolly good egg, so we don't mind giving her site a plug).